Just Money

Just Money

The Vision of Shalom

Wayne Kirkland

RESOURCE *Publications* · Eugene, Oregon

JUST MONEY
The Vision of Shalom

Copyright © 2012 Wayne Kirkland. All rights reserved. Except for brief quotations in critical publications or reviews, no part of this book may be reproduced in any manner without prior written permission from the publisher. Write: Permissions, Wipf and Stock Publishers, 199 W. 8th Ave., Suite 3, Eugene, OR 97401.

Resource Publications
An Imprint of Wipf and Stock Publishers
199 W. 8th Ave., Suite 3
Eugene, OR 97401

www.wipfandstock.com

ISBN 13: 978-1-62032-302-1

Unless otherwise noted, Scripture quotations are from THE MESSAGE. Copyright © by Eugene Peterson 1993, 1994, 1995. Used by permission of NavPress Publishing Group.

Scripture taken from the Holy Bible, New International Version. Copyright © 1973, 1978, 1984 by International Bible Society. Used by permission of International Bible Society. "NIV" and "New International Version" are trademarks registered in the United States Patent and Trademark office by International Bible Society.

Scripture quotations taken from the New Revised Standard Version Bible, copyright © 1989 National Council of the Churches of Christ in the United States of America. Used by permission. All rights reserved.

Manufactured in the U.S.A.

For Maria, Kellie, and Melody
May this book inspire you to pursue the blessing and joy
of God's shalom

Contents

Foreword by Tony Campolo | ix
Acknowledgments | xiii

Introduction | 1

1. Power | 7
2. Lenses | 14

Section A: Bible | 23

3. Blessing | 25
4. Land | 32
5. Wealth | 39
6. Justice | 48
7. Poor | 59
8. Mammon | 70
9. Giving | 77

Section B: Culture | 87

10. Capitalism | 89
11. Happiness | 103
12. Consumption | 110
13. Need | 119
14. Brand | 127
15. Choice | 135
16. Credit | 141
17. Affluence | 149

Section C: Counter-Culture | 157

18 Trusteeship | 159
19 Gratitude | 169
20 Generosity | 176
21 Contentment | 185
22 Simplicity | 195
23 Sabbath | 207
24 Hospitality | 214
25 Community | 225

Bibliography | 237

Foreword

WHAT WE SHOULD DO with money has always been troubling to Christians. Depending on who we listen to, the directives vary. There are some who like to tell us that we should set aside 10 percent of our incomes to support ministries that propagate the Gospel. That seems clear-cut, but then there are those who raise the question as to whether or not the 10 percent should be taken from the amount earned prior or after government taxes.

Adding to the confusion, there are those who preach a "prosperity theology," suggesting that insofar as we tithe, God will ensure us material blessings. In simple language, we are told that if we are faithful in our commitments to give to God, God will be generous in enabling us to enjoy economic wealth and well-being. But it doesn't end there! Some preachers even suggest that we should do what has been called "seed tithing." What this means is that if we give 10 percent of what we *hope* will be forthcoming in income in the upcoming year, then God will deliver nine times more as a reward for our faithfulness. Thus we can control how much we will be able to earn in the upcoming year simply by giving 10 percent of what we expect upfront.

The problem with prosperity theologies such as those cited above is that, in one way or another, they are built on teachings that come out of the Old Testament. However, as Wayne Kirkland makes clear, tithing is seldom mentioned in the New Testament, and when it is mentioned, it is mentioned in negative ways. Jesus, for instance, refers to tithing as a legalistic obligation that is carried out by the Pharisees, and he makes it clear that unless our "righteousness exceeds that of the Pharisees," we will not be part of the new kingdom of God he has come to establish. In the New Testament, there is little question that much more is required of us than just tithing.

Foreword

When we read in Mark 10 about the rich young ruler who comes to Jesus and wants to know how he can inherit eternal life, Jesus acknowledges that this young man has observed the teachings of the Mosaic Law with great care, but then adds that if he wants to be a true disciple, he will have to sell what he has and give to the poor. The disciples of Jesus immediately recognize the implications of what their Lord has said, and ask, "Who then can be saved?" Jesus responds by telling them that when he talks about this kind of commitment, he recognizes that people will look at this as impossible, but "with God all things are possible!"

Picking up the theme we find in Christ that the Christian is called to go beyond the tithe, John Wesley, founder of the Methodist movement, declared to his followers that, "a Christian should work as hard as he can; to earn as much money as he can; to spend as little as he can; in order to give away to those in need all that he can."

On a personal level, allow me to say that I am deeply troubled as I consider the way in which I personally have utilized the money that has been put in my hands over the years. I read the Sermon on the Mount and recognize that Jesus teaches that I should take no thought for the future as to what I shall eat, and what I shall drink, and how I will be clothed. In spite of claiming to be a follower of Jesus, I have failed to live up to that requisite. Instead, over the years, I have carefully put money away for my retirement and I have taken out insurance policies, all of which are attempts to lay aside treasure here on earth where moth and rust corrupt instead of utilizing that money for the work of Christ's Kingdom and trusting in him to care for me and my family in later years. In short, I am not about to live as Jesus suggested and be like the birds of the air and the flowers of the field that neither toil nor reap, but for whom God, nevertheless, supplies their needs. I could easily be judged for having a lack of faith, and I realize that I am far from being what Jesus called me to be. Fortunately, my salvation is dependent on God's grace instead of being dependent on my lifestyle.

On the other hand, I believe that what Christ expected was that Christians would live in supportive relationship to one another, much as we find in the second chapter of Acts, so that there would be no need for the kind of individualism in which persons would concern themselves with future needs, because the community of faith they were a part, would take care of their needs at such times. In the early church, the community was there for anyone who needed help or care. It was the community that took care of widows and orphans, but in today's society

Foreword

such Christian community as is found in Acts 2 seldom exists. Thus the necessity for individuals to prepare for their future and for emergencies as best they can.

Soren Kierkegaard, in one of his meditations, bemoans the fact that in the Sermon on the Mount, Jesus declares that a person cannot serve both God and Mammon at the same time. Kierkegaard wished that our Lord had said, "We *should* not try to serve God and Mammon at the same time." Sadly, Kierkegaard points out, Jesus creates an either/or situation and there is little room for some kind of compromising arrangement. Yet, it is in a compromising arrangement that almost all of us live. Granted, there are the likes of St. Francis of Assisi for whom material needs were completely ignored, and his service to Christ and to others in the name of Christ was undeterred by worldly concerns. But the numbers of Christians who have chosen to live like St. Francis are few and far between. In short, most of us try to serve God and Mammon at the same time. When we stop to think about that, we are deeply troubled.

In this book, Wayne Kirkland tries to call us to a realistic appraisal of how to live out our commitments to Christ while dealing realistically with the material demands that are made upon us so far as personal and family requisites demand. The book is not only filled with good biblical insights as to how to deal with money matters, but it also raises a host of questions which Kirkland calls Christians to reflect on and resolve as they seek to, in the words of Soren Kierkegaard, "work out their salvation with fear and trembling" so far as finances are concerned.

The Greek philosophers declared to the world that, "the unexamined life is not worth living." What Wayne Kirkland calls us to do is to live worthwhile lives by examining how we are going to utilize the financial resources we are privileged to possess, in ways that honor God and are faithful to the teachings of Scripture. The Bible also declares that each of us should be in a process of self-examination so that we are in a position to judge ourselves and not be judged by others and by God. This book will help any committed Christian on that journey to faithful, biblical stewardship.

Tony Campolo
Eastern University
St. Davids, PA

Acknowledgments

Thanks to:

Ian Dunwoodie—for your fine editing skills and ongoing friendship. I am indebted.

Friends who kindly read my manuscript and gave me helpful feedback.

John Crawshaw—for your insight and wise counsel. You're a true friend and colleague.

Regent College—for your generous hospitality in the Fall of 2009, allowing me the space to write.

Jill—my constant companion and partner through thick and thin.

Introduction

MONEY. SUCH A LITTLE word . . . with such explosive power. For love of money reputations have been ruined, marriages have been destroyed, lifelong friendships have been torn apart, whole nations have bled. For lack of money kingdoms have crumbled, corporations have foundered, lives have faded, dreams have died.

But what about us ordinary folk? You may not believe this, but I think I'm right in suggesting that we—you and I—spend more time thinking about money (worrying, planning, earning, spending, counting, hoping, envying) than about almost any other subject.

If that claim surprises you, listen to this: in the Gospels Jesus also talks a great deal about money.

Money is central to the way we live. And given the importance Jesus attached to it, I believe it's critical that we understand its role, and its value in our lives.

You've chosen to pick up this book. Am I right in thinking that you too have a feeling this topic is important as you live for God? Will you join me in exploring just how it is that this thing we call money has become so deeply rooted in our lives, in our thoughts, and in our emotions?

Where did it begin? Like so much in life, it's our early years that shape a great deal of what we think and feel about money, and of how we ultimately use it. In particular, how your family viewed, talked about, valued, and used money is likely to have left some indelible imprints on your own reaction to the "M" word.

I can certainly see that in my own growing–up years. As a child I was blissfully unaware of how much of a struggle life was for my parents. Dad worked for his father-in-law—in a retail business that ultimately he and Mum would own and run. They eventually were able to enjoy the fruit of their hard labor, but when I was young it wasn't easy for them.

They were careful managers of what they did have. And I don't ever recall them bemoaning what they didn't have. Though holidays were rare, and though I learnt from an early age that "Money doesn't grow on trees, you know!"—during my childhood there was always food on the table and I never felt deprived in any way.

The Presbyterian faith of my parents also shaped their attitude to money, with its strong emphasis on careful stewardship and regular giving to "God's work."

Dad and Mum had childhood backgrounds that were somewhat different from each other. Dad's parents were immigrants from Scotland. In the 1920s they arrived in New Zealand looking for a land of opportunity, and desperate to escape the hard and hopeless working–class life of Glasgow. What they found was how difficult it was to raise three sons in the middle of a worldwide depression and the World War that followed. For a few years they ran a small business, but eventually Grandpop became a union organizer. They managed to eke out a reasonable living from their endeavors, but never had much to come and go on.

Mum's parents were much better off financially. Nana came from a farm and her family had some resources. Poppa was an entrepreneur, full of life, personality, optimism, and generosity of spirit. After some years as a travelling salesman, he eventually found himself in business and did very well. While not extravagant, they enjoyed the "good things in life," building a new house on a prime piece of city land, taking in a Pacific cruise, and being quick on the uptake to purchase a new car or the hottest new gadgets—like a black and white TV and a radio cassette deck!

My parents and grandparents, then, were the ones from whom I initially learnt about money. The messages I picked up were implicit ones of working hard, saving hard (which meant delayed gratification), and giving to God what was "rightfully his." Money was not in unlimited supply. It therefore needed to be valued and managed carefully.

How does that compare with your experience? If you belong to a different generation, you may find you have some notable differences. As you read on you'll see that during the twentieth century dramatic changes took place in the way money was perceived, which may account for such differences. One way or another, be prepared to discover that your attitude to money is very much shaped by your background.

Introduction

Wider influences

Family background is of course not the only influence on how we think about and use money. Important messages also come from our peers and friends. And from the wider culture we are part of. Our culture sells us its values in many ways—through the advertising that surrounds us from morning to night, from the fashions and gadgets (clothes, cars, jewelry, watches, cell phones . . .) that we see everywhere we go, from the films and television we watch, from the people we admire.

And finally, of course—if we have a Christian faith, there's the Bible. We expect that what Scripture has to say about money, how it deals with the subject, will be a major influence on our lives. Spiritual growth is partly about learning to think the way God thinks, right? But here's the rub. When it comes to money (that precious commodity that is so near to our hearts) it is only too clear that many people read their own thinking into Scripture. Believe it or not, on this topic more than perhaps any other, *we may have projected our values onto the Bible.* We'll explore this reverse thinking in chapter 2.

Clearly, if we are genuinely seeking to follow Jesus and to live according to his values, on this topic of money we must be honest with God and with ourselves. Honest right down to how we live day-by-day.

This book unashamedly explores what role money has in the call of Christian discipleship. And my contention is that it's a big role—not some peripheral side issue. Which makes it all the more important that we think long and hard about it.

Are you up for it?

A road map—where we are headed

If you're someone who likes to have a map of where you're going, then here's an overview of the journey we'll be taking in the following pages.

There are twenty-five chapters in this book. Each deals briefly with a particular angle on money and wealth and possessions. The chapters are grouped in three sections—each one a building block for what lies ahead.

Before we proceed any further, there are a couple of (big) assumptions I will be making that you need to be aware of. Chapters 1 and 2 address these. They're important and fundamental starting points for what will follow. Miss these and you'll likely misunderstand what I say later in the book.

Section A: Bible

Scripture has an astonishing amount to say about money and resources—much more than we might first assume. So much so that we can easily get lost in the detail, or be overwhelmed by its at-times confusing messages.

So in this section I'll attempt what more sensible people would resist!—a quick view of some of the major themes in the Bible's take on money. It won't be a complete and exhaustive A-to-Z manual, but it *will* cover important biblical principles. As hooks on which to peg the broad themes, I'll use words such as Blessing, Land, Wealth, Justice, Poor, Mammon and Giving. With those insights we'll be able to evaluate how money is viewed in our world. Which leads to . . .

Section B: Culture

We must take seriously our culture's influence on our attitude to money. What does money represent in this world we live in? What do we mean by words such as Capitalism, Happiness, Consumption, Need, Brand, Choice, Credit, and Affluence?

I hope that as we explore these you'll grow in your understanding of what makes modern society tick *and* see how at crucial points there is a gaping chasm between the way the Bible and our culture value and treat money.

Section C: Counter-culture

Finally, in this last section we get to the crux of the matter: what it might mean to live as followers of Jesus in this world of ours. We'll explore eight "counter-cultural" practices that can help us live more faithfully—Trusteeship, Gratitude, Generosity, Contentment, Simplicity, Sabbath, Hospitality, and Community.

Getting the most out of this book

I'm honored that you've decided to read my thoughts and what I've discovered about money. But I must warn you —I've not penned these words just to inform. In fact, as I've written this book I've been freshly challenged to ask myself the question:

Introduction

So? What does this really mean for you, Wayne, and the people you are connected to?

I've realized it's the "therefores" that matter the most. So what will this mean for the way you and I live? What are the implications for the way you and I treat and use money every day?

Here's where the rubber hits the road. I'll try to give you some practical examples of what this might look like . . . *but* . . . I will emphatically *not* be laying down Christian rules and commandments about money! This is *your* life. Living it is *your* adventure with God.

To help you and me process what we discover and turn it into positive action, I've put some questions and exercises ("Up Close and Personal") at the end of each chapter. These will help you translate the conceptual ideas into the nitty–gritty.

While you can delve into these questions by yourself, you may find that grappling with the issues is easier and more fruitful in the company of others. In fact, one of the messages of my book is that we all desperately need companions for the journey—for discovering how to be "in but not of" our culture.

If you are planning to use this material as part of a group study series, you probably won't have twenty-five weeks to explore it together, so my suggestion is that you tackle it over a much more manageable twelve weeks, grouping the chapters as follows:

Week 1	Power and Lenses
Week 2	Blessing, Land, and Wealth
Week 3	Poor and Justice
Week 4	Mammon and Giving
Week 5	Capitalism and Happiness
Week 6	Consumption and Need
Week 7	Brand and Choice
Week 8	Credit and Affluence
Week 9	Trusteeship
Week 10	Gratitude and Generosity
Week 11	Contentment, Simplicity, and Sabbath
Week 12	Hospitality and Community

Up Close and Personal

1. What images/feelings/experiences/meanings does the word "money" trigger for you?
2. Can you identify where these have come from?
3. What can you recall of the messages you picked up as a child from your family?
4. Make a list of the words and images that our wider culture associates with money.

1

Power

"... money is not willing to rest contented in its proper place alongside other things we value. No, it must have supremacy. It must crowd out all else."
Richard Foster

It's 1756. A twelve-year-old Jewish boy takes a job at a bank in Hanover, Germany. Young Mayer surprises. He has abilities and ambition in generous quantities—despite his modest background.

His business apprenticeship finished, Mayer returns to his hometown of Frankfurt, armed with his growing expertise, his contacts, and his grand ideas. He begins trading in rare coins and medals.

Jews don't get many opportunities in Frankfurt, and life is hard for them. But one opening they do manage to exploit is business. Some even become "court agents"—financial dealers in the courts of German rulers. There are plenty of them; Germany of the 1700s is not a single state but a patchwork of states, mini-states, duchies, principalities, and "Free Imperial Cities."

It's not long before Mayer's fledgling business takes a fortunate turn. He manages to sell some rare medals to William, the Hereditary Prince of Hesse-Kassel. This first transaction quickly leads to others—and then in 1769 Mayer is appointed a court agent for William. A year later, at the age of twenty-six he marries, a strategic alliance, for his new bride is Gutle, the sixteen-year-old daughter of another court agent. The dowry is substantial. It greatly adds to Mayer's capital and it is not long before he is Frankfurt's leading dealer in medals, coins, and antiques.

By the early 1790s, Mayer's business has taken off. No longer is it just trading. Now he is extending credit to his clients; the world of merchant banking offers rich prospects. The name of Rothschild begins its climb to both fortune and fame.

Mayer and Gutle Rothschild are a fruitful couple. They produce nineteen children in almost as many years, though only ten live beyond infancy. Five are sons, and by the end of the eighteenth century they have joined the business. Mayer is determined to keep it within the family, and his sons are apt pupils. They too make strategic marriages.

Rapid wealth creation generally requires a measure of good fortune—and the readiness to capitalize on the events of the moment. For the Rothschilds, history served up two dramatic upheavals: one in France, one in Britain.

As to the first, the violent French Revolution spilled over into Germany and Austria. Mayer secured a contract to provide grain and cash to the Austrian army in their campaign against the French. Meanwhile in Britain something was happening which may have been less violent, but which was to change the world every bit as much. The factories of the British Industrial Revolution were beginning to pour out cheaper, mass-produced articles. Mayer's response was to send his third son Nathan to England in 1799.

Nathan showed himself to be the ideal person. Like his father, he had an eye for opportunity and for income. His establishment in London quickly began to reap the profits of trading in low cost English textiles. Mayer was encouraged to develop a Europe-wide enterprise. While Mayer's eldest son, Amschel, remained in Frankfurt, Salomon was sent to Vienna (Austria), Calmann to Naples (Italy), and Jakob to Paris (France). Their family influence mushroomed and their wealth ballooned.

Because Britain was the spearhead of European opposition to Napoleon, Nathan was perfectly positioned to funnel the financial support of the Rothschilds in their direction. He it was who found a way to both help fund the war effort and ensure the gold coinage got to the front lines. Then when Napoleon over-reached himself with his disastrous invasion of Russia, Nathan's opportunity came. To begin with, Napoleon was exiled to the island of Elba. Nevertheless, he soon escaped from there, returned to France as its hero, raised a new army, and faced the allies at Waterloo.

However, Napoleon's unexpectedly quick defeat at the hands of the Duke of Wellington nearly proved catastrophic for the Rothschilds. Having gambled on a long campaign, Nathan found himself with rapidly depreciating bonds. What saved the family from financial ruin was the way Nathan then audaciously ploughed their every last dollar into buying up more bonds, in order to manipulate demand for them. As a result, their price soared and when Nathan finally sold his huge stockpile of bonds two years later, the Rothschilds' fortune was dramatically enlarged. No wonder Nathan was soon hailed as "the Financial Bonaparte."[1]

It's a little difficult to separate fact from fiction when it comes to the Rothschilds. Over the years they have certainly been both credited with, and accused of, much greater influence than was ever the case. In fact, if you scour the literature you'll "discover" that apparently they have been responsible in the last two hundred years for most of the major events in the world—including the great wars, the stock market crash of 1929, and most recently, the Twin Towers tragedy of 9/11—as well as being leading lights in a secret society called the Illuminati!

The conspiracists have had a field day. So did the Nazis, who included the Rothschilds in their hate propaganda directed at Jews. Anti-Semitic attacks also account for other charges.

No doubt the over-imaginative speculation has been fuelled because so much of the Rothschilds' business has been done behind closed doors. Right from the word go Mayer determined that the family business would be exactly that—run by the family only, thus keeping the control of the growing fortune in the hands of the direct progeny. Even daughters and their children were excluded from ownership and decision-making. Everything was tightly managed and controlled. The magnitude of their wealth and the ways they have used it are shrouded in a great deal of secrecy. Because of this, we don't fully know how much power they were able to exercise over people and events down through the years.

But whatever the extent of their influence, Mayer Rothschild well understood that what he had was more than just money. In fact, he once said: "*Permit me to issue and control the money of a nation, and I care not who makes its laws . . .*"

Though he died in 1812, Mayer's statement has an ominous and prophetic edge to it.

Less than thirty years later a French journalist remarked: "There is but one power in Europe, and that is Rothschild." Another writer, the German poet Heinrich Heine, declared in 1841, "Money is the god of our time and Rothschild is his prophet." By then, it had become clear to

---

1. According to economic historian Niall Fergusson, it was the German writer Ludwig Boeme who coined this phrase. See Fergusson's book, *The Ascent of Money*, 86.

many in Europe that the family dynasty and its money had indeed begun to hold sway over the affairs of nations.

Their story demonstrates that money does talk. It is a powerful force—for both good and evil. It can influence, dominate, and manipulate us, even demand our allegiance. It can speak in ways that nothing else can.

Money is not peripheral

Few people will ever amass the kind of fortune the Rothschilds have. However, as we all know, none of us can live without money. It is part of the essential fabric of life.

Of course, I'm not just meaning cash—the banknotes and coins we carry in our wallets and purses. Money is a synonym for much more than "legal tender." It includes anything that carries economic value in our society: land and houses, shares and bonds, vegetables and luxury yachts, businesses and products, superannuation schemes, and real net worth.

All this "stuff" provides a medium of exchange. It can be traded for other things. And therein lies some of its inherent power. When we say that "Great-uncle Victor has money," we effectively mean he has the necessary resources to make choices—not only about what he owns, but where he lives, *how* he lives, and how he spends his time. Money means choices.

And it's not just the wealthy. For all of us, money plays a central role in our lives, no matter whether we are rich or poor, employed or unemployed, old or young.

We expect the Bible to address our lives. It makes sense, then, that it must also have something to say about this stuff of life. And indeed it does. Lots to say, in fact, as we'll discover in the following chapters.

Money is not neutral

Contrary to popular opinion, money is not *just* a medium of exchange. Money carries *power*. Even more, it *is* a power—all of its own.

Most of us are used to thinking that money is neutral. We believe that it only carries as much weight as we are prepared to give it. "It's just printed money, for heaven's sake!" But that is to dangerously underestimate money's seductive strength.

One theologian who understood this well was Jacques Ellul.[2] He suggests that money is in fact, one of the "principalities and powers" that the Apostle Paul mentions in the New Testament. And the way Jesus talked suggests that Ellul is right. In Matthew 6 he speaks of a strange creature called Mammon. In truth, mammon is just the Aramaic word for money/wealth, but it's as if Jesus pronounces it . . . with a capital letter. As if it's a real person. Mammon, he says, is a power that demands servitude. Our "master" is either Money or God.[3]

Do these sound like the words of reasonability and neutrality?

Building on Ellul's thinking, Marva Dawn explains: "Such things as money and technology are human constructions, but they both display a force that is more than human. The principalities and powers are created (ultimately by God) for good (Colossians 1:16). They have a vocation—that is, a rightful place in God's purposes for human well-being. But the powers share in the fallenness of all creation (Romans 8:19-22), and thereby always tend to overstep their vocation. Thus, money is not neutral."[4]

What indications do we have that this is so? The list is long and varied, but here are just a few:

- Most of us dream of having more of it.

- We lie awake at night worrying about it. More anxious energy is consumed on money matters than on anything else.

- Money is the cause of more arguments in marriage and more separations and divorces than any other issue. Plus, disagreements over inheritances cause many family relationships to splinter. Some siblings end up never talking to each other for the rest of their lives.

- Our "financial markets" are controlled by two heavily charged emotions—greed and fear.

- The prospect of making a fast buck or of losing what we have, is frequently enough to drive many of us to do things we normally wouldn't—like committing fraud, being less than honest, sacrificing a friendship, compromising our values . . .

These are all pointers to the importance and the power of the dollar. Money definitely matters. For most of us, far too much.

2 See Ellul, *Money and Power*.
3. I'll come back to this in chapter 9.
4. Marva Dawn, "Whom Do You Serve?"

And the most telling fact of all, perhaps, is that every one of these dysfunctional effects is experienced not just by those of us who are in the middle classes, not just by those of us who are poor . . . but by the world's millionaires too. *They* suffer from the very same complaints. John D. Rockefeller, one of the richest men in America through the late nineteenth and early twentieth centuries, was once asked how much money was enough. His answer: "Just a little bit more!"

"Just a little bit more . . . " The dark side of money.

Os Guinness declares: "Throughout history the most universally acknowledged problem with money is that its pursuit is insatiable . . . As we seek money and possessions, observers note, the pursuit grows into a never-satisfied desire that fuels avarice—described by the Bible as a vain 'chasing after wind' and by moderns as an 'addiction.' The very Hebrew word for money (*kesef*) comes from a verb meaning, 'to desire' or 'languish after something.'"[5]

It is a ravenous beast, capable of consuming us. Which is rather ironic really. Because we're often tempted to think that we are in control of our money—and of our attitude to money. That we are the consumers, not the ones *being* consumed.

The reality is that when it comes to money we are like a small boy taking a large dog for a walk. The youngster thinks he's in control. After all, he's been charged with the responsibility of leading the dog and ensuring that it doesn't wander where it shouldn't. But the dog has other ideas. It senses the child is not strong enough to handle it. It will go where *it* chooses to go and at the pace *it* wishes to travel. What's more, whenever the boy thinks he has at last got the dog under control, it only takes one lunge . . . !

Being in control is a figment of the child's imagination. So it is with money. Richard Foster notes that, "It is money's desire for omnipotence, for all power, that seems so strange, so out of place. It seems that money is not willing to rest contented in its proper place alongside other things we value. No, it must have supremacy. It must crowd out all else."[6]

With money—whether we have it or whether we don't—the battle for control never ends. Money is something you can never treat lightly.

And still people claim that they "don't have a problem with money"! Perhaps for a small minority that may be true. However, for the rest of

---

5. Guinness, *The Call*, 136.
6. Foster, *Money, Sex and Power*, 28.

us . . . we're just kidding ourselves. It has certainly been an issue for me. That's one reason I've written this book.

So what about you?

Up Close and Personal

1. I write that, "money is not *just* a medium of exchange. Money carries *power*. Even more, it *is* a power—all of its own."
   Do you agree? Why or why not?

2. What, in your terms, might determine whether the power of money is used well or poorly?

3. Can you think of other indications that money is "a power"?

4. People who have money have influence. Can you think of wealthy people who have used their "power" well?
   What about those who have abused their financial power and influence? (Think of both historical and current figures.)

5. Think back again to your experience of growing up. Do you have any personal memory of money being used in an unusually positive or supportive way? Or in a damaging or hurtful way?

6. In what ways is money a problem for you?

2

Lenses

"We do not see things as they are; we see things as we are."

MATT WAS SWEATING IT. Weeks ago his home group leader had asked him to prepare a bible study on money. It had been easy to say yes. Matt was well aware of the better-known Bible statements on the topic, and he hadn't found too much difficulty himself in striking a balance between them. He was confident he could make sense of the Bible's message.

But right now he was having second thoughts. Matt happened to be at the beach with three of his friends. They'd swum and volley-balled and barbecued, and were now sitting chatting over the last of the food. That's when Jessica asked how preparations were going for the bible study.

"We–ell, not too badly," said Matt. "I've got a pretty good idea of where I'm going on it." This was less than honest. In fact, he'd not done much more than toy with a few thoughts, and time was running out. Truth was, he was beginning to feel a bit anxious—the way you do when a deadline is getting too close for comfort and no clear directions are emerging.

Jessica, however, took his reply at face value. "So what particular line are you taking?"

Matt parried. "What do you mean, what line? I'll just deal with the Bible's teaching head on. It's all very clear really." Even to himself he sounded a little too emphatic. As you do when you're feeling a touch guilty.

Phil was obviously in a mischievous mood. "You're gonna push the health-and-wealth gospel, then?"

Matt felt a little easier. This at least was something he could talk to. "Well, obviously I don't go for that sort of stuff. That's taking Bible statements out of context. But there's nothing wrong with wealth as long as it's held in balance. You give generously and you don't get too attached to money. That would be worshipping it. *All in moderation* is really what it's about. You know—that passage in Proverbs: 'Give me neither poverty nor riches . . .'"

That's better. Listening to himself Matt felt just the slightest tinge of smugness. He certainly wasn't rich himself but, after all, he was comfortably well off. All told, he had the business of wealth in pretty reasonable perspective. Neither poverty nor riches . . .

"Oh, I see"—it was Janine this time, and there was the faintest edge to her voice— "Jesus got it wrong then, did he, when he told the rich young ruler to go sell his possessions and give everything to the poor?"

Matt smiled to himself, and began to feel even more confident. He could easily handle *that* one – if he'd heard it once, he'd heard it a thousand times. "Oh, *really*," he sneered (in a caring and loving way, of course; but Janine did tend to be rather intense about this sort of thing). "That's getting a bit carried away. What Jesus said then was a very specific word to a particular person. Obviously the rich young ruler happened to have a real problem with money. Think about it. If Jesus meant all of his followers to do that, we'd all be paupers and then we couldn't help anyone."

Ah, the fury of a woman scorned. Janine was too well studied on this topic to be knocked back by that sort of line. She launched into a recital of scorching verses from the Prophets—the ones that slammed people who had resources but didn't help the poor.

Matt countered: "But didn't Jesus say to Judas—'The poor will always be with you'?"

"Does that make it acceptable for us to be well-off when children are starving to death?" This was obviously something Janine felt strongly about.

Jessica, sensing that maybe some calm logic was called for, joined in. "Yes, but when you think about it, it's not all that clear-cut. Those great people of faith in the Old Testament—some of them were *unbelievably* wealthy. Guys like Abraham and Isaac and Job. *And* their wealth was viewed as a sign of God's blessing. God even said as much—remember how he told Abraham he would bless him, and when he returned Job's wealth at the end of the book. And, Matt, if you're saying 'everything in moderation,' where does that put those guys?"

"Perhaps the prosperity-doctrine people have got it right after all!" grinned Phil.

Which brought Janine back in. "But on the other hand, how do you fit that with Jesus' statement—and it couldn't be much clearer: 'It's easier for a camel to pass through the eye of a needle than it is for a rich person to enter the kingdom of God.' By the way, don't try explaining that away by saying there was a gate in the city wall of Jerusalem called the Needle, that camels had to get down low in order to go through. That's a myth. There never was any such gate."

Matt was sweating again. At least now he wasn't suffering from a shortage of material! But his neat, middle-of-the-road solution was looking pretty tattered...

Mixed Messages?

Matt's dilemma is not unusual. When we begin prodding the Bible we soon realize that its message on money is confusing and diverse.

We are sometimes apt to forget that the Bible is not one single, monolithic book. It is a *collection* of books, written by around forty authors, in three languages, spanning over fifteen hundred years of time, written to different people in a variety of contexts. And if that isn't enough to contend with, the sixty-six books involve several kinds of literary genres—history, poetry, wisdom, prophetic, gospel, letters, and apocalyptic material. The variety is enormous.

So it shouldn't be surprising that there is no uniform, one-size-fits-all perspective on the issue of money. Finding a unified message on this subject is not impossible. But it *is* challenging. Different writers and books express slightly different perspectives. This has a lot to do with the different contexts from which they are writing and the different literary genres they use.

There is diversity—however, there is also a real unity. The Bible's take on money is like dealing with a multi-sided object. Each view gives us one perspective from a particular angle, but it's not until we attempt to reconcile this with the other views that we begin to see a consistent picture emerge, one that has a clear shape within its different lines. Forget that and you'll make the Bible say what you want it to say. On the matter of money, it's only too easy to manipulate it.

To put it another way, if you are determined to make biblical texts support a particular view on wealth, you will have a field day.

Reading in Context

So how do we counter this tendency?

The starting point is reading the text carefully and attempting to be open to what *it* says – rather than what *we* would like it to say. To help us do this, learning to read it in context is a must.

Real estate agents have a saying that goes something like this: "When you want to buy a house to invest in, what are the three most important things to look for? Answer: Location, location, location."

Biblical scholars could well offer a similar reply to the question, "What are the three most important principles for interpreting a bible passage? Answer: Context, context, context."

A verse or a statement may well be *from the Bible*, but without reading it in context, it may not be *biblical*. Such "proof-texting" can be misleading and dangerous.

We must therefore be very careful to read something in its "context" (a word meaning literally: *with the text, alongside the text*). This includes:

- Understanding the type of literature and literary devices the author is employing.
- Understanding something of the history and culture that forms the backdrop to what the author is writing.
- Reading the complete chapter from which the verse comes.
- Reading the whole book.
- Reflecting on other verses and passages in Scripture that deal with a similar issue, and looking for consistent themes and emphases. This is sometimes referred to as "the whole counsel of God." Chapters 4–9 of this book will help us do this.

Seeing Scripture through our own view of the world

All of us come to the Bible with an already existing set of assumptions. Assumptions about the world and the way it operates . . . about God . . . about ourselves.

Another way of putting this is to recognize that we all read the Bible through the lenses of *our own* "context." When we see scriptural words we see them from the angle of what is important to *us*, from our own particular experiences, and our own particular environment. As the Talmud (the ancient Jewish law book) puts it: "We do not see things as they are; we see them as *we* are."

In other words, it is as if we are viewing the world with spectacles on. The focal length of our lenses will allow us to see certain things sharply. But anything closer than that will be fuzzy; anything further away will be blurred. What we see best is what our spectacles condition us to see. Same with the way we read the Bible. We read it through the "lenses" of our own particular experiences; our own interests, insights, and enthusiasms; all the combined ideas and values that we have accumulated through our life and (particularly) our upbringing. Sociologists call this our "worldview."

With that in mind let's re-word the Talmud's statement, as it relates to our reading of Scripture: "We do not read and understand the Bible as it is; we read and understand it as *we* are."

When we read Scripture we are filtering the words through what we know and experience. Whether we like it or not, our spectacles are already coloring what we read according to our pre-existing view of the world. We are automatically interpreting the words without even being aware of it.

This has a big influence on what we "see" and what we subconsciously screen out, particularly (though certainly not exclusively) as it relates to money. The reason for this is partly that the Bible has so much to say about money, possessions, and related subjects. In fact, one out of every ten verses in the synoptic gospels (Matthew, Mark, and Luke) has to do with wealth and poverty.

This is not just a New Testament emphasis. In the Old Testament, the pattern is just as strong—next to idolatry, poverty is the most prominent theme.

No wonder Matt was having so much trouble!

Jim Wallis, leader of the Sojourners community, recounts how when he was a seminary student one of his friends took a pair of scissors to an old Bible one day, cutting out all the verses and passages that referred to riches or the poor. "It took him a long time. By the time he was finished the Prophets were decimated, the Psalms destroyed, the Gospels ripped to shreds and the Epistles turned to tattered rags. The Bible was full of holes."[1]

Money is no peripheral issue in Scripture. It has an exceedingly prominent place. If this surprises you, you are not alone. Most of our church gatherings, conversations, bible studies, and prayers don't come anywhere near reflecting this prominence. An outsider could easily assume by our talk that money was a very private matter, largely unrelated to following God—or to our "salvation."

This all suggests that we are not reading Scripture as it really is. Something very important is missing. Subconsciously we are filtering out large chunks of the Bible. It's as if we have an enormous blind spot in our vision.

Why do we not see that following Jesus has significant economic implications? Why, as Wallis contends, do we continue to carry around a Bible full of holes, quite unaware that we have metaphorically cut out great chunks? The short answer is that each of us has a view of the world and ourselves that makes sense to us. In order to keep on living, acting, and thinking the way that we're comfortable with, we need to defend and protect that worldview. When it seems to be contradicted by data from the Bible, our lenses automatically filter what we're reading. We make the awkward pieces "fit" . . . and usually have no idea we're doing it.

This filtering process happens all the time—not just on the issue of money. The way we justify our position is often by subconsciously saying to ourselves, "Oh, that doesn't apply to me." Or, "The writer is using over-the-top language just to make his point." Or, "Jesus didn't really mean it that way"!

It all depends on how you see yourself

Let's take another angle on this, to get some more perspective . . . Most of us reading this book are, by world standards, rich.

We may not *feel* rich, but the fact that we have a home to live in, good meals to enjoy, a regular income, and a range of choices, indicates that by global standards we are wealthy. (And being able to purchase and read this book is another indication of our fortunate status!) However—being human—we are always comparing ourselves with others, and that natural tendency dulls our appreciation of how rich we are. Bill Gates or Warren

---

1. Wallis, *The Soul of Politics*, 162–63.

Buffett is wealthy—not us. Several of our friends obviously have plenty of money . . . they can afford overseas trips . . . *they're* wealthy—not us.

Yes, they may all have more money than you or I, but the fact we have choices that most others in the world don't, places us in the ranks of the wealthy.

As we've seen, the Bible has much to say to the rich. But if we don't consider ourselves wealthy we will miss this. Or skip over it, thinking that Scripture is talking to billionaires and corporate masters—and perhaps those well-travelled friends of ours. But not to us.

Most of us, me included, have a natural pre-disposition to justify our own situation and actions. And to exempt ourselves from statements that seem a little challenging or unsettling.

For example, as Tony Campolo once noted, the way we see ourselves will affect the way we read passages like Mary's Magnificat in Luke 1:46–55: "He [God] bared his arm and showed his strength; Scattered the bluffing braggarts. He knocked tyrants off their high horses, Pulled victims out of the mud. The starving poor sat down to a banquet; The callous rich were left out in the cold."

Or, in another translation: "He has brought down the powerful from their thrones, and lifted up the lowly. He has filled the hungry with good things and sent the rich away empty."[2]

I cautiously suggest that when you read this you did not put yourself in the category of the "rich" that God has "sent away empty." It's our natural inclination to think, "Me, rich? No—never. I identify with the victims and the poor. Not with the bluffing braggarts and callous rich. Nor with the mighty and powerful. They're rightly damned for their arrogant behaviour!"

But could it be that God might be speaking *about us*—you and me?

This is a very uncomfortable place to find ourselves in. And most of us would prefer not to be there—me included!

Hope for us all

One could easily assume that given our natural predisposition to reading and interpreting the Bible through our own filtered lenses, we are hopelessly at sea without any chance of seeing clearly the distant headland, let

---

2. Luke 1:52–53 (NRSV).

alone reaching it. And it is certainly true that it's not easy to remove our blind spots, or even identify them.

We definitely can't hope to to do this alone. Thank God for the Holy Spirit. For it is the Spirit's role to break through our filters—to allow us to read with increasing clarity.

And we also need help from one another. That's one reason reading and reflecting on this book in the company of others is a helpful thing to do. For that purpose I've added some thought-prompting questions to each chapter. Don't just pass over them, will you!

Prayer

Lord, we are finite beings and very limited in our perspective.
You are infinite and unlimited.
We are broken and sin-ridden creatures.
You are the whole and holy creator.
We see through a glass dimly.
You see things in their completeness.
We see things as *we* are.
You see your universe and us as they *really* are.

So we ask for your help.
We want to hear and see you more clearly.
Break through our filtered lenses, we pray.
Open our eyes to help us see with increasing clarity *your* perspectives, *your* truth, and *your* direction.
Holy Spirit, we desperately need your enabling in this.
Amen.

Up Close and Personal

1. If you had to sum up the Bible's perspective on money in one or two sentences—on the basis of what you already know, how would you describe it?

2. Were you surprised to realize the prominence of the subject of money in Scripture? If you were, why do you think you had never spotted this?

3. What assumptions can you identify that you already carry regarding what the Bible says about money? Where do you think these assumptions have come from?

4. It's true, isn't it, that we don't see the warnings and condemnations given to the rich in Scripture as applying to us. Why do you think that might be the case?

Section A

Bible

Considering seven major themes of the Bible on money

God's intention was to bless his people in order for them to be a *Blessing* to the world. For the Israelites, their *Land* was a central part of this covenant relationship with God. It was a gift to be evenly distributed, providing the means for abundance and *Wealth*. However, when Israel disobeyed God, the Prophets sought to challenge them about issues of *Justice*. For the covenant carried with it certain responsibilities, including care for those who might become marginalized—the *Poor*. When Jesus came, he brought a stark choice between worship of God and *Mammon*. Money was not neutral to him, nor was it peripheral to his core message. In the early church, a natural implication of this was that *Giving* and sharing became central to the life of discipleship and Christian community.

3

Blessing

"I'll make you a great nation and bless you. I'll make you famous; you'll be a blessing. I'll bless those who bless you; those who curse you I'll curse. All the families of the Earth will be blessed through you."
Genesis 12: 2–3

Pastor Mike was at full throttle. It was just before noon on a warm spring Sunday. His message on faith had gone down a treat. It was time to nail it home.

"God wants to bless you. He *wants* you to be prosperous and wealthy."

Amen's sprinkled the auditorium.

"In fact, I'll go so far as to say that if you're not succeeding financially, you're not living within God's will.

"We are, after all, the King's kids. The wealth of the Kingdom is ours. God wants the very best for you—and for me.

"The problem, people," pausing slightly for effect, "is that we do not *expect* God's blessing to be on our finances. We are not exercising faith. If we truly believed, the blessing of God would rain down upon us. Those amongst us who are struggling with not having enough money, those who are not enjoying the abundant, prosperous life Jesus talked about . . . you need to hear this message today. It is God's will that you experience his blessing in your bank account."

Section A: Bible

Close to fever pitch, Pastor Mike reached his climax—"So reach out and claim his blessing today!"

A wave of applause washed over the auditorium.

"We're going to take up the offering now. We're going to give to God so that he can give to us. God is no man's debtor. God will bless you a hundredfold when you give to him. So bless God with your offering today and I can promise you that you will be blessed financially like you've never been blessed before. Let us pray."

God's blessing

The so-called Prosperity (or Health-and-Wealth) Gospel has been around for a while. And it comes in various shapes and forms, not all of them as blatant as Pastor Mike's. In fact, the problem with heresies is that they are rarely black-and-white obvious. Generally they take the subtle form of a twist on the truth. That's why heresies are often called "half-truths."

It *is* true that God wants to bless us. And, as we'll see, this *is* about more than just a "spiritual rejoicing." That's the half that is truth.

So what is the full truth, and what is it about the Bible's message on money that such characters as Pastor Mike omit? How do they manufacture their "Prosperity Gospel"? How do they manipulate Scripture to claim that if we live in a certain way God will bless us with hard cash?

This is an important question, and we're going to look into it. But first, let's focus on those words "bless" and "blessing." What do they refer to when used in the Bible?

While this word group covers a wide range of uses and situations, three broad types of blessing tend to dominate:

God blessing us

In the Old Testament, God is seen as the true source of all blessing. When God blesses us he bestows favor and goodness on us, contributing to our well-being—physically, socially, emotionally, environmentally, and economically.

Us blessing God

When we "bless" God we give God praise. We adore and worship him. We honor him. It's because of God's loving-kindness and faithfulness toward us that we can, in gratitude, bless him.

Us blessing others

When we bless others we commend them to God, interceding for them, or praising them for something they did or said or modeled. Sometimes a person blesses others by giving money or possessions to them—like a gift from a benefactor to someone in need, or like a legacy you might leave to your children.

Original intentions

In the beginning, God's blessing was intended to be central to our life here on earth. The creation account of Genesis makes it very clear that God planned for humanity to enjoy the beauty, abundance, and fruitfulness of creation. In the idyllic setting of the Garden, the first humans were commanded to "be fruitful and multiply," and to "till and keep" the land. This was a richly fertile place, and humanity was intended to prosper in every sense.

As the writer of Genesis states early on in the story: "When God created the human race, he made it godlike, with a nature akin to God. He created both male and female and *blessed* them, the whole human race."[1]

Part of the blessing of relationship with God was very definitely tangible, in-the-hand stuff. And these material blessings were thoroughly integrated with the other benefits of knowing and loving the Creator.

So in the first two chapters of Genesis we find a vision of a harmonized world—where all relationships are complete and whole. That is, intimacy and community with God spills over into the other fundamental relationships of life—our relationship with ourselves, with each other, and with the wider created order.

The Jews would later describe this kind of integrated life and world as *shalom*. The words harmony, peace, wholeness, and completeness all provide windows into the full range of this blessed state.

---

1. Gen 5:1–2. Italicised emphasis is mine.

Section A: Bible

Disaster

Of course, as we all know, this shalom did not last for long. The rebellion of the first humans had a catastrophic effect not only on their relationship with God but also on themselves—psychologically, emotionally, socially, ecologically. And certainly economically.

As a result of the Fall, people begin to live more under a curse than a blessing. The land, and therefore its productivity and fruitfulness, is deeply impacted by the breaking of relationship with God, prompting the Creator to say to Adam: "[As a result of your disobedience] The very ground is cursed . . . getting food from the ground will be as painful as having babies is for your wife; you'll be working in pain all your life long. The ground will sprout thorns and weeds, you'll get your food the hard way, planting and tilling and harvesting, sweating in the fields from dawn to dusk . . ."[2]

The Fall has many lessons for us. One is that when we break our relationship with God we set in motion a whole raft of problems. Because God is the source of blessing, being no longer close to him affects all aspects of life—including the economic.

Fortunately, as we know, the story doesn't end there. God persisted with the human project, in spite of the depressing saga of the Flood. However, even when he began again with Noah and his extended family, wickedness and rebellion soon took hold, resulting in the Tower of Babel (described in Genesis 11). This was really the nadir of God's relationship with humankind; it was the last straw for God. The people decided they no longer needed God to bless them, they could quite happily bless themselves, developing their own great enterprise independent of God. Such was their egotistical arrogance.

A new initiative—covenant community

And then the story unexpectedly turns a corner and shifts gear. In Genesis 11–12 we are introduced to Abram (soon to be Abraham). We read that God chooses to make a covenant—an agreement—with this man. God directs him: "Leave your country, your family, and your father's home, for a land that I will show you. I'll make you a great nation and bless you. I'll make you famous; you'll be a blessing. I'll bless those who

---

2. Gen 3:17b–19a.

bless you; those who curse you I'll curse. All the families of the Earth will be blessed through you."[3]

The apparent absurdity of all this must have struck Abram and Sarai, his wife. He was already seventy-five years old and childless! What was the point of God promising that he would be the father of a great nation, when he didn't have any children to start with?

Nevertheless, the covenant Yahweh[4] makes with Abram forms the foundation for a succeeding covenant he makes with Abram's descendants—the people of Israel—at Mount Sinai. And then ultimately it leads to the new covenant Jesus establishes with his disciples at the Last Supper.

Yahweh restates his commitment to Abraham in Genesis 17, saying, "I am the Strong God, live entirely before me, live to the hilt! I'll make a covenant between us and I'll give you a huge family."[5] He then goes on to give more details regarding the covenant.

Covenant is not a word that we use a lot these days. However, it occurs 287 times in the Old Testament and is critical to the biblical story—as well as to understanding the nature of God's blessing. A covenant is quite different from a contract. It is not simply a business deal, but involves a mutual desire for intimate relationship. While Scripture mentions various types of covenants, generally the word describes an agreement between two parties involving promises, obligations, and reciprocal responsibilities.

An important element of this covenant is that God envisages a "people" of his own, not just an individual or even a series of individuals. In other words, God was establishing a *covenant community*. Within the context of that community his blessings could be experienced. If the people of the community joined with him in intimate relationship and obedience, they would enjoy the blessing of shalom. So that they would understand the requirements of this community, God gave his people the Law (Torah). It unpacked the specifics of *how* they (and the nations through them) could experience God's blessing.

So in what way did Yahweh intend to bless Abraham and his descendants through this covenant?

---

3. Gen 12:2–3.

4. Because, as we will see, the biblical material on wealth is so closely woven into God's covenant with Abraham and his descendants, I frequently use the more personal name "Yahweh," by which God chose to identify himself to the Israelites.

5. Gen 17:1–2.

Section A: Bible

When the words "I will bless you" are spoken here, they certainly include *physical* blessing. Yahweh's intention was that Abraham would become the first of a family with growing numbers of descendants, all of them with a strong sense of identity and belonging to Yahweh. And, as we will see in the next chapter, they would have a fertile land to dwell in and make their own, a land "flowing rich with milk and honey."

Furthermore, God's plans extended to the whole world. The covenant was to bring blessing *through* Abraham as much as blessing *to* Abraham. We see Yahweh signaling that Abraham and his family are going to be God's instrument in reversing the curses of the Fall, and bringing about salvation to the whole of creation. The narrowing down (or particularizing) of God to one family was not a rejection of everyone else. Far from it. It was the beginning of something huge. Universal blessing was to flow from this particular covenant relationship.

Look into God's covenant with Abraham and you will see that it is full of promises. That's because it is focused on the future. We know from the Genesis story (and also from Hebrews 11) that Abraham needed to be a person of faith—and faithfulness—because only a small portion of these promises of blessing was fulfilled in his own lifetime. Indeed, it took several hundred years for the people of God to possess the land Yahweh had promised them and to enjoy the blessing of self-government under his rule. Even then, the fulfillment of these covenantal promises was not complete. In fact, the unfolding fulfillment continues to this day.

This highlights a very important point—and one that Pastor Mike needs to understand. Yahweh's blessing is able to be partly experienced in the here-and-now . . . but there's a broad aspect of it that won't be fulfilled until the end of this age. The whole range of God's blessing—his complete shalom—won't occur until God's rule is fully present or realized. Even though we may experience elements of prosperity and good health, they are only an incomplete foretaste of what is still to come.

So to sum up . . .

- God's intention from the very beginning has been to bless humankind.
- This blessing is thoroughly tied to covenant relationship—with obligations and responsibilities on both sides. God's blessing in the Old Testament is experienced by the covenant community (that is, by the Israelites) as they live in loyalty and faithfulness to their God.

- God's blessing very definitely includes the economic side of life, as it does every other dimension.
- Some of the blessing of God can be experienced now, but it won't be fully realized until the end of this age.

Pastor Mike has it only partly right—and therein lies the problem. It's one we'll return to in chapter 5 on Wealth. But before that we'll turn, in the next chapter, to the role that land plays in God's covenant promise of blessing to Abraham and his descendants.

Up Close and Personal

1. Have you heard a sermon similar to Pastor Mike's? If so, can you recall how it made you feel at the time? Did it prompt you to any particular actions? Looking back on it, what do you think?

2. The idea of "blessing" is a word that's hard to pin down. When you hear it, what does it bring to mind for you? What about the phrase "the blessing of God"?

3. Think through two or three blessings in your own life that flow from your love of God. What practical behavior on your part have these blessings led to? (If you're reading this book with a group, share one of your blessings.)

4. Read Genesis 12:1–What does the passage mean when it says, "All the families of the Earth will be blessed through you"? What "blessings" will those families experience?

4

Land

"God claims Earth and everything in it, God claims World and all who live on it."
Psalm 24:1

IN THE 1860s, NEW Zealand became embroiled in what are usually now called the Land Wars. The conflict began when indigenous Maori tribes reacted to persistent violations of the original treaty they had signed with the British Crown in 1840.

Pressure had been building for some years. With increasing numbers of European settlers desperate to buy farmland and real estate, questionable land deals were completed. As a result, many Maori found themselves disenfranchised from their traditional hunting, fishing, and agricultural areas.

Inevitably, the grievances finally came to a head. Fighting flared up, troops were called in, and soon campaigns were being waged in parts of the country. At first Maori tactics won them numerous successes but eventually the colonial forces, with their superior weaponry and numbers, quelled Maori resistance. As a result of these "rebellions," the European government of the day began confiscating large tracts of tribal territory. This land grab continued in waves for several decades.

In 1975, a court named the Waitangi Tribunal was finally established to hear the grievances of Maori, and to arbitrate on historical land claims. This proved to be a deeply complex process—one that is still continuing more than thirty years later. Much of its challenge has been determining who had claim to what, more than a century after the fact, especially since Maori land was communally owned. It is further complicated by the number of ownership transactions on much of this land since confiscation.

At the heart of all this has been a difference over the role of land in the life and understanding of two different peoples.

The Maori word for "land"—*whenua*—is also their word for "placenta." This is more than just coincidence. It indicates a strong tie between the Maori people and the land they inhabit. The territory a particular Maori *iwi* (tribe) occupies is intimately connected with the identity of its members. It is like an umbilical cord, tying people and land together in a symbiotic and somewhat spiritual relationship. Traditionally, Maori view themselves as *kaitiaki* (guardians) of the land, the sea, and the sky. This caretaking role is also generational. That is, one's identity is rooted not just in the land, but also in one's *whakapapa* (genealogical/ancestral lineage).

And, of course, since Maori knew little, if anything, of private ownership, the land was "owned" by the *iwi* or the *hapu* (the extended family group), not by the individual.

For those who have grown up in European cultures, this is all somewhat unfamiliar territory. We are used to viewing land in much more utilitarian and individualistic ways. It is there to be used. It is a resource. And its value has to do primarily with its potential for producing. We might think nothing of selling land and buying another property somewhere else. Our identity is rarely tied up with our land—though some farming families would have elements of this kind of generational attachment and connection to "place." And the idea that we might have to consult others before deciding to sell would not normally is a consideration.

When Maori looked for some form of redress of the wrongs of the past, their concern was not primarily about the economic value of the land. Though that is a factor, for them the issue was, and still is, much deeper. Their ties to the land go to the heart of their identity and their history as a people. And in that sense they have a lot in common with the people of Israel.

The people of Israel

Land forms a crucial piece in the puzzle of the Old Testament's take on money and possessions. In fact, we cannot gain an understanding of

Section A: Bible

God's covenant relationship with the people of Israel (and of their sense of identity) without appreciating the central role the land played in this. Old Testament scholar Chris Wright portrays this three-way relationship in the form of a triangle:[1]

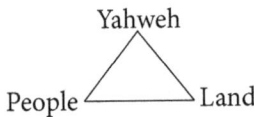

Their identity as a people was (and still is, in many ways) tied deeply to the land. As we noted in the last chapter, the starting point was the covenant Yahweh made with Abraham.

The land as promise, gift and blessing

Yahweh's promise to Abraham and his descendants included the provision of a specific land (hence the phrase: Promised Land, referring to Canaan). Of course, after a few short generations the ties with Canaan were cut. Jacob and his family, faced with a disastrous famine, made the decision to immigrate to Egypt.

It was not until several hundred years later—following enslavement in Egypt, the Exodus, and the Wilderness experience—that the Israelites returned to Canaan. But even then, the promised territory was only partially occupied. What's more, that too was eventually lost. The persistent breaking of the covenant by the people and their kings finally led to their exile. There was ample warning. Successive prophets railed against Israel for decades. But sadly, the people and their leaders did not change their ways, and so they were dragged off to Babylon.

When your identity as a people is connected so strongly with the earth you inhabit, being torn from it is a viscerally painful and disorienting process. No wonder they so deeply lamented and longed for their homeland while in exile: "By the rivers of Babylon, we sat down and wept, when we remembered Zion."[2]

---

1. See Wright, *God's People in God's Land*, 105. Wright goes further by noting the role of family as the basic unit of Israel's system of land tenure.

2. Ps 137:1 (NIV).

Land

Ownership and trusteeship

The Promised Land was a gift from Yahweh to the people. However, Yahweh did not give the land absolutely—it remained his (as is the whole earth) and he gave it to his people "on trust." The land was an essential provision for their well-being, and the covenant was the "trust deed." It set out how they were to act in relation to God, to one another, and to the land, in order to experience the blessing Yahweh intended. The people's failure to keep covenant meant they were not being faithful trustees of this Promised Land.

Leviticus 25:23 puts it dramatically, in a way that comes as an unexpected jolt to those of us with European thinking about property: "The land cannot be sold permanently because *the land is mine* and you are *foreigners*—you're my *tenants*."[3]

One of King David's psalms reinforces this: "God claims Earth and everything in it, God claims World and all who live on it."[4]

So on the one hand, the land was part of God's generous provision for his people, intended for their blessing. On the other, this wonderful resource was to be used according to God's direction. The people were trustees, answerable to God.[5] When they lived faithful to the covenant—faithful to God—the land produced great blessing.

Why "foreigners"?

The Leviticus statement that we've just seen introduces language that seems at odds with the promised gift of the land. The surprise comes from two words: *foreigners* (or *aliens* or *sojourners* depending on which Bible translation you choose), and *tenants*.

Walter Bruggemann notes: "'Sojourner' is a technical word usually described as 'resident alien.' It means to be in a place, perhaps for an extended time, to live there and take some roots, but always to be an outsider, never belonging."[6]

A "foreigner" in your own land? The phrase is pregnant with paradox. It's like saying: "I've given you this land as a people, so make

---

3. Italics are my emphasis.
4. Ps 24:1.
5. I'll look specifically at the concept of trusteeship in chapter 18.
6. Bruggemann, *Interpretation and Obedience*, 294.

Section A: Bible

yourselves at home here, enjoying the fruit of its earth. But don't make yourselves too comfortable. It's not your real, ultimate home. Remember you're just passing through. So you'll always be living with a certain degree of ambiguity. For your ultimate inheritance, your full blessing as my people is in the future. This means that my promise to your forefathers is yet to be fulfilled completely. And by the way, this is *my* land—you're just managing it for me."

Laws relating to property and possessions

Given the role of the land as a key element of God's covenant promise, gift, blessing, inheritance, and identity, it is not surprising that a fair chunk of the Jewish Law relates to matters of property.

In an agrarian-based society, land is absolutely fundamental to being able to live. If people are dispossessed of their land, either through fair means or foul, the results are disastrous for them and their family. That is why significant attention was given in the Law to providing mechanisms and safeguards for protecting people's livelihoods.

Some of these related to ensuring the land wasn't over-farmed, like the provision of a sabbatical year for resting the ground from production, in order to revitalize the soil and pasture. Other laws were concerned with protecting what was, in one sense, the only relatively reliable asset they owned. For example, the year of Jubilee (to be observed every fiftieth year) was established to help protect the capacity of *all* the people of Israel (every household and "clan") to thrive economically, and to assist the passing down of land title from generation to generation. Its purpose was to relieve the economic pressure on the poor, and to counter a tendency that is constantly seen in history—the tendency over time for property to accumulate in the hands of a wealthy few. Though there are questions as to whether it was ever seriously practiced, the year of Jubilee sought to realign assets, and in doing so to maintain the vision of shalom.

Tentative implications

So how should we interpret the centrality of land in God's covenant with Abraham—and how should we make use of its principles in the twenty-first century?

We have to be tentative here—for two important reasons. As we have seen, the promised land and its role in God's blessing was particularly tied to Israel's covenant relationship with Yahweh. In this sense it was unique. Additionally, we clearly live in a very different cultural and economic environment—one where, for a start, the means of production is tied far less directly to the land.

However, there are some general implications we can make from Israel's context, which also apply to our own situation. They are worth pondering. According to the Bible:

- *All* that we have and are is first and foremost, *gift*. Pure and simple.

- Ownership of land and property is ultimately *God's*, not ours. Any claim we have to land, money or possessions is provisional, not absolute.

- Because God is the owner, our role is to be *stewards*—managers or trustees of the resources that have been entrusted to us. We'll explore this more fully in chapter 18, but suffice to say, the concept of stewardship is fundamental to a biblical view of resources. Plus—and this is important—such a role should not be viewed in solely individualistic terms. Stewardship is a communal responsibility. Part of our role is cultivating and conserving ("to till and keep") the land as the economic source/base of human, and indeed all, life.

- Everybody on our planet has a right to a share in the planet's resources. While personal wealth is recognized in the Bible—as part of God's gift and generosity to us—it cannot claim priority over the rights of other humans to participate in life at a meaningful level.

- As much as we are to make ourselves at home in this world and to revel in the goodness of God's earth, we need to remember that we are *sojourners*—resident aliens—with our eyes on the future fulfillment of God's promises. This brings a perspective to our lives and dreams and schemes. It should cause us to hold lightly the material things of this world.

Up Close and Personal

1. How do you think about land? For example, for you is it a resource which you are happy to freely buy and sell, or is it a part of your life

Section A: Bible

    to be treasured? Or something else . . . ? Where do these attitudes of yours come from?

2. Discuss your views on the role of "private property." How consistent are they with Old Testament principles?

3. Describe an experience where you have been a stranger or alien. How did it feel?

4. If you have lived as a "resident alien" in another country for a period of time, share your experiences with the others in your group. What freedoms did such a status give you? What limits did it impose on you? How did this affect the way you lived there?

5

Wealth

"Make sure that when you eat and are satisfied, build pleasant houses and settle in, see your herds and flocks flourish and more and more money come in, watch your standard of living going up and up—make sure you don't become so full of yourself and your things that you forget GOD, your God . . ."
Deuteronomy 8:12–14

CATHY IS CEO OF her own IT company. Specializing in web design and graphic art, this innovative firm has grown quickly in what is a competitive but highly profitable industry. Cathy employs twenty-two staff, and the company's regular clients include government departments and several publicly listed corporations.

Cathy lives in an expensive home on the upmarket west side of the city, with her husband Brad who is a deputy principal of a high school. They are both in their late thirties and are unable to have children. Together, they attend a large, inner-city church that is led by an entrepreneurial pastor who seems to value people in business, and corporate high fliers. At any rate, he values the money they bring with them. In her worst moments, Cathy feels that her contribution is measured by how many dollars she gives to the church and its big-budget projects.

She knows she has a gift for making money and that she is fortunate to be in an industry that pulls the big bucks. That said, Cathy is a very generous woman. She loves to contribute to causes that are making a difference. And yet when she sits in church services and meetings, she doesn't feel valued for her other gifts which could contribute to the life of the church community. And she gets virtually no help working through how her faith might impact on her work. Any interest in her role in the market place is all one-dimensional—nothing much beyond how well her company is doing and therefore (though, of course, no-one is quite so crass as to put this in words) how much she will be able to give to church schemes this year.

That question about "how her faith might impact on her work" is getting to be a bit of a niggle these days. Cathy has now been in the business long enough for the glow of success to be dying down a bit. Questions are beginning to surface in her mind that she would never have thought of ten years ago. Questions about herself and her faith and her wealth and her involvement in life . . . Or, more precisely (since Cathy is nothing if not precise):

- Is my growing wealth a blessing from God or is it just because I'm good at making money and have got some breaks? Or perhaps I should be feeling guilty about all the money I have . . . Is my rather "sheltered" and "upmarket" life, which consists of mixing it with prosperous and well-to-do clients, workers, neighbors, and friends—in other words, people just like me and Brad—is that all that I'm called to be involved in? I live in a bit of a bubble, enjoying a life of privilege that few others enjoy. People defer to me and treat me as special because of my money. I remember how I used to think that was silly—but I notice that I'm now taking it for granted. Is that healthy?

- Are my church friends right when they say that "the rich need Jesus too," and that in order to reach these people God has put folk like me in their world—people who have a similar lifestyle and standard of living? But are they the *only* ones I'm called to influence? And if they are, *how* should I influence them?

- Should I feel uneasy (I *do* feel uneasy) about one or two of the corporates and businesses that we do work for? Like the company we help actively market their high-end, luxury goods for outrageous prices, when I know they are sourcing their products from sweatshop labor in Asia? Should I just turn a blind eye to this? And anyway, what *can* I do?

As you can see, Cathy is grappling with some tough questions. And like all tough questions, there are not likely to be any simple, easy answers.

When we looked at the Bible (and especially the Old Testament), we found a remarkable picture of God's plans for our world. What might we find if we (and Cathy) were to look at how the Bible views wealth?

Depending on the circles we mix in, we may have received very different messages about wealth. For some people in the church being rich is a sign of God's blessing; for others it's something to be avoided; for those in the middle it's something to be cautious about—or at least wise and restrained. But that's hardly surprising, since the Bible itself *seems* to communicate mixed messages.

Many of the Old Testament characters we most revere were wealthy. That is, they had more than they "needed"—an abundance of resources; a surplus to their daily requirements.[1] They include Abraham, Isaac, Jacob, Joseph, Boaz, Job, David, Solomon, and Nehemiah. Remember that in ancient times the primary means of wealth was land and livestock, which accounts for most of these men's wealth.

In the New Testament we have a handful of others such as Joseph of Arimathea and Nicodemus who are identified as wealthy, along with the "rich young ruler." Plus one or two whom we meet in passing. Like Lydia, the dealer in purple cloth.[2]

Let's look at some of these characters—to see what they did with their wealth and what it had to do with their faith in Yahweh.

Abraham

The "father" (or grand-daddy) of the Jewish nation, Abraham was a very wealthy man. He owned substantial livestock and had numerous servants in his household.[3]

While it is implied that Abraham and his wife Sarah were already well off when Yahweh first called them, God's covenant to "bless" Abram and his descendants led to the amassing of some serious wealth. This fits in with what we saw in chapter 3, where God's blessing of the "patriarchs" (Abraham, Isaac, and Jacob) very much *included* material prosperity.

---

1. Of course, I'm aware that the word "need" is somewhat problematic because of the way we've lost touch in recent years with a healthy distinction between needs and wants. This is an issue I'll explore in chapter 13.

2. Acts 16:14–15.

3. Gen 13:2.

Section A: Bible

Abraham was not only very wealthy, he was also very generous. For example, he allowed his nephew Lot to choose the better land when they reached Canaan. He also gave a "tithe" to Melchizedek, the king of Salem, and he offered generous hospitality to travellers (Gen 18).

Boaz

In the book of Ruth we meet Boaz, a wealthy and prominent landowner. We don't know a lot about him, but the account gives a very clear insight into how he used his wealth.

When Boaz went out one day to greet his workers and check on progress with his harvest, he discovered Ruth, a young Moabite woman, gleaning in his fields. Ruth had courageously accompanied her Jewish mother-in-law Naomi back to Israel, after both Naomi's and Ruth's husbands died. Since both were widows—and Ruth was also a foreigner—neither of them had legal access to land. Life was a real struggle for these two women. And that's where we discover that Boaz was a compassionate, hospitable, and generous man who considered that what he had been blessed with was not just there for his own pleasure. He went well beyond societal expectations in providing Ruth and Naomi with more than enough to feed them.

In this sense, Boaz represents the very best of what the covenant intends faithful Yahweh-worship to look like. And his actions led to a non-Jew (Ruth) becoming included in the covenant community, and experiencing all the blessings that went with this.[4]

Job

In the first chapter of the book named after him, Job is introduced as being "totally devoted to God" and also being "very wealthy—seven thousand head of sheep, three thousand camels, five hundred teams of oxen, five hundred donkeys, and a huge staff of servants—the most influential man in all the East!"[5] Even in today's terms Job was very well off. And it was both his wealth and his commitment to God that attracted Satan's attention. Right at the beginning of the story it is fascinating to see how

---

4. In fact, Ruth became part of the generational line to King David, and ultimately Jesus.

5. Job 1:3.

confident God was that Job's "righteousness" was not dependent on his wealth and health.

We also discover through Job's lengthy discourse how Job has lived and why God thought so highly of him. One of the striking features was his involvement in the public affairs of his community, and in the care of the poor.[6] Job's life intersected with the poor of his district on a regular basis. He was not isolated from them but lived in close proximity to his servants, widows, the fatherless, and the stranger/traveller (to whom his "door was always open"). He "knew" the poor, treated them as equals, and his relationship with them led to a deep compassion and care for them.

At one level, the story of Job is a serious knock to the belief that wealth is an automatic result of faithfulness to God. In fact, it is this issue more than any other, which Job's "friends" tripped over. Their counsel was built on the flawed theology that sickness and poverty are the result of our disobedience to God. This common view among the Jews continued into New Testament times. Jesus encountered it on a number of occasions.

However, at another level, Job demonstrated that it *is* possible to love God faithfully, act justly toward people, and be rich.

Solomon

When we think of wealthy Old Testament characters our minds are immediately drawn to King Solomon. And there's good reason for that. Solomon became unbelievably rich and it is in his reign that Israel's wealth and power reached its zenith.

However, given that he is also known for his wisdom, it seems ironic that Solomon's conspicuous and over-the-top consumption not only contributed to his rejection of God's covenant, but also laid the foundation for tearing Israel apart. What began as a reign of wisdom, generosity, and devotion to Yahweh, descended into one of excessive opulence and idolatry. Solomon's wealth (along with his foreign wives) became a corrupting influence. Read in context, this is a sobering tale of how seductive and dangerous wealth can be.

---

6. See Job 29:7–25; 31:13–34.

Section A: Bible

Is wealth an Old Testament sign of blessing by God?

Remember Pastor Mike from chapter 3? He's our "health and wealth" preacher who forged a link between faith and finance. In essence, Pastor Mike was insisting that if we live in a certain way God would bless us materially. At its most extreme such teaching contends that God wants you and me to be rich and healthy. And if we aren't, there are only two possible explanations—either we are not being obedient to God, or we are not exercising enough faith.

Of course, we can see where Pastor Mike gets his prosperity doctrine. The Old Testament provides him with plenty of quotable people and statements. For example, Abraham and his descendants *appear* to model this viewpoint. And then the Wisdom literature—that's books such as Proverbs, Ecclesiastes, and Psalms—often connects righteousness with prosperity. For example, in Proverbs 3, we get the well-known saying: "Honor GOD with everything you own; give him the first and the best [in other translations: 'the first fruits']. Your barns will burst, your wine vats will brim over."[7]

Pastor Mike couldn't have said it better himself! But then, choosing a single verse is the best way to oversimplify. As Craig Blomberg points out in his study on material possessions in the Bible: "Wealth *can* be a sign of God's blessing, even if it is not always related to an individual's or a nation's obedience. But the unique covenantal arrangements between God and Israel prevent us from generalizing and saying that God *must* materially reward his faithful people in other nations or eras."[8]

Blomberg argues that most Old Testament promises of prosperity must be viewed through the framework of God's covenant with God's people. Such wealth is invariably connected to the Promised Land, the sacrificial form of worship and the expectation that the people would, as a result of their blessing, bless the nations. We don't live in quite the same context so we can't automatically assume that wealth is the result of God's blessing.

In fact, we need to be extremely careful in assuming a *quid pro quo* link between righteousness and prosperity. The link is even more tenuous in the New Testament, as we'll see in chapter 8. Biblical scholar Gordon

---

7. Prov 3: 8–9.
8. Blomberg, *Neither Poverty nor Riches*, 51.

Fee argues that in the New Testament possessions are *never* related to a life of obedience—even though they sometimes are in the Old.[9]

Even with characters such as Joseph, Job and David, who were all wealthy at some stage in their lives, their life trajectory and circumstances don't mirror how faithful they are to God. For example, Joseph's integrity led him to a prison cell. Job found himself losing his considerable wealth for a time, to say nothing of his children and his health. David was tormented by Saul and run out of town.

And there are many other men and women of God in the Old Testament who weren't "blessed" with any such riches, in spite of their commitment to Yahweh.

On the other side of the equation, there are also more than enough people of wealth who prosper through their wickedness. We've already noted Solomon. Several of his descendants continue the trend, including Ahab. In 1 Kings 21 we read that the king lusted after Naboth's land and when he failed to acquire it by fair means, his wife Jezebel had Naboth executed. This, even though Ahab was already unbelievably wealthy.

The dangers of wealth

So even though some Old Testament scriptures link wealth to God's blessing, there are other passages that alert the reader to the truth that wealth is dangerous. Riches can cause all kinds of negative side effects...

Firstly, wealth often leads to pride and arrogance. Proverbs 28:11 notes: "The rich think they know it all, but the poor can see right through them." It is easy for those with wealth to believe they have gained it through their own cleverness. Ezekiel warns the King of Tyre, "Your sharp intelligence made you world-wealthy. You piled up gold and silver in your banks. You used your head well, worked good deals, made a lot of money. But the money has gone to your head, swelled your head—what a big head!"[10] "Self-made men and women" are particularly susceptible to this insidious self-belief.

Secondly, wealth frequently leads to self-sufficiency, complacency, and a false sense of security. One extreme example of this is Ephraim's boast in Hosea 12:8: "Look, I'm rich! I've made it big! And look how well I've covered my tracks: not a hint of fraud, not a sign of sin!" And

---

9. See Fee, *The Disease of the Health & Wealth Gospels*, 9.
10. Ezek 28:5.

the prophetic words of Hosea a chapter later are also very poignant—describing Israel's abandonment of Yahweh—"I took care of you, took care of all your needs, gave you everything you needed. You were spoiled. You thought you didn't need me. You forgot me."[11] It is only too easy to think that we have no need of God when our bellies are full, life is good, and the future seems assured.

Thirdly, wealth can also dull our senses to the deep needs around us (Solomon being a good example), draining compassion and mercy from us.

Fourthly, and most seductive of all, is the lure riches have in capturing our hearts and dividing our loyalties. Here we see the Bible's acknowledgment of the power that money wields. The Psalmist warns us of this when he writes: "Though your riches increase, do not set your heart on them."[12]

This danger is also carefully spelled out for the people of Israel in Deuteronomy 8:10–20:

> After a meal, satisfied, bless GOD, your God, for the good land he has given you.
>
> Make sure you don't forget GOD, your God, by not keeping his commandments, his rules and regulations that I command you today.
>
> Make sure that when you eat and are satisfied, build pleasant houses and settle in, see your herds and flocks flourish and more and more money come in, watch your standard of living going up and up—make sure you don't become so full of yourself and your things that you forget GOD, your God . . .
>
> If you start thinking to yourselves, "I did all this. And all by myself. I'm rich. It's all mine!"—well, think again. Remember that GOD, your God, gave you the strength to produce all this wealth so as to confirm the covenant that he promised to your ancestors—as it is today.
>
> If you forget, forget GOD, your God, and start taking up with other gods, serving and worshipping them, I'm on record right now as giving you firm warning: that will be the end of you; I mean it—destruction.

Sobering words.

---

11. Hos 13:6.
12. Ps 62:10b (NIV).

And very consistent with the New Testament's perspective which we'll consider in chapters 8 and 9.

A mixed review

So money and wealth get a mixed review in the Old Testament. While there are some wonderful examples of wealthy people employing their prosperity for the good of others, the Bible also reveals a very dark side.

We've seen some of that dark side in this chapter: the way riches can destroy their possessor. In the next we'll see how wealth can lead to the bitter oppression of others.

Up Close and Personal

1. How many possessions do you need to be considered wealthy? Would you call yourself rich? Affluent?

2. Discuss the various dangers of wealth that are mentioned in the Old Testament quotations toward the end of this chapter. Can you see examples of any of these in our culture? What about closer to home—do you recognize any of these temptations in yourself?

3. When Christians think about King Solomon, do you think they see him in a more *positive* or more *negative* light? Why do you think this is?

4. Re-read Cathy's story at the start of the chapter—and particularly her questions.

    - What are some of the factors you think would be important for her to consider?

    - Do you identify with any of her challenges or questions? In what way?

    - How would you answer Cathy if she asked you your opinion?

5. Read through Job 2What do you notice most about Job's attitude and relationship with the "poor" in his neighborhood? If we were to learn from his example, what do you think might be some of the implications for the way we live?

6

Justice

> *"Do you know what I want? I want justice—oceans of it. I want fairness—rivers of it. That's what I want. That's all I want."*
> Amos 5:24

I WAS A LITTLE anxious. There were just a handful of white faces on the plane, but my unease had nothing to do with being outnumbered ethnically. The real reason was that this was only three weeks after the bloody pro-democracy demonstrations, and I still wasn't sure it was the most sensible thing to do, continuing with my short visit to the Asian hotspot of Myanmar—Burma that was. Even though my visa application had been miraculously granted (or so it seemed to me), I was a little nervous about what to expect. A few more tourists would have eased my anxiety.

But here I was, nonetheless. My Burmese friend met me at the airport. His smiling face was a welcome sight. I had expected a tough interrogation at the immigration and customs desks, but it took only a few minutes to get through the officials. We left the extravagant (and nearly empty) new terminal and headed for a taxi, for the ride into Yangon.

The next few days were a strange mix of the familiar and the disorienting. To all intents and purposes, the city looked like many another Asian metropolis, though it didn't have the in-your-face poverty and barrenness of a Kolkata or a Manila. But neither was it an affluent and immaculate Singapore. However, it *was* very green and, in a run-down kind of way, very beautiful. Stunning Buddhist pagodas (temples) dominated the skyline and the vegetation was lush.

But beneath the surface I could tell that things were not well. The stress and tension were palpable.

Trying to make sense of how this country worked was not easy. There was no banking system. Cash ruled the day—either US dollars or the local currency converted at exorbitant government-set exchange rates. I stayed at a fancy hotel just down the road from my hosts—feeling deeply uncomfortable with my "digs." Not only were they a radical contrast to the conditions of my friend's apartment, they were also flasher than anything I'd previously stayed in, bar the hotel in Singapore on the way over. My friend explained that it was illegal to have people to stay in homes. A hotel or guesthouse was the only option.

To my surprise (call it naivety!) I noticed that most of the guests in the hotel and restaurant were Burmese. Clearly there were some locals who were doing very well economically. Yet out on the streets it was evident that most people were barely scratching out a living. I talked to a man who was a teacher. He explained that his government pay had recently been cut, and was far from sufficient for even basic survival.

Meeting me for dinner that evening, my host casually remarked that the owner of the hotel was in prison, and had been for several years. Evidently he had refused to "pay off" the military junta with the necessary bribes and favors required to stay in business.

Fear and anxiety was never far from the surface in my conversations with Burmese. Many seemed to live with perpetually high levels of stress—no doubt amplified even more by the events of the previous month's demonstrations and the subsequent clampdown. Rumors flew around the city; thousands of people were thought to be missing.

One evening a young man whom I enjoyed a meal with opened up about what it was like to be unexpectedly found in the middle of one of the demonstrations. He was returning home from study, but got caught in the gunfire. The young man saw people shot and killed alongside him. Thinking he was going to die, he ran and ran, somehow miraculously managing to escape the fast-closing ring of soldiers. The trauma was clearly visible in this young man's eyes, speech, and tears.

On another evening my host failed to appear for dinner. I discovered late that night that the military had unexpectedly turned up at his apartment and taken him away for questioning and the usual threats.

One day we took a taxi out of Yangon to the countryside, to visit a village. The wide roads of the city were potholed and most of the houses and shacks dilapidated. But every now and then we passed flash housing estates that wouldn't have looked out of place in Florida or Hawaii. My friend explained that they were houses for the military.

At one point we passed a heavily barricaded and armed side road. My friend leaned over to me and said, "The democracy leader, Aung San Suu Kyi, lives down there." I was familiar with the years she had been under house arrest and the "reasons" for it.

My visit to Myanmar was only a few days long. Driving back to the airport I pondered the unfairness of it all. Here I was, free to exit this oppressive city—back to a life of liberty and ease, while my friend remained.

If there was one word that summed up my impressions of this beautiful land and its beautiful people, it was *injustice*. How could it be, I thought to myself as the plane lifted off, that the people I met had to endure such deprivation and hardship? This country, after all, was for many centuries known as "the rice bowl of South East Asia," a land rich in natural resources—rice, timber, minerals, and natural gas—now ruled with an iron fist by a brutal military dictatorship. These officers lived in luxury and unimaginable extravagance, while their own people eked out a miserable existence.

We climbed above the cloud band. At thirty-thousand feet, soaring south toward home, I was reminded that just a few hundred miles to the north and east, hundreds of thousands of ethnic minority Burmese were being forced from their homes in the thick and mountainous jungle, by their own country's army. Villages and crops pillaged and burned, stragglers picked off for rape or forced labor. What a life.

The words of the prophet Amos, written centuries before, rang in my ears: "Do you know what I want? I want justice—oceans of it. I want fairness—rivers of it. That's what I want. That's *all* I want."[1]

Justice, so taken for granted in my homeland, so wretchedly absent here.

What kind of justice?

Justice is a slippery word. It means different things to different people. For some it represents one of our culture's highest aspirations. At the other end of the spectrum it's a negative idea, confused with the "criminal justice system" and with the idea of punishment—often, in moods of

---

1. Amos 5:24.

vengeful anger, punishment of the "lock him up and throw away the key" sort. Consider the emotions stirred up by these situations:

- While his assailant is being tried the victim of a vicious assault sits in court thinking to himself, "I want justice." What he really means is, "I want him punished for what he did to me."
- In the next courtroom, the man who killed with his car because he was two-and-a-half times over the alcohol limit is given two hundred hours of community service. The woman sitting in the fifth row, who in a single moment lost four members of her family, wonders what justice means.
- A mother and two terrified children watch as their father is shoved roughly into the army van. The same thing happened several months ago, and he came back that time, beaten and bleeding. What chance they'll ever see him again, or ever know his fate . . . ?

Fairness

All of us have an innate sense of fairness, reflecting something of God's image in us. For however warped our own reflection of this aspect of God's character, it is still a clear sign that deep down true justice counts for us too. Yes, we view fairness through our tinted lenses of self-absorption, but it is there, nonetheless.

Most of us dream of a world where everyone gets a "fair go," where all people regardless of race, gender, or socio-economic background are able to have a decent crack at leading the kind of "abundant life" Jesus talked about.

But life is not fair. It's not just. In fact, for a majority of the world's population, their daily lives are an ongoing experience of *in*justice. Some of it vicious.

The reasons for injustice are many and complex. But it almost always has economic implications. The accumulation of power and wealth in the hands of the few inevitably results in the exploitation of others.

But even *relatively* (notice the choice of word) fair societies such as our own are full of injustice. Examples abound. Whether it is the ongoing legacy of oppressive policies against indigenous peoples (such as the New Zealand Maori, mentioned in chapter 4) or exorbitant interest rates on loans to the poor by financial institutions, if we open our eyes we will discover all kinds of small injustices . . . and many not–so–small.

Justice in the Promised Land

The nation of Israel was in many ways no different to any other country that has ever existed. While it was certainly true that Israel was a more just and fair society than any of its neighbors, the longer things progressed, the more the cracks of injustice began to appear. This happened despite the principled demands of the Law, despite its moderating effect on the human tendency toward unfairness and injustice.

As we've seen, that Law included several mechanisms to bring a leveling effect economically. The main ones were:

- *The year of Jubilee.*[2] Every fiftieth year was designated as a year of "new beginnings." All land sold during the intervening years was then to be returned to its original ownership—effectively meaning that any land sales were "leasehold," not "freehold." In addition, any Israelites who had been forced by poverty to sell themselves into "indentured labor" were to be automatically freed from their obligations.

- *The sabbatical year.* Every seventh year the people were instructed to let the land take a break from production. But the sabbatical year was more than that. It was also a time for all financial debts between Israelites to be cancelled and, like the year of Jubilee, for emancipation of Jewish servants.[3]

- A *tithe* (tenth) of the harvest for the Levite (priestly tribe), sojourner, widow, and orphan. This particular tithe was legislated for every third year.[4]

- *Gleaning.* This was the practice whereby landowners (such as Boaz) were to leave some of the harvest uncollected, so that those who were without means (such as Ruth and Naomi) could, with a little work, gather food to live from.[5]

---

2. Lev 25:10–24.
3. Lev 25:1–7; Deut 15:1–18.
4. Deut 14:28–29.
5. Lev 19:9–10.

However, these laws fell into disuse even though they were fundamental to living within God's covenant. Ultimately the same sort of inequity arose as was widespread in the nations round about. In the generations after King David, more and more land was concentrated into the hands of the few. The gap between rich and poor increased accordingly, and the powerful abused their position and status to the detriment of the majority, who were left to scratch out a living under the weight of oppressive practices and high taxes.

Clearly, this was not how God intended his covenant community to live. So Yahweh sent his prophets—people like Jeremiah, Hosea, Ezekiel, Micah, and Amos. All attacked the injustices in uncompromising words. Some went to extreme lengths to communicate Yahweh's anger. Nowhere in the Old Testament is the demand for economic justice more vigorously stated than in the Prophets. It is a dominant theme of their messages.

An important emphasis they made was that our relationship with God has social and economic implications. If we say we love God, then this should be reflected in the way we treat others. Conversely, if we engage in acts of injustice and exploitation, our behavior reflects a poor relationship with God, and our piety is consequently worthless.

Typical of the Prophets' message is the book of Amos. It makes a no-nonsense challenge to those with the power and the means to oppress others. Amos is really the first of the biblical writers to go public with the truth that our worship walks hand-in-hand with our lifestyle—that the way we treat money can't be separated from the way we relate to God.

Here are some of the blunt things Amos says—made contemporary by Eugene Peterson:

> People for them are only *things*—ways of making money.
> They'd sell a poor man for a pair of shoes.
> They'd sell their own grandmother!
> . . . I can't stand your religious meetings.
> I'm fed up with your conferences and conventions.
> I want nothing to do with your religion projects, your pretentious slogans and goals.
> I'm sick of your fund-raising schemes, your public relations and image making.
> I've had all I can take of your noisy ego-music.
> When was the last time you sang to *me*?
> Do you know what I want?
> I want justice—oceans of it.
> I want fairness—rivers of it.

Section A: Bible

That's what I want. That's *all* I want.[6]

Amos is unequivocal—our worship is meaningless if we are accumulating wealth through the exploitation of others.

A contemporary of Amos, the prophet Micah, pursues a similar theme: "Listen, leaders of Jacob, leaders of Israel: Don't you know anything of justice? Haters of good, lovers of evil: Isn't justice in your job description? But you skin my people alive. You rip the meat off their bones . . ."[7]

Micah declares that God has, ". . . already made it plain how to live, what to do, what GOD is looking for in men and women. It's quite simple: Do what is fair and just to your neighbor, be compassionate and loyal in your love . . ."[8]

Jeremiah too proclaims the same message, haranguing the people of Israel:

> Don't let the wise brag of their wisdom.
> Don't let heroes brag of their exploits.
> Don't let the rich brag of their riches.
> If you brag, brag of this and this only:
> I'm GOD, and I act in loyal love.
> I do what is right and set things right and fair,
> And delight in those who do the same things.
> These are my trademarks.[9]

What are God's trademarks? His loyal love (*hesed*), his setting things right and fair (*mishpat*), and his doing what is right (*sedeqah*). These are contrasted with wisdom, exploits, and riches—echoes of the very things Solomon was known for.

Walter Bruggemann suggests that throughout the Old Testament these three attributes (loving-kindness, justice, and righteousness) are features of covenant living.[10] They were meant to be marks of Jewish society.

---

6. Amos 2:6–7; 5:21–24.

7. Mic 3:1–3.

8. Mic 6:8. Or in the more familiar language of older English translations—"act justly and love mercy."

9. Jer 9:23–24.

10. My source for this are the Laing Lectures given by Bruggemann at Regent College, Vancouver, Canada, in 2008.

Steadfast love means caring for and supporting all partners of the covenant, standing in solidarity with one another, honoring commitments to all.

Justice involves the distribution of resources to ensure that all members of the community—particularly the weak—have access to goods for the sake of a viable life of dignity.

Righteousness refers to active intervention in social affairs in order to respond to social grievance and correct every activity that diminishes or demeans a person or group of people.

God epitomizes steadfast love, justice and righteousness. They are core to who he is, and therefore, by implication, they must also be central to what his covenant community lives out. So when Israel—in particular her leaders—act in ways that actually exhibit the opposite, God reacts in anger. Nothing is more abhorrent to him than religious garb and rituals when they are used to cover social and economic injustice. For, as Hosea proclaims, it is steadfast love God really wants from his people, not sacrifice.[11]

Sadly, the warnings of the prophets remained largely unheeded. The inaction of the powerful and rich led first Israel and then Judah to be dragged off into captivity, far away from their promised land.

Justice and righteousness intertwined

One of the difficulties we have in appreciating the centrality of *justice* in the prophets (indeed, in the whole Bible) is the way this word has normally been translated into English.

The Hebrew adjectives *saddiq* and *misphat*, and the Greek adjective *dikaios*, are the words most frequently used to describe what we have been examining. All three words can be translated "upright," "righteous" or "just." However, in most English Bibles they are generally translated "righteous." William Tyndale began this trend, back in the very earliest of translation attempts.

The real problem for us, though, is not the translation *per se*, but rather what we have been taught to understand as the meaning of "righteous" or "righteousness." For most Protestants one of three images comes to mind:

---

11. Hos 6:6.

Section A: Bible

1. A law court where we have been pronounced guilty by the judge but because of the work of Jesus on the cross, we have now had our relationship with God restored. (While this interpretation is not inaccurate, it captures only one element of these words.)

2. "Self-righteousness"—a word that carries thoroughly negative connotations of puffed-up and inflated self-importance along with a judgmental attitude toward others. It usually involves a smug assumption of moral superiority, and is often used to justify outrage at the failure of others to live up to a particular standard of behavior.

3. "Works-righteousness"—the practice (identified in the New Testament) of striving for salvation by good works.

However, as biblical scholar Colin Brown points out: "Righteousness in the Old Testament is not a matter of actions conforming to a given set of absolute legal standards, but of *behavior* which is in keeping with the two-way relationship between God and man."[12]

Righteousness is primarily concerned with *right relationships* and *right behavior*. It involves "justice." That's why, for example, crime is viewed in the Bible primarily as a violation of relationships. It is taken seriously because it undermines the kind of relational peace and harmony inherent in shalom. Whenever the Bible deals with a case of "criminal justice" it is therefore mainly concerned with the putting right of relationships, not the meting out of punishment.

The strong tones of justice implicit in the word "righteous" are reflected in such phrases as Amos 5:24: "But let *justice* roll on like a river, *righteousness* like a never-failing stream!"[13]

The poetic device Amos employs here is parallelism—a device that is used regularly in the Hebrew poetry of the Bible. Simply put, the writer expresses a thought in one line, and then repeats it in the following line, using words that vary slightly. (Old Testament poetry is almost always in the form of "couplets": pairs of lines.)

The second line is intended to reinforce, and often to expand, the first. It is a way of bringing emphasis or depth to the statement. A clear example (using "righteousness") is found in Job's discourse where he

---

12. Colin Brown, "Righteousness," *Dictionary of New Testament Theology* Vol.3, 355.

13. NIV. This is the same passage as previously quoted from *The Message*. Italics are mine.

states, "I put on *righteousness* as my clothing; *justice* was my robe and my turban."[14]

Here, righteousness and justice are really so intertwined that they are almost one and the same thing.

In the Greek New Testament, the word *dikaios* is open to the same double translation.[15] For example, in Jesus's parable of the sheep and goats (Matt 25) the righteous could as easily be called "the just." The message is clear—these people are declared just, because of their actions.

When Paul uses *dikaios* translators have most often opted for the English word *righteous*. But of course Paul is using the same word as Jesus did, and the same two shades of meaning apply. For example, see what happens when you replace the word *righteous* with the word *just* in Romans 2:13: "For it is not those who hear the law who are *just* in God's sight, but it is those who obey the law who will be declared *just*."[16]

John, too, follows this line of thinking, particularly when he states: "It is the person who acts right [read: *justly*] who is right [read: *just*]."[17]

Justice and our money

As the Prophets make clear, God's justice and righteousness have an awful lot to do with economics—with money. The way we earn, spend, and invest our money can support either justice or injustice. In this sense, our money is not neutral. For instance, if I choose to buy cheap clothing or footwear from a business that is getting these goods made in developing world "sweatshops," where local labor is paid a pittance for long hours in pitiful conditions, my money is, in reality, supporting injustice.

Of course, not all injustice is economic. Racial or ethnic prejudice, for example, is not in itself a money issue. However, it almost always has economic consequences. In Burma's case, the active persecution of some of the ethnic minorities by the military, leaves these communities scattered, traumatized, and debilitated, leading ultimately to economic

---

14. Job 29:14. Italics are mine.

15. See for example, the parable of the sheep and goats (Matt 25:31–46) and the resurrection of the righteous (Luke 14:14).

16. I am using the NIV translation here.

17. 1 John 3:7. John is explaining that the right actions will automatically result from a righteous person. They are the evidence. The Book of James takes the same approach, but uses the words *faith* and *works* to illustrate that true faith results automatically in good works.

ruin. (If they observed what is now happening in the state of Burma, the Prophets would be outraged.)

Invariably, true justice and money are closely aligned.

Up Close and Personal

1. Make a list of injustices you are aware of in your local community, your nation, and globally.
2. How many of these have economic implications or consequences?
3. What/who are the causes of these?
4. Read through either Amos or Micah in one session. Note down your overall impressions of what is being communicated. (If you are meeting with a group, discuss your observations.)
5. In Micah 4, an alternative vision is painted. Have a read through this chapter and discuss what are some of the features of this vision.
6. If we live as Christians, as people of the new covenant, what implications might the messages of Amos, Micah, and Jeremiah have for us today, regarding our money?

7

Poor

> *"[Yahweh] rescues the poor at the first sign of need, the destitute who have run out of luck. He opens a place in his heart for the down-and-out; he restores the wretched of the earth. He frees them from tyranny and torture—when they bleed, he bleeds; when they die, he dies."*
> Psalm 72:12-14

It was a typically hot, steamy Manila afternoon. Not the kind of day that you'd pick for sunbathing—at least not where I was. As I stood there, in the heart of those sprawling slums, a vast mountain of rubbish was on fire.

But that was common, I was told, in the middle of the hot season. The heat had created natural combustion—enough to turn the huge scrap heap that was the Manila city dump into a mass of thick smoke. No wonder the locals called it Smokey Mountain.

It was 1986 and my wife Jill and I, along with three others, had already spent five weeks assisting the nearby YWAM base, feeding malnourished kids and caring for badly underdeveloped babies. I had just finished the rounds of the many shacks where the kids on the feeding program lived, when Jeremiah, my Filipino friend and co-worker, said to me, "Come on, Wayne, I want to take you somewhere."

Warming with intrigue to his request, I began to follow him over the open sewer ditch and around the side of the mountain. The path was super-spongy—like walking on extra-padded Nikes. The ground

Section A: Bible

was countless thousands of tones of rubbish gradually compressing together. We fought our way through the armies of flies that descended on anything and everything that stood still. "I want to take you up to the scavenging area," explained Jeremiah.

It wasn't long before we reached the top. I'd never been up here before. Day after day I'd mixed with the people in their poor excuses for houses, chatting freely about life, sharing both laughter and pain, but never had I gone to see why ten thousand people lived on this grotesque accumulation of stinking, filthy, rotting, and disease-ridden rubbish.

As we reached the top I looked around. Between the thick banks of wafting smoke I could see for miles. It was a great view of Manila. But the people about me weren't interested in the scenery, and I suspected Jeremiah hadn't brought me here for that reason either. I dropped my eyes, forgetting the view, and looked instead at a large group of squatters, scratching their way through the freshly dropped rubbish, searching for anything that might prove of some value for the scrap dealers.

A garbage truck tipped its load and then chugged away, and the groups scurried over to rake through the garbage with their metal hooks. Picking up wood, metal, bottles, and plastic, they dropped the scrap into large cane baskets strapped across their backs, before the bulldozer came to heave the rubbish over the edge.

We stood there in silence. I turned to Jeremiah and asked him how frequently he visited this spot. "Not often," he replied. "I don't like coming here."

"Why not?" I asked.

"See over there—look at those men. Do you recognize any of them?" As I looked closer I realized I knew three or four of those scavenging. They were local men I had come to know over the weeks. They all attended a Bible study group where I had assisted Jeremiah. "Have you noticed that none of them has acknowledged us? Not one of the men we know has smiled or said hello to us."

I thought about that. It made no sense. The way they were ignoring us was totally different from their normal behavior.

"You know why that is? It's because they're so ashamed to be here. They hate what they have to do for a living. It's humiliating. But they know that if they don't scavenge, their families will starve to death. They have no choice."

My heart broke. Not for the first time had I begun to feel something of the pain of the lives of these men.

Seeing such poverty up close and personal made a huge impact on me. This daily struggle for survival is indelibly printed on my heart; it was an unending reality for people such as my friends in Manila. I had choices they didn't. I was "rich." They were poor.

Poor?

That word carries a lot of baggage. Its use is often highly emotive and charged with undercurrents and insinuations: *destitute . . . pitiful . . . helpless . . . lazy . . . beggars . . .*

Who are the "poor"?

This planet is home to countless millions of people who live on the edge of disaster. That is, they have no capacity to provide the basic necessities of life for themselves or their dependents. They lack some or all of: adequate food, clean water, shelter, sanitation, health, and education.

Of course, these words encompass a very broad range of situations. Because of that, when we use the words "poor" or "poverty" we often have to qualify what we mean.

Extreme or absolute poverty

The World Bank estimates that 1.1 billion people currently live in "extreme" poverty. That is, they live on less than US$1 a day. Of course, the one-dollar a day marker is arbitrary, but it does give us a sense of the desperate state huge numbers of our fellow humans live in.

What we're talking about here has sometimes been referred to as "stupid poverty." By "stupid" we're not referring to the people who are poor, but rather the senselessness of others having the resources to remedy this tragic situation, but not doing so. It is stupid because it doesn't need to be this way. People are dying of diseases that have long since had vaccines and treatments available; they are dying because they lack simple basics like clean water. In fact, an estimated twenty-five thousand people living in extreme poverty die *each day* of hunger or hunger-related causes. That's nearly ten million people every year!

A further 1.6 billion people live on less than US$2 per day—a kind of hand-to-mouth or "subsistence" poverty. This latter group is highly borderline in economic terms. They are just one unexpected setback away from disaster. A bad harvest, a family death, a squatter fire or flood, or numerous other regular occurrences can in one swift stroke send them tumbling into the ranks of the destitute.

Relative poverty

Compared with such absolute poverty we may think that countries in the "developed" world have nothing to be concerned about. And while that's true to some extent, poverty is nonetheless also a very real issue in the West. However, it's rarely of the extreme variety. Generally it is a kind of "relative" poverty. That is, when we talk about the poor in our society we do so with the knowledge that such folk are, compared with most people, limited in their capacity to live life well.

Homelessness (or lack of adequate shelter), unemployment, major health issues, severe mental or physical disabilities, isolation, an absence of support structures or people, severe addictions, prejudice, traumatic or abusive experiences—all of these are either symptoms or contributing factors to such poverty. Those who suffer from these conditions are not only poor economically, but also lacking in the psychological, social, emotional, and spiritual resources to do something about their situation.

Features of being "poor"

Whatever kind of poverty people experience, there are some consistent characteristics of their state. They include:

Vulnerability

The poor are the ones who are most exposed to the storms of life—physical disasters, economic downturns, and all the other unexpected trials that come our way. Since they have so little chance of recovery, they are also the ones who suffer most from being taken advantage of or ripped off. In the face of such challenges they find themselves largely helpless and defenseless. This was certainly the case with my friends in Manila. They were particularly vulnerable to sickness, disease, fire, flood, and cyclone.

Resourcelessness

Because of their lack of resources, the poor also have little or no capacity to improve their situation. They lack the very wherewithal—tools, skills, education, seed money, job openings—to climb out of their poverty.

Powerlessness

Vulnerability and resourcelessness present a huge hurdle, but other barriers stand in the way of the poor, too. Extreme poverty brings with it internal factors such as a crippling lack of confidence and a debilitating sense of hopelessness, both engendered by endless disappointments. External factors add to this weight of despair. The poor are powerless in the face of decisions made by others, decisions that affect their prospects but over which they have no influence; decisions that sometimes crush them.

Poverty in the Bible

In the Bible, the words "poor" and "poverty" generally, but not exclusively, refer to the economic state of people. Access to land was for a long time the critical factor in people's livelihoods. However, over the centuries the urban centers of Israel gradually developed, and wealth became less exclusively tied to land ownership.

By the time of Jesus, the poor were the majority of the population in Palestine. There was only a relatively small group of people who were wealthy, and they, of course, owned the majority of land and resources. It's estimated that King Herod, his family and their "hangers-on" may have between them owned as much as 50 percent of Palestine. The rich also included the high-priestly clans, partly because they controlled the considerable commerce around the Temple—which may have added fuel to the anger of Jesus against the moneychangers in Mark 11.

In contrast, the poor came to represent a very wide range of economic situations. Best off were those who owned a small parcel of land, though their lives remained precariously balanced. One bad harvest or two and they could easily lose their land to a wealthy neighbor, leaving them to face starvation as beggars. Then there were tenant farmers—people who were renting the land and therefore had to pay their landlord first.

Section A: Bible

There were also fishermen and tradespeople—it is out of this group that Jesus and many of his disciples came.

The worst off in Palestine were the myriads of hired laborers or beggars—those without land or skills—and their families. Their hand-to-mouth existence was the most precarious of all.

We can see from this that in spite of the Law, the words of the Prophets, and the experience of the Exile, little had been learnt. In fact, life had become even more burdensome in the few hundred years between the re-settlement of Jerusalem and the Roman occupation. Great inequities resulted from constant covenantal disobedience by Israel. These inequalities were compounded by a series of oppressive imperial powers that ruled their land—the Persians, Greeks, Seleucids, and eventually the Romans.

God's special concern for the poor

It is difficult to see how someone could possibly read the Bible and not be struck by God's special concern for the poor. He has a genuine soft spot for them! It's written all over Scripture. For example, in the Psalms we read: "[God] rescues the poor at the first sign of need, the destitute who have run out of luck. He opens a place in his heart for the down-and-out, he restores the wretched of the earth. He frees them from tyranny and torture—when they bleed, he bleeds; when they die, he dies."[1]

Furthermore, "[GOD] always does what he says—he defends the wronged, he feeds the hungry. GOD frees prisoners—he gives sight to the blind, he lifts up the fallen. GOD loves good people, protects strangers, takes the side of orphans and widows . . ."[2]

The Law of Moses showed special concern for the fatherless, along with the widow and the alien.[3] This is not surprising given that all these groups were clearly the most obviously helpless, defenceless, and vulnerable in such an agrarian-based society. In fact, when the people of Israel lament their situation following the fall of Jerusalem in 586 BC, they actually describe *themselves* as orphans and fatherless.[4]

---

1. Ps 72:12–14.
2. Ps 146:7–9.
3. See for example, Exod 22:22; Deut 10:18; 24:17–22.
4. See Lam 5:3.

God is so fiercely protective of such people that he is described by the Psalmist as "a father to the fatherless, [and] a defender of widows."[5] As we noted in the last chapter, under the Law provision was made for them to glean some of the harvest from fields and vineyards,[6] and furthermore they were to share in one of the tithes, along with the Levites.[7] Their debts were also supposed to be cancelled in sabbatical and Jubilee years.

The Prophets continue the expectation that caring for these particular underprivileged groups is exceptionally important to God. Zechariah is typical among the Prophets when he states: "Thus says the LORD of hosts: Render true judgments, show kindness and mercy to one another; do not oppress the widow, the orphan, the alien, or the poor . . ."[8]

Reasons for poverty

It's easy to think simplistically about the causes of poverty. On the one hand, we can subconsciously assume that people are poor because of their own bad choices, even stupidity. On the other hand, it is also possible to naively think that all poverty is the result of oppression and injustice.

The Bible spends most of its time dealing with *how we should respond* to the poor, not with the *reasons for* poverty. Nevertheless, it is true that at times the Bible suggests causes. And its reasons are not all one-way traffic.

Proverbs is a book that has an enormous amount to say about money and possessions. So it's not surprising that we find in it several pointers to the causes of poverty (and wealth). Such as: "You lazy fool, look at an ant . . . All summer it stores up food . . . So how long are you going to laze around doing nothing? Do you know what comes next? Just this: You can look forward to a dirt-poor life, poverty your permanent houseguest!"[9]

However, as Craig Blomberg notes, "Fewer than one third of the proverbs dealing with rich and poor teach that people get what they deserve, whereas the rest recognize the presence and problem of socio-economic justice."[10]

---

5. Ps 68:5 (NIV).
6. Deut 24:19–22.
7. Deut 14: 28–29.
8. Zech 7:9–10a (NRSV). See also Jeremiah 7:5–7.
9. Prov 6: 6–11.
10. Blomberg, *Neither Poverty Nor Riches*, 65.

Section A: Bible

A level playing field?

In a world that was entirely "level" and "fair," establishing a strong and consistent link between good choices and wealth, and linking poor choices to poverty would be easy and straightforward.

In such a cause–and–effect world the truth of proverbs such as Proverbs 14:23 would make perfect sense: "Hard work always pays off; mere talk puts no bread on the table." Laziness, wasteful indulgence, poor self-discipline, and addictive behavior would all lead naturally to poverty. On the other hand, hard work, careful consumption, healthy self-discipline, and freedom from addictions would result in wealth.

However, the truth is that we don't live in a world that is anything close to a level playing field. It is neither fair nor even–handed. To begin with, none of us start life from the same position. Our family, community, and societal circumstances dictate much about our place in the world. Some of us are fortunate to be born into loving families and prosperous countries, with a myriad of abilities and opportunities. Sadly, others are born into worlds that are resource–less in every sense of the word.

And, even for those of us born with plenty of advantages, there are other factors along the way that display the apparent unfairness of life. A natural disaster happens, wiping out a community's livelihood. A husband becomes abusive, reducing wife and children to disempowered victims. An investment fails because of fraud, leaving the family who had saved hard for the future, without means.

We must be very careful then, not to make assumptions about the reasons for anyone's material status—rich or poor. So many factors are at work, some of our own making and some outside our control.

Responding to the poor

So while the Bible doesn't say much about the reasons for poverty, it does proclaim—loud and clear—that those who live in abundance are obliged to care for the poor.

We have already observed in chapter 5 that characters such as Abraham and Job, who are noted for being rich, were also very generous. They were considered righteous (or just) because of their interactions with those in need.

Harold Stigers points out that in the Old Testament: "The man who is righteous tries to preserve the peace and prosperity of the community by fulfilling the commands of God in regard to others. In the supreme sense the righteous man is the one who serves God (Mal. 3:18). Specifically, he, like Job, delivers the poor and the orphan, helps the blind along the way, supports the weak and is a father (provider) to the poor (Job 29:12-15) . . . The *saddiq* [just person] gives freely (Ps. 37:21), without regard for gain."[11]

It is worth noting here that what is true for the righteous individual is also true for the just community or nation. The Prophets made it clear that the nation of Israel would be judged according to how well they looked after those on the margins of their society: the alien, the orphan, and the widow. It is a strong indicator of how just (or righteous) they are as a nation. This responsibility was very much a part of Israel's covenantal obligations.

The same measurement can be applied to any group of people—including a church. The health of the group or the society is shown by how well they care for the poor and powerless around them. Those who occupy positions of power—if we are to base our judgments on biblical standards—are not there to receive increased privileges, but increased responsibilities.

Nehemiah—governmental, organizational, and personal response to the poor[12]

That's certainly how Nehemiah saw it. He was the governor of the city of Jerusalem, working as a delegated leader for a foreign government—Persia. A significant aspect of his work was to oversee the rebuilding of the city walls.

As a high-level public servant, Nehemiah was well rewarded materially. It would have been easy for him to just enjoy the privileges that went with his position. Instead, he made deliberate choices to use his influence and wealth so that he could (in the words of the prophet Micah) "act justly and love mercy."

For example, in chapter 5 of the Book of *Nehemiah* we are told how he is approached by a group of Jews who are finding themselves

---

11. Stigers, "sedeq—justice, rightness" *Theological Wordbook of the Old Testament* Vol.2, 753.

12. This section on Nehemiah has been adapted from a previous book I co-authored with Alistair Mackenzie: *Just Decisions*.

oppressed by their own brothers and sisters. These people complain that through exploitation they have lost everything:

> Some said, "We have big families, and we need food just to survive." Others said, "We're having to mortgage our fields and vineyards and homes to get enough grain to keep from starving." And others said, "We're having to borrow money to pay the royal tax on our fields and vineyards. Look: We're the same flesh and blood as our brothers here; our children are just as good as theirs. Yet here we are having to sell our children off as slaves—some of our daughters have already been sold—and we can't do anything about it because our fields and vineyards are owned by somebody else."[13]

Nehemiah was furious when he heard this. He gathered the leaders together and denounced their injustices in public. He challenged them to give back what they had gained from the people they had exploited.

Believe it or not, they agreed to do so!

Then Nehemiah arranged a relief program providing food and money for those who were in distress, encouraging others to do the same. However, knowing that this kind of help usually only provides temporary relief, he also tried to work on some longer-term solutions. He challenged those Jews who had taken land to give it back. Not only that, but he suggested they also give back olive trees to help their impoverished neighbors develop a livelihood again. And he urged them to lend out money at no interest for those who needed assistance to get restarted in business.

However, Nehemiah's response to the poor within his jurisdiction didn't just stop at the governmental and organizational level. It also included a costly and very personal response.

He saw the danger of adopting a lifestyle that can only be supported while others live in poverty. His solution: Nehemiah decided to identify with the needs and aspirations of the oppressed rather than the oppressors. He chose to live in a way that expressed this concern, so that his own lifestyle could echo his ideals and be an example to others.

Having observed how his predecessors and their assistants "placed a heavy burden on the people" and lorded it over them, Nehemiah deliberately chose to limit and forego his rights and privileges. With the intention of relieving the burden on others, he restricted his income, thus

---

13. Neh 5:2–5.

choosing to live more simply than previous governors. He also turned down the opportunity to buy land, and chose not to take food and wine from the people that he was entitled to. Beyond even this, Nehemiah expressed generous hospitality to one hundred and fifty Jews, officials and foreigners—inviting them to eat with him at his table, and presumably at his cost.[14]

Nehemiah is an outstanding model of what the Bible teaches as a meaningful response to the poor. He doesn't hide behind his status, position, or wealth. Instead he engages the poor at both the structural and personal level.

Up Close and Personal

1. Think about your own community. Who would be considered "poor"? (Remember, three features of being poor are being powerless, vulnerable, and lacking in resources to change one's situation.)

2. What contact do you personally have with any of these groups of people?

3. In your group share as honestly as you can any assumptions you have made about poor people. Can you think of what experiences/conversations/literature contributed to these assumptions?

4. I make the claim that how a society cares for those who are most vulnerable determines the health of that society. Do you agree? (If you do, how do you think your own nation rates?)

---

14. See Neh 5:14–18.

8

Mammon

"You cannot serve both God and Money."
Jesus

MANY YEARS AGO I decided to spend some concentrated time reading through the New Testament and noting everything that was written on the subjects of money, possessions, and giving. I can't recall what inspired me to undertake this exercise, but I do remember how surprised I was at how long it took me!

To aid me, I wrote out longhand all the verses involved. It filled pages and pages of my refill pad! One of the main benefits of this exercise was being able to gain an overview of how Jesus and the New Testament writers viewed money. It allowed me to feel the full weight of their teaching. Some of its impact has remained with me, even to this day.

Money in the Gospels

The topic of money was not inconsequential to Jesus. After the kingdom of God, money is the theme that dominates the gospels. It far exceeds the topics of heaven and hell, new birth, and salvation.

With so much material, I find it hard to select a starting point. Discussing the attitude of Jesus to money is not easy; there is just so much he has to say. But perhaps the best place to begin is by considering one of the most quoted of his many utterances on the subject, found in Matthew 6:24: "No one can serve two masters. Either he will hate the one and love the other, or he will be devoted to the one and despise the other. You cannot serve both God and Money." Or, as most Bible versions render it: *You cannot serve both God and Mammon.*

So what is "Mammon"? And why is it capitalized?

It is pure myth that "Mammon" was some kind of pagan god in the ancient world, as some people have made it out to be. Mammon is derived from the Aramaic word for money or wealth. And translators capitalize it because Jesus is intentionally personifying for effect. Jesus pits Mammon against God.

As I noted in the first chapter (on Power), in doing so he is emphasizing that money is not neutral. It is a competing god, one that calls for our allegiance. There is an inherent "power" in money. One that can easily consume us. Money—and the pursuit of it—is intensely addictive.

Os Guinness observes that: "Individuals and societies who devote themselves to money soon become devoured by it. Or, as the Bible reiterates, we become what we worship. Money almost literally seems to eat people away, drying up the sap of their vitality and withering their spontaneity, generosity and joy."[1]

We just can't get enough of it. And the more we get, the more it seems to squeeze out the other parts of our life.

The dangers of wealth

This is why the New Testament tends to major, even more than the Old Testament, on the dark side of money. Wealth is a dangerous thing to have, says Jesus. It is like a stick of dynamite. While it has the potential to do much good, it can also do a great deal of harm. And the more you have, the greater the risks.

This attitude to wealth is evident in the way Jesus relates to the "rich young ruler." Jesus says to the man, "If you want to give it all you've got . . . go sell your possessions; give everything to the poor. All your wealth will then be in heaven. Then come follow me."[2]

The Master knew very well what barrier stood in the way of this man who wanted to follow him. It was his wealth. It had created a divided heart. As Craig Keener writes: "The kingdom is not meant to be an extra blessing tagged onto a comfortable life; it must be all-consuming, or it is

1. Guinness, *The Call*, 137.
2. Matt 19:21.

no longer the kingdom. For that reason, *it appeals more readily to those with less to lose.*"³

Little wonder then that Jesus turns to his disciples and declares, "It is easier for a camel to go through the eye of a needle than for a rich man to enter the kingdom of God."⁴ His hyperbole is not lost on the disciples. They are so taken aback that they ask, "Then who has a chance at all [of being saved]?"

The widespread view of the day—one that the disciples clearly shared—was that wealth gave evidence of God's blessing. Yet what Jesus had just said stood in stark opposition to this. Rather than expecting the rich to inherit eternal life, he was highlighting the inherent spiritual dangers of wealth. A person's riches are more a liability than an asset. For the disciples, this was a significant paradigm shift.

However, we must be careful not to assume that Jesus is anti the rich and wealthy. Far from it. In Mark's equivalent telling of the incident we read that, "Jesus looked him hard in the eye—and loved him!" This is not a response of judgment. Nor of distaste at the man's wealth. As his subsequent challenge reveals, Jesus perceived where the young man's first allegiance lay.

One assumes that it was not just the rich young man who walked away sad. Jesus too, would have been heartbroken.

Blessed are the poor

Jesus *does* display a preference for those at the other end of the economic scale. But by "preference" we are not meaning a greater love. The point is that Jesus went to special pains for those who were hurt or damaged in any way at all.

He made this clear right from the start of his public ministry. His mandate, he said, was to fulfill Isaiah's words: "God's Spirit is on me; he's chosen me to preach the Message of good news to the poor, sent me to announce pardon to prisoners and recovery of sight to the blind, to set the burdened and battered free . . ."⁵

3. Keener, *The IVP Bible Background Commentary (New Testament)*, 98. Italics are my emphasis.

4. Like the contention that "Mammon" was a pagan god, the notion that "the eye of the needle" was a gate in the wall of Jerusalem is entire myth. As Jessica pointed out in chapter 2, there is no basis for such a belief.

5. Luke 4:18.

Mammon

Poor, imprisoned, blind, burdened, or battered—the worse their suffering, the more Jesus' heart went out to them. So, given the world he lived in, the emphasis he lays on those who are poor is not surprising. As I noted in the last chapter, it is estimated that by his day most people in Palestine were in various levels of poverty—from destitution to subsistence living. And the oppressive Roman occupation only added to this burden.

We can do all the spiritualizing we like here, but it still can't draw us away from the clear bias toward the poor, the marginalized, the underdog.

Other statements reinforce this. Such as: "Blessed are you who are poor, for yours is the kingdom of God."[6] This seems somewhat of an oxymoron. Blessed poor? The two words don't seem to belong together. How on earth can someone who is totally destitute be considered fortunate? Matthew's better-known version sheds some light: "Blessed are the poor *in spirit* . . ."[7]

Jesus is clearly not "blessing" poverty itself. There is nothing romantic or virtuous about being resource-less. Rather, he is suggesting that those who recognize their total destitution have one great advantage—for this is the first vital step in discovering our need of God. Our desperation can lead us to God-dependence.

Matthew's version gives some encouragement to those of us who are wealthy. For it hints that the rich can also develop the desperate dependence on God that is a more natural consequence of poverty. As I have already noted, wealth tends to seduce us into self-reliance rather than God-reliance. It blinds us to how spiritually bankrupt we really are. However, those who are poor and have no options are not so easily self-deluded. Their destitution is obvious for all to see.

In other words, "You're blessed when you're at the end of your rope. With less of you there is more of God and his rule."[8]

In this sense, the poor can teach the rich what both poverty of spirit and dependence on God are all about. Chris Sugden makes the point that "the wealthy need the poor, to learn from them the nature and meaning of the deliverance God brings to both."[9] Seeing this has the potential to

---

6. Luke 6:20 (NIV).

7. Matt 5:3 (NIV). Craig Keener points out that "the term poor could encompass either physical poverty or the faithful dependence on God that it often produced . . ." Keener, *Matthew*, 56.

8. Matt 5:3.

9. Sugden, "Poverty and Wealth" *New Dictionary of Theology*, 524.

drastically alter the rich person's attitude to, and relationship with, the poor. Both suddenly find themselves on an equal footing before God. So instead of being in a position of strength, the rich person who is "just" takes the stance of a learner—eager to learn from his/her poor neighbor what it is to rely on God.

Of course, this is not to suggest that all financially poor people develop a strong trust in God. Simply that they may be more open to this relationship.

Eternal destiny

Perhaps the most shocking element of Jesus' approach to money is the connection he draws between the way we handle money and possessions . . . and our salvation. This is enough to cause most of us evangelical Christians to choke on our food! For any suggestion that how we handle our resources might be related to our eternal destiny is just too much like "works-righteousness"—that roundly-condemned old doctrine of being saved by our own efforts.

In Matthew 25 two parables sitting side by side provide insight into how faith and money are related. The first is the parable of the talents. The second is the "parable" of the sheep and goats.[10]

We are so familiar with the parable of the talents and now so used to thinking of our "talents" solely in terms of gifts and abilities that we can easily forget Jesus was actually talking about *money*. A "talent" was the highest denomination of money in the currency of his day—a particularly large amount. In today's terms, many thousands of dollars.

While it is fair to conclude that Jesus was intending his listeners to interpret the call to stewardship in terms *wider* than just money, it nonetheless *includes* our money and possessions. Financial resources are at the core of this parable. Jesus was essentially saying: "What you have—your money, possessions, gifts, heritage, and time—are not yours. They are God's. Therefore you will be judged on how you steward/invest what you have on behalf of the Master."[11]

---

10. This is not a parable in the true sense of the word, though it is often referred to as one.

11. For the Jewish leaders, it seems fair to assume there would have been an added and more immediate inference—regarding their stewardship of the Law and the Temple. As Tom Wright states, "They had been given wonderful promises about how God would bless not only Israel but, through Israel, the whole world. And they had

Hard on the heels of the talents is the "parable" of the sheep and goats.¹² Here Jesus talks about the final judgement—contrasting two groups of people who come before him. While the "goats" are taken aback when Jesus castigates them for their lack of initiative toward those in need, the "sheep" are equally surprised by his commendation. The explanation Jesus gives for welcoming them into his kingdom is: "I was hungry and you fed me, I was thirsty and you gave me a drink, I was homeless and you gave me a room, I was shivering and you gave me clothes, I was sick and you stopped to visit, I was in prison and you came to me . . . I'm telling you the solemn truth: Whenever you did one of these things to someone overlooked or ignored, that was me—*you did it to me.*"¹³

This story should send a shiver down our spines. For the "goats" also profess Lordship. Yet ultimately they are rejected because their lifestyle doesn't reflect their beliefs and convictions.

It is important to clarify that this passage is not saying that *if* we care for others, we will be considered "righteous" or "just." Rather, it is affirming that when we live in a "right" or "just" relationship with God, this will lead us to respond in care for those who are marginalized and poor. Right relationship is revealed by right or just actions. And this will involve our personal resources—not simply time and abilities, but money and possessions as well.

The encounter Zacchaeus has with Jesus (in Luke 19) continues the same theme. His time with the Master is clearly a transformational experience. For Zacchaeus volunteers to provide generous restitution to all the people he has ripped off through his tax collecting over the years. In response Jesus announces: "Today is salvation day in this home!"

The spontaneous decision Zacchaeus makes is proof to Jesus that true repentance has occurred. Conversion has reached as deep as his pockets.

Through all these encounters and parables we can see that Jesus proposes a thoroughly different perspective on wealth and possessions. Their role in our lives as disciples is radically redefined and transformed.

---

buried them in the ground . . . And now, when their master was at last coming back, he was going to call them to account." Wright, *Matthew For Everyone Part Two*, 138.

12. The Jews viewed themselves as Yahweh's sheep and Yahweh as their shepherd. The choice of sheep here is therefore very deliberate by Jesus. Those who have been obedient and faithful to Christ are considered the true "sheep."

13. Matt 25:35–36, 40. Italicised emphasis is mine.

Section A: Bible

Up Close and Personal

Exercise (highly recommended)

1. Read carefully through all four gospels, looking for any passages that refer to money, possessions, or giving. Highlight them, or better still, write them out. As I comment above, this is a striking exercise because it allows us to focus on the full weight of Jesus' teaching on money. It *is* a large assignment, but I encourage you to undertake it. Your life may never be the same again.

2. Craig Keener notes that the kingdom "*appeals more readily to those with less to lose.*" As a personal exercise, think about how much you "have to lose" by embracing the all-consuming kingdom. What in particular do you find hard to off-load?

For discussion

3. It's a revolutionary thought that we have lessons to learn from the poor. What kind of lessons?

4. It's not easy to discuss money with others. What are the reasons for this?

9

Giving

"No one said, 'That's mine; you can't have it.' They shared everything . . . And so it turned out that not a person among them was needy."
Acts 4:32b

Pastor Mike was at it again. It had been several months since his sermon on God's blessing. Most folks had been very responsive and affirming about the teaching. In fact, initially giving to the church jumped a massive 35 percent. This was a great sign that the congregation was really taking the message on board.

However, in the last month there had been a severe turnaround. Giving had plummeted nearly 20 percent. Of course things were tight for some families, what with the global financial crisis biting deep now, and a couple of people had lost their jobs. Still, overall they were in good heart. Every week there were testimonies of how God had blessed individuals—one with a new car and another with a pay rise.

But even so, Pastor Mike's computer printout showed it wasn't good enough. Tithing figures divided by the number of families in the church produced a CGACIpw (Current Giving Average per Congregation Income per week) of only 8 percent— disappointingly short of break–even. And the monthly special offerings (for the building project, missions, Mike's apostolic trips to Africa and Asia, and love offerings for visiting speakers) were well below budget.

The problem was clear: people weren't being obedient to the call, and they certainly weren't exercising the kind of faith that Pastor Mike

Section A: Bible

was exhorting them have. They needed a rev-up. So he carefully planned a message on giving. He had a pretty good idea of what he wanted to say. It just needed a catchy and memorable title. Mike brainstormed a few options on the computer:

"Those who tithe, thrive." Had a nice crisp ring to it.

"How to avoid your finances going pear-shaped: giving your first-fruits to God" People always liked sermons starting with "How to . . ." Good and practical.

"Don't rob God blind: three easy steps to giving the Lord his dues." The allusion to cheating God was always a healthy guilt-string-puller.

But eventually Mike settled on *"Give to The Storehouse, where everyone gets a blessing."* This was a play on the local retail chain's well-known advertising slogan— "Go to The Warehouse, where everyone gets a bargain."

"Very clever," he thought to himself. "And memorable. That's what effective communication is all about." He could even get the worship band to play the little jingle that went along with it.

Pastor Mike already had the key scripture he would use—Malachi 3:8 and 10: "Will anyone rob God? Yet you are robbing me! But you say, 'How are we robbing you?' In your tithes and offerings! . . . Bring the full tithe into the storehouse, so that there may be food in my house, and thus put me to the test, says the LORD of hosts; see if I will not open the windows of heaven for you and pour down for you an overflowing blessing."[1]

He'd used it before, of course, but it had all the right phrases: "robbing God," "full tithe," "storehouse," "open the windows of heaven," "overflowing blessing."

Pastor Mike looked through his ending. "If you want to receive God's blessing, then you need to give the *full* tithe to God. Not 5 percent, not 8 percent, but 10 percent! Don't rob God. Give him his dues. And when you do, people, God will open the windows of heaven and bless you like you've never been blessed before."

"Do you want his blessing? Then bless God with your tithes and offerings today. Make a commitment now to give him your first-fruits, not just today but every week, every year. And then God will give *you* richness and blessing, every week, every year, for all your life!"

Excellent. Still a couple of days for fine-tuning. Just the right level of appeal and emotion was needed. God's work depended on it.

1. NRSV.

Giving and Sharing

Giving (and its partner, sharing) is one of the pervasive themes of the Bible. On this point, Pastor Mike has it right.

Scripture is the story of a self-giving God. A God who displays an unfathomable capacity for generosity. And a God who is our constant example. In both Testaments, the faith-full *are* called to give the first-fruits of their labor back to Yahweh and to support others less fortunate.

For the people of Israel this meant giving out of the produce they had harvested and the livestock they had raised on the land. Much of this prescribed giving was intimately tied in with the obligations around the Temple cult and its system of sacrifice.

Tithing

Many discussions about giving in the Bible begin with the tithe (literally: tenth). And this is understandable. It forms the cornerstone of the Law's commands on giving.

Abram and Melchizedek

However, the first mention of a tithe is actually found in Genesis 14:20.[2] Abram has just battled the four kings who had captured his nephew Lot, along with the kings of Sodom and Gomorrah. When Abram recovers the plunder he gives a tenth of it to Melchizedek, variously described by the writer as the "king of Salem" and "priest of The High God." It's just a passing reference—and without any real explanation or qualification.[3]

The Law

It's not entirely clear exactly how many tithes were prescribed in the Law.

At the end of Leviticus (27: 30–32), a tenth of whatever is produced from the land or the herd and flock is mandated to be God's. However,

---

2. The fact that "tithing" pre-dates the Law is often used by proponents of tithing to argue that this practice is important throughout the whole course of salvation history—not just the Old Testament.

3. That is, until the writer of Hebrews gave it some context, many centuries later. See Hebrews 7.

Section A: Bible

there's no indication here as to how this tithe was to be distributed. We have to turn to Numbers (18: 8–32) for that information. Here, the Levites are instructed to tithe the tithe that they receive from the people. That tenth goes to the High Priest; the remaining nine-tenths are for the Levites' own use, regarded as payment for their work.

However, in Deuteronomy (14: 22–29) there is mention of another tithe. It is an annual offering that is to be consumed as a sacred celebration—an extravagant party it seems—with God!

Additionally, every third year, a tithe was to be gathered and taken to the storehouses, to then be distributed to the Levites and to "the foreigner, the orphan, and the widow who live in your neighborhood." It's unclear whether this triennial tithe was in addition to the annual one or a variation of it every third year.

However, by the time of Jesus, it is likely that this tithe was practiced in addition to the other two. If this was so, it all amounted to giving of around 23.3 percent annually. On top of all this, other sacrifices and offerings were prescribed for specific purposes. (Some of these are mentioned in Deuteronomy 12.)

So as we can see, establishing how many tithes there were in the Law is not entirely straightforward, though it is likely there was more than one. And each tithe served a different purpose. Collectively the tithes and offerings seemed to operate as part temple tax and pay for the Levites, part support for the poor and marginalized, and part "holiday pay"—or rather, savings for the special day(s) of celebration!

What about the New Testament?

Interestingly, tithing is mentioned only four times in the New Testament. And three of these references are in the Gospels.[4]

In Luke 11:42, in the middle of a tirade against the Pharisees, Jesus declares: "I've had it with you. You're hopeless, you Pharisees! Frauds! You keep meticulous account books, tithing on every nickel and dime you get, but manage to find loopholes for getting around basic matters of justice and God's love. Careful bookkeeping is commendable, but the basics are required."

In this outburst, Jesus is not criticizing the Pharisees for tithing. Rather, his focus is on fulfilling the more important matters of the Law.

---

4. And two of these three are parallel passages—Luke 11:42 and Matt 23:23.

Giving

Similarly, in the parable of the tax collector and the Pharisee, Jesus condemns the pious and pretentious utterances of the Pharisee's prayer—"Oh God, I thank you that I am not like other people—robbers, crooks, adulterers, or, heaven forbid, like this tax man. I fast twice a week and tithe on all my income."[5] Again, tithing is not dismissed outright, but it's very definitely put in its right context.

Is tithing relevant for us?

A fair question to ask is why there is such an absence of reference to and support of tithing in the New Testament documents. And when it *is* mentioned, why is it so negative?

It's reasonable to assume that while tithing was not actively discouraged among the early church members,[6] it *is* largely superseded in the new covenant by the greater principle of generosity.[7] People are encouraged to give freely and according to their means. Rather than a set percentage being prescribed, the New Testament indicates that different people should give different amounts according to their own circumstances.

Having made it clear that simply carrying out the requirements of the Law does not amount to true obedience, Jesus regularly calls on his listeners to go well beyond the Law's commands.

It's at this point that tithing can become something of a problem. The reality for many of us is that we are frequently able to give away far *more* than 10 percent of our income. So setting aside our tithe can easily lead us to pat ourselves on the back for doing it right. In the process we also subconsciously presume that what is left is for us to do with as we please. The result looks uncomfortably like both self-indulgence and self-righteousness!

Furthermore, tithing takes no account of the huge variety of ways we can give to the cause of the Kingdom. For example, what if you choose to be employed for only twenty hours per week, in order to give the rest of your time to unpaid service? Or what about the couple who use their home as a place of refuge and support for vulnerable women and children, without asking for any financial remuneration? Are these not

---

5. Luke 18: 11–12.

6. It is likely that the Jewish believers continued to practise tithing, but unlikely that the non-Jewish ones instituted it.

7. I'll spend a whole chapter looking at the practice of generosity. See chapter 20.

examples of giving? And if so, how can they be "calculated" as part of the tithing equation?

Ironically, most people who champion tithing as a necessary requirement for Christians today, generally only do so on the basis of it being 10 percent of their income. However, as I've already noted, for the Jews it was never one tithe—but several. So if we really want to continue the practice of tithing, then perhaps we should set aside, say 25 percent of our earnings!

Another practical and realistic way of structuring regular giving into our finances is that suggested by Ron Sider in his book *Rich Christians in an Age of Hunger*—a "graduated tithe" where we increase our percentage of giving as our income rises.

My own preference is to maintain regular, planned giving, but not be limited by the concept of tithing. The primary issue to me is not, "is tithing right or wrong" but "will tithing help us to be generous and faithful givers"? For me, tithing doesn't help answer this question.

Giving to whom?

Another challenge for those promoting the continuation of tithing is working out *where* or to *whom* their tithes should be given.

It is common to hear people quoting Malachi's words—just as Pastor Mike did: "Bring the whole tithe into the storehouse, that there may be food in my house"—and implying that the modern equivalent of the "storehouse" is the "local church" and that fulltime pastors are comparable to the Levites. This brings problems. To begin with, as I've already noted, the Law involved a wider framework of sacrificial worship, which in order to be maintained, required one of the tribes—the Levites—to operate as priests and administrators of the system. More than one tithe was set aside for support of these people. It acted like a kind of religious tax.

Today, no such system exists. The complexities of animal sacrifice and elaborate ritual focused around the Temple are not part of our world (neither Jewish nor Christian).

So, it is drawing a very long bow to make a local church out to be the equivalent of "the storehouse," or to argue that by implication paid pastors are analogous to the Levitical priests.[8]

---

8. However, the Apostle Paul does draw a link between the Levites and those "who proclaim the gospel" in his first letter to the church in Corinth (10:13–14).

However, there *is* plenty of support in the New Testament for all members of the Body taking responsibility to contribute to the ongoing communal life and mission of the church. As we pick our way through the developing practices of the first believers, we see that sometimes this meant giving in order to provide for those members of the church who had limited means of support (see, for example, the widows mentioned in Acts 6:1). Other times, this involved providing for people outside the church. There are also examples where particular people were set aside to play a specific role or task in God's mission, and financially supported in order to do so.

The Apostle Paul's own ministry and teaching demonstrates that there was a great deal of liberty and diversity, remarkably free of rules or demands. Where possible, Paul attempted to support himself financially and he encouraged others to do similarly. However, he wasn't opposed to receiving gifts in order to fulfill his ministry, and indeed he received support from the Philippian church—though probably not while he was working among them. It seems that Paul's practice of supporting himself as much as possible was because he wanted his preaching of the gospel to be free of any personal greed or obligation to others (see 1 Cor 9). For Paul, God's mission was paramount and shouldn't be compromised by mixed motives. Self–support was his preference, but it wasn't a rule.

So to summarize the early church's experience:

- Is it likely that regular, planned giving was encouraged? Yes.[9]
- Did members and congregations engage in spontaneous, liberal giving? Yes.
- What about compulsory, percentaged giving? Was it mandated? No.
- Was there freedom to set aside and support particular people for particular tasks? Yes.
- Was regular pressure applied to congregations to give more and more money to "support God's work"? At least, on the evidence of the New Testament . . . No.

Once again, Pastor Mike has conveniently twisted the Bible's teaching on money and giving, making it out to say something that it simply doesn't.

---

9. See, for example, Paul's instructions to the church at Corinth in 1 Cor 16:2.

Section A: Bible

Spontaneous acts of giving

It seems clear then that in the New Testament there is a less prescribed approach to giving, than in the Old. So it is not surprising that we observe two significant acts of spontaneous and voluntary overflows of Spirit-driven generosity in the recorded story of the New Testament church.

The first of these is in its very early days. We read about it in Acts chapter 2. In describing the heady days after Pentecost, Luke notes: "They [the believers] committed themselves to the teaching of the apostles, the life together, the common meal, and the prayers. Everyone was in awe—all those wonders and signs done through the apostles! And all the believers lived in a wonderful harmony, holding everything in common. They sold whatever they owned and pooled their resources so that each person's need was met."[10]

This financial *koinonia* (communal sharing of resources) is repeated in Acts 4. Here we are told that: "The whole congregation of believers was united as one—one heart, one mind! They didn't even claim ownership of their own possessions. No one said, 'That's mine; you can't have it.' They shared everything . . . And so it turned out that not a person among them was needy. Those who owned fields or houses sold them and brought the price of the sale to the apostles and made an offering of it. The disciples then distributed it, according to each person's need."[11]

There is some debate among scholars regarding the exact details of this extraordinary display of generosity and solidarity. Was it an example of absolute collectivism? Or did a place for private ownership still exist? Certainly, there is little other suggestion in the New Testament that complete economic equality occurred within the church.

Nevertheless, however it happened, the early church was clearly very committed to taking Deuteronomy 15:4 seriously: "There should be no poor among you." Remember, this was part of what it meant to be a covenant community. And it is also significant that in both chapters (Acts 2 and 4), the sharing of resources is noted as a clear response of the Holy Spirit's work among the believers. It seems that such powerful works of God have economic implications and outworkings.

The second significant act of giving noted in the records of the New Testament church, can be found in Paul's second letter to the church at Corinth, chapters 8 and 9. According to Paul, the churches in the province

---

10. Acts 2:42–45.
11. Acts 4:32–35.

of Macedonia spontaneously began financial aid toward their brothers and sisters in Jerusalem—struggling with the devastation of an ongoing famine. This, even though the Christians of Macedonia were also battling with "fierce troubles" of their own that had "pushed them to the very limit."[12]

In this letter, Paul challenges the Corinthians to follow the example of their sister churches in Macedonia and give generously to this relief operation. It seems that they have previously been inspired to contribute, but have so far failed to act on their good intentions.

Some time later, Paul travels with a number of companions from these churches to Jerusalem, carrying with him the relief money that has been raised. As it transpires, this is his last trip back to Judea; it results in his arrest. In his defense to Governor Felix in Acts 24:17, Paul alludes briefly to the raising of the money: "While I was away I took up a collection for the poor and brought that with me, along with offerings for the Temple."

We'll explore this contribution from the Macedonian churches more fully in chapter 20. However, it's worth noting here that the passage in 2 Corinthians, which deals with this money-raising project really forms the core teaching on giving in the New Testament. It has important things to say about both *why* and *how* we should give.

Finally...

In summary then, we can safely assume the following about the theme of giving in the Bible:

- God is a self-giving God. Therefore, giving and sharing of financial resources is core to what it means to be part of the covenant community (both Old and New).

- While the tithe was a central part of the Law's requirements for giving, it never involved just 10 percent of a person's income—the Jews gave far more than this.

- Tithing is hardly mentioned in the New Testament, and when it is it's generally viewed in a more negative than positive light.

- Giving generously and freely according to one's circumstances supersedes the Law's prescribed tithes and offerings.

12. 2 Cor 8:2.

Section A: Bible

- The intention of leaders such as Paul is to ensure that within the church everyone has enough for their needs—a minimizing of the gap between rich and poor.
- Wherever there are common purses, or special offerings are taken up, they are distributed with this purpose in mind and the early church creates mechanisms to do this (e.g. Paul's journey to Jerusalem with the relief fund, and the appointment of deacons in Acts 6:1–7).

There is also great encouragement to care for the poor outside of the church.

Up Close and Personal

1. Discuss what you have been taught regarding the place of tithing?
2. Is tithing taught and/or practiced in your church tradition? If so, how? What advantages or limitations do think such an emphasis has for us today?
3. What unexpected and spontaneous communal acts of giving have you observed (or been part of)—either in a church/Christian group setting or in your community? What sparked it? How was it received?

Section B

Culture

An exploration of the way our culture treats money

CAPITALISM IS THE IDEOLOGY that drives the economic system we live in. The goal of this vision for human life is individual *Happiness*, which is mainly found in the *Consumption* of more and more things, and the freedom to have maximum *Choice*. Producers encourage us to consume more by convincing us that what they have, we *Need*. They promote their *Brand* through advertising and marketing. Our financial system persuades us to take advantage of *Credit*, so we can purchase things now rather than later. Our resulting *Affluence* is more like a disease than a blessing.

10

Capitalism

> "*Capitalism is not merely a description of an economic arrangement based on markets. Rather, it is a moral vision based explicitly on utilitarian philosophy, materialism and individualism.*"
> Paul Williams

IN 1995 I BECAME involved, somewhat unexpectedly, in the business of buying and selling cars. A colleague and I had been looking for a small business opportunity that would allow us to become involved in the marketplace, while also producing revenue for our charitable enterprises. For the next dozen or so years I attempted to do business in this challenging industry.[1]

Now let me say right from the start that I'm fully aware of the low esteem my "profession" (an overly generous term?) is held in. We've done particularly poorly on the "most trusted professions" annual survey, rating just above politicians who carry the perennial tag of "least trusted." I'm comforted by the fact that only just above us are lawyers, and that the ongoing behavior of some politicians means that we're not likely to supplant our not-so-honorable Members at the bottom of the pile—at least not any time soon. Though I write from our New Zealand context, I'm sure the same is largely true across the world!

I've also learnt to live with the jokes—like the one that asks when you can tell that a car dealer is lying. (Answer: when he moves his lips.)

---

1. It's only relatively recently that I decided not renew my dealer's licence—so I'm now an "ex" car dealer!

Section B: Culture

Nevertheless, my experience as a car dealer taught me a great deal about the economic system we are part of. I came to understand the realities of trading in a market economy, buying secondhand vehicles in Japan, and then shipping them to New Zealand in the hope that I would be able to sell them to customers for more than they cost me. Most times a profit was made. However, sometimes I lost out.

I remember my first venture into this world of trading vehicles. I had gone to a local auction house and got carried away with the bidding. The minute the auctioneer brought down the hammer, pointed at me and shouted "Sold!," I had that sinking feeling in the pit of my stomach. Had I just bought a "lemon"? Would I be able to resell it? (I eventually did—for a miniscule profit—but the experience was a daunting rite of passage.)

I learnt quickly about the principle of supply and demand, the rapidly changing car market, and the problem of unsold vehicles losing value. There were financial rewards for risks taken, but also the potential to go backwards very quickly.

My practical experience in the car business taught me much about capitalism from the bottom up. And that venture—putting Bible and business together and learning from both—lies behind many of the lessons of this book.

This is a difficult chapter to write, but if we are to understand the way our culture views and treats money, and if we are to apply the Bible's lessons about money to this century that we live in, we must understand clearly the economic system that drives us in the twenty-first century: namely, Capitalism. For it is Capitalism that shapes the majority of our financial aspirations, attitudes, and behavior.

The *economic* swamp is bad enough, but there's worse. I'm only too aware that our Christian world is as split over economic theories as it is over theological beliefs. To dot an economic i incorrectly, or cross a financial t at fractionally the wrong angle risks condemning me in the eyes of some of my fellow believers and casting me into outer darkness. So, with poisoned chalice in hand and metaphors crashing round my ears, let me venture across this snake pit of fiscally ferocious serpents, and into this den of doctrinally dangerous lions!

Which "capitalism" are we talking about?

The first step is to clarify what we mean by capitalism, and this is a much harder task than you might think. Phrases such as "free market," "democratic capitalism," "consumer capitalism," and "market economy" get bandied about. Do they have special meanings, or are they simply different words for the same thing?

While these terms do overlap, they refer to slightly different matters. And how they look varies substantially from one country to another.

British economist and theologian Paul Williams argues that any discussion about capitalism needs to distinguish between "capitalism as an *ideology* of the market" on the one hand, and "the market economy as a *system for organizing our economic behavior*"[2] on the other.

I think this is a really helpful distinction. But what exactly does he mean? And why is it important for us to understand it?

Let's begin with the second description: "the market economy" that is "a system for organizing our economic behavior." This, says Paul Williams is "a way of organizing the production and distribution of goods and services which is more efficient and more effective than any of the alternatives." Alternatives like:

- Each one of us producing for ourselves everything we need—all our food and clothing and shelter and whatever, or

- Having the government tell us what to produce, and then distributing everything to everybody, or

- Violently grabbing what we want from our neighbor or the nation next door.

The trading of goods and services in a "market" economy is a very efficient way for a society to operate. It creates a system of matching what is produced to what is desired. You think you've come up with a clever new product? Then you'll soon learn that if there is no demand for it you either have to stop making it or find ways of convincing people they *need* what you've produced.[3] In this way, your innovative ideas are tailored to the market. It's very efficient. The law of supply and demand is what makes it work. No demand by customers for a product means that that product won't be worth producing.

---

2. Williams, "Free markets do foster the decline of virtue."
3. I'll look more closely at the role "need" plays, in chapter 13.

Section B: Culture

A market economy does something else: it gives *sellers* an accurate way to determine the merit of their product—and it also helps *buyers* to calculate how much they want it. Money is the mechanism. It allows us to measure what is worth producing, consuming, or investing in.

Capitalism – with a big 'C'

So much for the market economy, the efficient system that connects producers with consumers. Williams also points out that Capitalism is something else. It is an ideology— "a moral vision based explicitly on utilitarian philosophy, materialism and individualism." Let's call it Capitalism—with a big "C."

So Capitalism, the ideology, is a *particular* way of understanding how and why a market economy should operate. It is a specific belief system that provides the logic for our particular form of market economy. That's why understanding this chapter is important. This is the ideology that drives much of our economic behavior—as individuals, businesses, governments, and whole societies.

So what are the core elements of Capitalism?

At its epicenter, the goal of Capitalism is individual happiness. Fairly ordinary, you may think—happiness for individuals is hardly a new idea. Well, you're wrong. It is! At least, in the sense that whole societies should base their behavior on such a belief. The idea was formulated in the 1700s as the notion that the moral worth of a particular action can be determined solely by the degree to which it maximizes happiness or pleasure for the greatest number of people. If you set up a society with this sort of thinking, freedom is everything. Humans are seen as rational beings, able to determine for themselves what is best and good.

If we give people as much choice as possible, the assumption is that they will then make the best choice for themselves, and that taken over the whole economy these individual choices will bring about what is best for society. Furthermore, says Williams: "Mainstream economists argue that more effective individual choice and more competitive [free] markets will produce greater economic efficiency and faster economic growth. Since greater production is bound up with greater happiness for more and more people, any barrier to the expansion of choice must be removed."[4]

4. Williams,"Free markets do foster the decline of virtue."

This belief develops a natural impetus. It comes to assume that the market should extend to almost *every* area of life—so that people can make their own choice about not just what car they will drive but what type of health care they will receive, which school they will send their child to, which church they will attend, how long they will stay married, and whether they will keep alive the fetus they've just conceived.

Free market, free trade, profit maximization, unrestrained choice, maximum individual happiness, economic growth—these are the bywords of our Capitalist system.

Where does democracy fit into all this?

In order for Capitalism to develop the way it has, it turns out that a stable and supportive political system is necessary. And the one that has provided the ideal conditions for capitalism (small "c": the free market) to flourish is democracy—of the universal suffrage type, where every person has a vote. What democracy has done is provide a system where personal rights and ownership are guaranteed and where every person, regardless of his or her station in life, has a say in the economic and political life of the state and the opportunity to produce, buy, sell, and invest. (At least, that's the theory!)

When people know that a feudal lord or a modern dictator isn't going to forcibly confiscate their capital or stop them from trading, or engage in monopolist practices, they become confident and free to innovate, experiment, and trade. Entrepreneurship flourishes. And when products and services are traded, both parties involved do so freely, believing that the trade is fair value for them.

It's no real surprise then that Capitalism has evolved hand–in–hand with the development of modern democracy. The two are very much linked—each feeding the other. Because of this, our system is often called democratic capitalism.[5]

---

5. It is also often called "consumer capitalism." And for good reason. We'll look at the critical role consumption plays in our system in chapter 12.

Section B: Culture

How do Christians view our economic system—good or bad?

As I suggested back at the beginning of this chapter, when it comes to discussions about our economics there's an enormous spectrum of views amongst followers of Jesus.

Some Christians believe that Capitalism is ordained by God. It is God's preferred system! They'll vigorously defend it until the cows come home, and even back up their arguments by quoting Scripture—but in a way that betrays more about the tinted lenses they're seeing through than what the Bible actually does say.

Meanwhile, other Christians consider Capitalism to be inherently evil—a rotten system we would be better off without. It seems to me that these people really want to have their cake and eat it too. That is, they pick holes in the system, arguing that there's nothing worth redeeming from it, but generally still choose to enjoy all or most of the great benefits it provides.

It is dangerous and somewhat shallow to paint Capitalism in either totally black or white colors—as though it's thoroughly bad and rotten (on the one hand) or the best thing since sliced bread (on the other). I believe that identifying a distinction between our market economy and Capitalism helps to clarify things. Our market economy, our free market system, has brought undeniable benefits to our lives. However, at the same time, it also threatens our very future—and certainly is a corrosive influence on our capacity to faithfully follow Jesus. To understand this clearly, we need to see the ideology behind our market economy; that is, Capitalism.

These two sides must be held in tension. Developing a balanced assessment of our economic system is not easy. So let's reflect, ever so briefly, on some of the positives and negatives, keeping in mind that we're more likely to be debating about features of Capitalism (the ideological framework) than about features of capitalism (the existence of markets).

The positive side

In the white corner . . . we have clear evidence of the remarkable difference Capitalism has made to the lives of billions of people over the past few centuries—including yours and mine.

It is easy to assume things have always been the way they are, and to take for granted all the huge advantages of living in the twenty-first century. Idealizing life in past centuries is always a popular trap to fall into. (For example, we often view the New Testament church through rose-tinted spectacles.) We like to think that life was simpler in bygone days, and therefore less complicated, less rushed, less stressed. In a word, *easier*.

There are elements of truth in this . . . but most of it flies in the face of the brutal realities of pre-modern life. The full truth is that materially life for most people in most countries and in most centuries has been appallingly hard. Life expectancy was abysmally low. Disease was rife. Economic survival was deeply unpredictable and dependent on the greed of the ruling class, the prevalence of war, and the fickleness of the seasons. Hard work didn't necessarily correlate with reward. In fact, most people toiled long days, with little if any disposable time or money. There were few opportunities to improve one's lot—that largely depended on one's station in life.

Capitalism has brought unbelievable improvements to our standard of living. Innovation and creativity have thrived. A flood of technological breakthroughs have resulted in enormous leaps forward in health care, communication, transportation, and housing. And while there are still numbers of people in our Western nations who miss out on some of these benefits, there are many more beneficiaries than any other system has ever produced.

There's also no doubt that the arrival of Capitalism has meant more people having the opportunity to chart their own course economically than was formerly the case. Coupled with democratic freedoms, Capitalism has enabled a significant majority of men, and now increasingly women, in the West to make choices about what work they will do, how long they will work, where they will live, and how they will spend their money and time—all of them choices that were previously unthinkable for the masses.

The negative side

Meanwhile, in the black corner . . . we have unmistakable signs of unease about the way Capitalism corrupts and undermines our capacity to live out God's intended vision for his world. Here are four such concerns:

Section B: Culture

The problem of growth

A consequence of the free market has been to fuel the myth that economic growth is always good. According to our system, more is always better. Bigger is always best.

In fact, Capitalism only works well when more and more is being produced. To do this, more and more stuff has to be sold. Which means that more and more "desires" have to be created—or at least manipulated. It's as if we have stepped on an escalator that we just can't seem to get off. Confidence in the market requires stimulus when growth slows down.

Capitalism is, because of its very vision, incapable of putting limits on growth. Or of discerning when enough is enough.

This is not to say that economic growth is in itself unhealthy. The flood of products and services that Capitalism has stimulated has been the fuel of the market economy. But Capitalism is voracious. It is committed to increasing the productivity. It must always grow. If the growth ever stops, as it does from time to time, crisis sets in. And this is the problem: you can't just feed more and more into a body. The more food you pump in, the more bloated and unhealthy it becomes.

There's another problem too with Capitalism's fixation on product growth: to measure our quality of life in such narrow, economic terms is to focus on and aspire to the wrong things. It highlights the very lopsided and limited vision Capitalism has for life. To be sure, charting the growth by GDP (Gross Domestic Product—what we produce) can be useful—but by itself it fails to take into account other valuable indicators of a society's health.[6]

The problem of equity

In spite of the fact that billions of people are now living above a subsistence level, there are still significant numbers in the countries that embrace Capitalism who continue to miss out on the "party." These underclasses of the poor and marginalized look on in envy, growing more resentful by the day. And the gap is getting wider—not narrower. At an alarming rate. Significantly, in times of increased prosperity, like that

---

6. GPI (General Progress Index) is a broader measuring stick that has traction among some economists. It includes issues such as unemployment, crime rates, and environmental factors. However, even GPI is still measuring a society's health or well-being in largely economic terms.

Capitalism

experienced around the turn of the century, the "trickle-down" theory[7] has had little or no effect. Some might even say that what we've had is more of a trickle–up!

Furthermore, although the means now exist to eradicate absolute poverty in the world, those who have thrived and benefited most from capitalism have displayed minimal interest or *will* for sharing their overwhelming surplus with the "have-nots." This is compounded by the sad irony that much of the great wealth of Western nations has been built on the back of poor nations. The dramatic growth of the West in the last few centuries has been through exploitation of the developing world—particularly by way of raw materials and cheap or expendable labor.[8]

In spite of some wonderfully generous mega–philanthropists, and large numbers of compassionate but more modest givers, the rates of charitable giving have decreased. The same can be true at a state level. Though numerous pleas, campaigns, and pledges have been made, assistance by wealthier nations toward poorer states is pitiful. And forgiving of developing–world debt is still some distance away.

To be fair, there are at least two qualifiers to this concern. Firstly, as I've already noted, the vast majority of humans have *always* lived at subsistence level or below for most of history. Capitalism has dramatically decreased (at least as a percentage of the world's population) those who are physically poor.

Secondly, some of the huge inequities in the world, it could be argued, are precisely because the kind of "liberation" that democratic capitalism can bring to a nation is sadly missing. Burma and Zimbabwe provide two such tragic examples. Both countries were, until recently, considered the "rice bowls/bread baskets" of their particular continents. Rich in natural resources, they would be expected to support vibrant and healthy economies. Instead, a combination of tyrannical rule, confiscation of private property, unfair monopolistic laws, and the erosion of democratic processes have all led to both countries becoming "basket cases." The majority of their people live in abject poverty, fear, and uncertainty. No enterprise except that which is government-run or sanctioned will thrive in this context.

---

7. The idea that the benefits of wealth–creation will "trickle down" from those in society who are most benefiting from it, to everyone else.

8. This is a huge, ongoing issue, and while the "fair trade" movement has grown substantially in recently years, it still is only a small fraction of the market of products from the developing world into the West.

97

Nevertheless, it is the largely unwilling nature of the "haves" to share with the "have-nots" that draws big question marks on how "good" Capitalism is for us.

The problem of sustainability

Coupled with this apparent unwillingness to share is the growing realization that the kind of lifestyle Capitalism has now made possible for significant numbers of the world's citizens, is actually unsustainable. Even if all countries fully embraced democratic capitalism, there is no way that all seven billion residents of the earth could share the kind of standard of living being experienced by most of us in the West. There are simply not enough resources to go around.[9] And, even more concerning, the ecosystem itself will not sustain it. Our environment is already hemorrhaging from the rape and abuse that industry and our own lifestyles have brought on it. As political theorist Marius de Geus contends, "unlimited production and consumption are at the roots of our current environmental decay."[10]

One of the contributing causes of this unsustainability is what economists call "externalities." This is where some group, company, individual, sector of society (or even a whole society) doesn't pay the full costs of a particular service or product. A vivid example is the driving of our private cars. We pay fuel, maintenance, purchasing, and roading costs, but many of the biggest costs are hidden or unable to be easily calculated. Social dislocation, commuting time, greenhouse gases, pollution—these are just some of the other real costs of our driving lifestyle. If the true cost of such activity could be calculated and then charged to us, it would force us to limit our use of private vehicles (or at the very least, fuel-inefficient ones) because the cost to us personally would be astronomical.

Of course, some of these costs *can't* be measured in economic terms—costs such as visual pollution, the social and community implications, and the individual implications (like the increase in our levels of stress that comes from the speeding up of our lives). Because the real cost is not factored in—or able to be calculated—the long-term

---

9. I recognise that there are some who dispute this—particularly those economists who claim we don't have to worry about resources running out, since technology will always get better at using what we have. They are more optimistic than I am.

10. de Geus, *The End of Over-Consumption*, 13.

Capitalism

consequences of our choices fail to carry the moral weight they should in our decision-making.

So Capitalism has so far shown itself incapable of placing economic and environmental constraints on the consumption of resources. Either we are too blinded by self-interest or too addicted to our affluent lifestyles to significantly change our ways.

The problem of commodification

Perhaps most disturbing is the subversive way Capitalism has changed how we value things.

Our system is made possible because of the belief that anything can be given an economic value, and exchanged. This makes it a commodity. Skye Jethani points out that, "as a result, an object's value is not linked directly to what it is, but what it can be exchanged for."[11]

When we are so used to asking how much something is worth (in dollar terms) it becomes a very short step to reducing *all* of life to a monetary value. This is called "commodification." Os Guinness explains:

> [Commodification] describes the process whereby money assumes such a dominant place in a society that everything (and everyone) is seen and treated as a commodity to be bought and sold. The term may be new, but the problem, as the Greek legend of Midas shows, is old. Among notorious early examples of commodification are the moneychangers in the Jewish temple and the papal selling of indulgences by Johann Tetzel in the medieval era.
>
> ... The charge of commodification is not a criticism of the marketplace itself—buying, selling, merchandizing, and marketing are all legitimate in their place. But not everything can or should be given a market price. The line drawn between "For Sale" and "Not For Sale" is a prime indication of a nation's or group's values.[12]

(Curiously, Karl Marx recognized well over a century ago that the end result of Capitalism is that everything becomes saleable and purchasable!)

Unfortunately, over time Capitalism has so coloured our view that even things of greatest value are now vulnerable to being commodified.

11. Jethani, *The Divine Commodity*, 36.
12. Guinness, *The Call*, 137.

Section B: Culture

Like, for example, our bodies, which are increasingly an open market. While prostitution has always been a tawdry selling of human sexuality, the commodification of our bodies has now extended to offering body parts for sale (including sperm and fertilized eggs for reproduction). Surrogate babies too—and even the renting of people's bodies for advertising purposes! All these matters are now "products and services." They can be exploited for economic gain. And our culture seems largely happy to allow this.

Even our relationships with others fall into this category. Marriage is now often viewed as an economic commodity, with some couples determining whether or not they get married according to the financial costs and benefits. The "time is money" equation leads us to wonder, based on some form of cost/benefit analysis, how much time to "invest" (a financial term!) in a particular relationship. "Spending"[13] time with someone is costly, so that it seems we need to weigh it up against other purposes we might put the time to—including creating income! Of course, the most extreme form of the commodification of relationships occurs when we consider certain individuals as valuable to us because knowing them will help us make money.

Australian economists Clive Hamilton and Richard Denniss put it this way:

> Market values have increasingly colonized all other values, so that ethical decisions have become economic decisions, despite a nagging feeling that putting a price on some things actually devalues them. Even the most intimate and precious aspects of being human have been subtly transformed into their antithesis. Becoming a parent used to be something we did because it was part of the human condition; now it is a "lifestyle choice" . . . In the richest societies humanity has ever known, people are asking whether they can afford to have a baby.[14]

Tragically, this has also spilled over into the way we determine matters of faith and God.[15]

---

13. Yet another money term!
14. Hamilton and Denniss, *Affluenza*, 142–43.
15. We'll explore this further in chapter 12.

Limit–less

All the black marks I have noted here against our capitalist system have one thing in common. They all demonstrate Capitalism's inability to place *limits* or constraints on our economic endeavors. Capitalism shows itself unwilling to limit economic growth, or the accumulation of wealth, or the use of resources, or the areas of life that should be valued by an economic calculation. All these indicate the insidious potential of Capitalism as an ideology to overwhelm all the positive benefits our market economy has brought.

Some might say that this inability to place limits is not so much a fault of the system, but rather of the people who inhabit the system. The two *are* related. However, fundamentally it is the overriding worldview of Capitalism that leads us to throw off the shackles of restraint. To return to my earlier metaphor, Capitalism is too busy devouring food to notice the signs of its obesity.

Ethic–less

A further problem: Capitalism fails to support an ethic beyond that of personal happiness. To be sure, concern for "the common good" is often expressed—but in practice does this mean any more than the sum total of everyone maximizing their own happiness? That is, what is "good" for me is "good" for our society. (This is what Adam Smith—often considered the father of Capitalism—called "enlightened self-interest.")

In many ways, Capitalism is actually built around a lack of self-control. In fact, the system depends on it. Several astute commentators have noted over the years that all the "seven deadly sins" have, under consumer capitalism, been transformed into a positive virtue. Greed, lust, envy, gluttony (over–consumption), sloth, anger, and pride are the driving force of our economy.

No wonder Gordon Gekko could so unselfconsciously proclaim: "Greed is good." Within the ideology of Capitalism his statement makes perfect sense.

However, even though Capitalism lacks an ethical framework, it is certainly not "value–free." Its vision for life is built on the core values of personal happiness, consumption, need, and choice. They undergird Capitalism. Which, as my experience as a car dealer taught me, makes it

Section B: Culture

a real challenge to seek to live by an alternative vision—one shaped by the Bible—while still being an active participant in the market economy.[16]

So it is to these values that we'll turn, beginning in the next chapter with the role that the pursuit of happiness plays in all of this.

Up Close and Personal

1. Prior to your reading of this chapter, how have you personally viewed the value of the free-market capitalist system? (Rate your position 1–10, with 10 being unquestioning acceptance.) Where have your views come from?

2. Discuss the positives and negatives raised in this chapter.
   - Which ones do you think are particularly pertinent?
   - Which ones do you think are questionable?
   - Which ones hadn't you considered before?
   - Can you think of other positives or negatives?

3. Try thinking of an advertisement for a product or service that has transformed each of the following vices into a virtue.
   - Greed?
   - Lust?
   - Gluttony (over-consumption)?
   - Pride/Vanity?
   - Envy (coveting)?
   - Anger?
   - Sloth?

---

16. I've written elsewhere about these challenges—particularly in two books co-authored with my friend Alistair Mackenzie—*Where's God on Monday?* and *Just Decisions: Christian ethics go to work.*

11

Happiness

"Whoever said money can't buy happiness isn't spending it right."
Lexus advert

In chapter 6 I mentioned the weeks I spent in the Philippines. Over twenty years later I can still recall many of the sights and smells that confronted me each day in the Asian heat and humidity. Decomposing mounds of trash. Smoldering fires, the result of spontaneously combusting rubbish. Flies by the hundreds, hanging off every available space. Dogs, lean as skeletons, roaming the alleyways. Shelters made from pieces of cardboard, corrugated iron, and plastic, all arranged in some kind of order—poor excuses for houses to protect against the harsh elements of tropical Manila.

But what I most recall are the people. Toothless grins from dear old women. Scantily clad children playing in the "streets" with old deflated soccer balls. Laughter and chatter in the common areas of the slum. The warm smile and welcome from people I hardly knew, ushering me into their shacks for a drink or something to eat. Giving of their best, even though that meant going without themselves.

These humbling experiences left a deep impression on me. I remember being struck by the stark contrast when I returned home. While I knew better than to romanticize in any way the harsh conditions that my new-found friends in Manila lived under, I noticed the presence of a great deal more happiness and joy there than I found on the streets of New Zealand. The simple pleasures of life and community were celebrated. At home I noted the sour faces, trite complaints, intolerance,

Section B: Culture

and moans about anything that might have "spoilt" a person's day—like traffic jams, a shower of rain or having to queue in the supermarket for a couple of minutes.

The contrasts were vivid. Even more so because I noticed how many of these trivial concerns were part of my own life and experience. I had to be honest and admit that in spite of the deprivation and pain in their lives, my friends in the Philippines seemed to be much happier than the average Westerner.

Years later, a friend of mine who visited us from India would say to me, "In your country Wayne, people have full stomachs and empty hearts. In my country, people have empty stomachs but full hearts."

The elusive state of happiness

Happiness. It's the thing we want more than anything else. And our culture is very good at promising it . . . just around the next corner. Generally in the form of a new car, the latest gadget, lotteries win, an overseas holiday, or a fashion accessory. In fact, as I noted in the last chapter, it is really the goal of Capitalism. When we extend freedom of choice to cover more and more spheres of life, we do it in order to maximize individual happiness. Our economic system is meant to make us all happy.

So in our consumer culture money and happiness go together like love and marriage. Or so we believe.

But do the facts support this? Let's consider the last fifty years of life in the West. It's undeniable that we are now more affluent than any other previous generation. We have more gadgets, disposable income, and lifestyle options. Real income has risen dramatically since 1960. We now have much more purchasing power, more educational opportunities, better nutrition, and better health care. We also have more chances to see the world and experience things our grandparents could only dream about.

However, depression is now ten times more common than in 1960. Plus, it strikes at a much earlier age. The mean average of a person's first depressive episode was 29.5 years in 1960. Now it is 14.5 years! Coupled with this are our suicide rates, which although leveling off, are still substantially higher than fifty years ago.

In 1957 the percentage of Americans describing themselves as "very happy" reached a peak. It's been in decline ever since. In other words, these days we have a lot more "stuff" but the feeling of well-being is less than it was.

Two experts in different fields reinforce this. Clive Hamilton is an Australian economist who heads up the Australia Institute. The belief that economic growth means better or happier lives for all of us is, he says, hollow. It simply can't be supported by the evidence.[1]

In fact, he suggests that our political fetish of economic growth and the marketing society lies at the heart of our social ills. It corrupts not just our social priorities and political structures, but also produces enormous alienation.

Martin Seligman is a psychologist who has studied happiness for more than thirty years. His research suggests that when looking for life satisfaction, you needn't bother with making more money, staying healthy, getting as much education as you can, or moving to a sunnier climate![2] There's no doubt that a certain amount of money or health helps, but once we get past survival level, more money, it seems, doesn't make a lot of difference. It's like the law of diminishing returns.

In short, he discovered that circumstances don't create happiness. Nor do things. They may help a little, but they're not a significant factor in true, enduring happiness.

Seligman contends that one reason we as a culture are less happy than our parents' generation is because of our over-reliance on "shortcuts to pleasure" such as shopping, fast-food meals, TV, drugs, spectator sports, and loveless sex. We're a culture that is more concerned with short term pleasurable feelings than long term happiness. True fulfillment, he suggests, is not the sum total of a whole lot of pleasurable experiences. We're focusing on the wrong thing.

That makes a lot of sense. For some of the products and experiences we purchase do indeed give us a good feeling. At least, for a time. When we buy a new appliance we may actually feel "happier" for a couple of days—until the warm fuzzy from the novelty of having something new begins to wear off.

However, this is very different from true contentment—and yet our culture masquerades these pleasurable experiences as the path to well-being. In fact, as media critic, Jean Kilbourne notes, "[Advertising] teaches us that happiness can be bought, that there are instant answers to

---

1. See Hamilton, *Growth Fetish*.
2. See Seligman, *Authentic Happiness*.

life's complex problems, and that products can meet our deepest human needs."[3]

Consequently, it's not a surprise that this tenuous connection between money and happiness has spawned a mini joke industry all of its own. Here are a few classics to chuckle over:

"It isn't necessary to be rich and famous to be happy. It's only necessary to be rich." Alan Alda

"Money can't buy you happiness but it does bring you a more pleasant form of misery." Spike Milligan

"Whoever said money can't buy happiness didn't know where to shop." Gertrude Stein

Hidden beneath the humor are some unnerving and conflicting thoughts. On the one hand, we know the foolishness of expecting that more wealth and more stuff will increase our sense of satisfaction with life. Yet, at another level, so much of our energy is spent dreaming what it would be like if we had more money. So many of our aspirations come with a price tag.

Few of us would ever admit to swallowing the "money buys happiness" line. And yet our lives often tell a different story. We are Jekyll-and-Hyde's. We are split personalities. We live life on two levels. In short, we are creatures of our culture. Intellectually we know that beyond a certain point more money will not bring contentment, but we are too deeply immersed in our culture to completely sever the link.

The result is that when we think about it . . . sure, we reject the line. But when we're involved in the business of daily living . . . well, *then* we just take it for granted. It's a social given. Of course we want more.

What is the "good life" we think will make us happy?

At the heart of this is our dream of the "good life." The form the dream takes comes courtesy of the culture we belong to, with slightly different features depending on where you live. But the global village has defined the furniture pretty consistently.

In New Zealand, for example, the "great Kiwi dream" goes something like this:

---

3. From the transcript of the documentary DVD program, *The Ad and the Ego* (Parallax Pictures).

I want to own a nice house on a good-sized section (kiwism for lot/yard), preferably with a view and with all the mod cons—high definition TV, spa pool, etc. —in a "safe" area of town. I'd be able to buy the new car I've always wanted to own but could never afford.

I want a bach or crib (kiwisms for cottage, cabin or holiday house) by the beach or lake. This is where I'll spend the lazy days of summer, soaking in the sun and relaxing. With the bach will come a boat. With the boat will come fishing and waterskiing to my heart's content.

Once a year we'll take an overseas holiday—exploring the parts of the world we haven't yet seen—like Thailand (I mean Phuket), India (that's Agra), Greece (the Greek Islands), and South Africa (the wildlife parks).

I'd like to take up a hobby or two like golf and theatre and spend a lot more time eating out and enjoying the finer things of life.

By age sixty I'd like to "retire" (read: stop paid employment) and enjoy the hard-earned benefits of a life of work. In order to do this, I need a good superannuation/retirement scheme with a diverse range of investments that allow me to live at a really good standard of living. A portfolio of somewhere around a million dollars or more should do.

When I have all this I'll be really happy.

Common features of the great Western dream

You'll need to change a few of the specifics above to suit the country you live in and your own personal tastes. But for our voiced or unvoiced dreams of the good life, the recurring themes are all there.

First, our dreams usually rely on the accumulation of more and more "stuff." In fact, in aiming for the *good* life, we really find ourselves settling for the *goods* life.

Second, they invariably emphasize increased choice. That is, the good life involves the freedom to do what we want to do. Anything that increases this choice is included. Those things that might restrict our freedom are discarded.

Third, the great Western dream usually involves a withdrawal from society. We see ourselves as being happier once we've dis-engaged from the "rat race," for we think that it is our immersion in the complexity of modern life (the need to juggle multiple balls, the pressure to perform and to get ahead, etc.) that causes the stress and alienation we feel. (On this we are *partly* right—but we'll leave that for a later chapter.) Climbing off the merry-go-round will finally, we assume, create the kind of balance and de-stressing that we've been dreaming of for years.

Fourth, inherent in our hopes and aspirations is often a belief that the last third or quarter of our lives should be a reward for good behavior and hard work. After all, we've earned our right to take it easy, retire, and enjoy the fruits of our labor.

An alternative dream?

The kind of dream we follow after will determine the type of "happiness" we experience. Our culture's great dream relies on money to buy our way to happiness. And of course, if it's just some short-term pleasurable experiences then money may do the job. But not, as we've seen, when it comes to finding the kind of happiness that involves long term well-being.

For that we need to aspire to an alternative dream. One that doesn't rely on the accumulation of more "stuff," one that isn't taken in by the lure of unlimited choices, or the belief that we'll achieve it by extracting ourselves from the hurly-burly of life.

We need a dream that will sustain us for the long-haul.

Up Close and Personal

1. How would *you* describe the "great Western dream"? What particular things in our culture most promote this dream and how do they do it?

2. Read Matthew 5:3-1 The Greek word used here for "blessed" is *makarios*, which could also be translated "happy"—and is so rendered in some Bible versions. Clearly happiness, or the state of being blessed, meant something definite to Jesus.

   Now look again at the section "Common features of the great Western dream" toward the end of this chapter. In it I have surveyed the specifics of our modern dream, and identified four longings that lie behind them.

   In the same way that I have done for the twenty-first century "good life," survey the specifics that Jesus lists in the passage from

Matthew's Gospel. That is, stand back and identify the principles on which Jesus bases *his* "good life." What do you see as the themes of this "blessed life"?

3. On a sheet of paper list the ingredients that made up happiness for you *up to the point when you began reading this book*. For this exercise you need to be as honest as you dare!

   Then, either in personal pondering or by sharing in a group:

   a. First, identify where you gained this view of happiness.

   b. Then choose the two or three items in your list that best fit what you see as the *true* goals in your life.

   c. Finally, is there any new item you might now add to your list? (Hang lightly on this question. There's a lot more that you will be thinking through as you continue to read this book.)

12

Consumption

"Consumerism envelops us as surely as the air we breathe..."
Rodney Clapp

Mike's day had started well. Lying in on a Saturday morning was the world's best gift to a sensitive, highly-trained-though-severely-underrated father. (Mike was not one to withhold credit where credit was due.) Newspaper, coffee, and toast in bed were unbeatable.

We–ell, perhaps if one of the kids could be trained to make it and bring it in on a tray...? Nah, that would be flying in the face of Nature. Mike was a reasonable man.

But when, on the southern side of 9am, he wandered outside... suddenly he was hit with an overwhelming feeling of exhaustion. All round him his property shouted, *"Work!!"* The hedge was long past time for trimming. The boat and both cars needed cleaning. Sarah had pressed him to repair the collapsing trellis that was being held up by the jasmine. And then there was the rubbish. Ah yes, the rubbish. It had been piling up for some time. More than just the garden and kitchen variety—this was a mound of old furniture, computers and garbage from their back-room renovations of six months earlier. It all needed carting off to the tip.

Sarah had been running a campaign for the last three or four weeks. "It just can't sit round the side of the house any longer," she would say, tears welling in those beautiful brown eyes. A pre-marital career in amateur acting had made her irresistible. On this point the nation would vote in her support.

Consumption

What can you say when the whole country is against you? Mike made the big decision. Today will be workday. Today the property will be beaten into shape. Today the world will change.

A tui's call rang out from the pohutukawa.[1] Not a bell note; just a guttural cackle. The sod was sneering at him. Mike squared his shoulders. Instead of returning to the kitchen for the support of a second coffee, he opened the door to the double garage.

And his shoulders drooped. It was a mistake. He shouldn't have. He could see that now. No wonder they couldn't get their cars in there these days. The place was chocker.[2]

Just getting to the garden tools would need a map. He gazed across to the home gym he and son Simon had set up a year or two back. It was now stashed into a corner, next to the camping gear. Aha, but with careful planning he might be able to achieve access. He mentally mapped out the route. Take the track to the beer fridge, veer left, climb over the suitcases . . .

Mike felt tired just looking at it all and thinking of the day ahead. "Who needs a gym?" he groaned, turning his mind back to coffee. "Cleaning up will keep me fit."

Back in the house around mid morning, Mike made Sarah a coffee—and fixed himself another one just to be sociable. In truth, he'd earned it. The cars and the boat were gleaming. But once again his shoulders gave him away. The state of the garage weighed heavily. Mike—who was a fast learner—shared his dismay with Sarah, weeping pitifully. She grinned and kissed him gently before clipping him over the earhole.

"But seriously, Mike, what *are* we going to do?" she said. "It's not just the garage. This house doesn't have enough storage room." She was right. Of course, this was no surprise to Mike. She was always right, and he regularly said as much to his mates over a barbecue.

They *had* talked about moving to a bigger place. Then they'd looked at adding on to their current house. Problem was, things were a little tight money–wise. The overdraft, as always, was stretched. They seemed to be only just getting by, even with Sarah now working fulltime at the local medical center.

But they had to do *something*. It was intolerable the house being so cluttered. Mike had been putting it off for months. A friend had told him

---

1. New Zealand native bird and tree.
2. Colloquial for absolutely full!

about the storage unit he'd hired down the road. "They don't come cheap, but it's taken all the pressure off. I can pull down the roller door on the lockup and it's out of my hair."

Yep. That was probably the best option, though it would eat up his next pay increase and they'd have to put it on the card till then. Even so, he still kept wondering, "Where on earth did it all come from? When we got married we could have packed what we owned into a van."

Consuming as a way of life

At the heart of free-market Capitalism and of our great Western dream is consumption. Put simply, we find happiness through consuming.

Consuming, in itself, is not wrong or bad. Far from it. Indeed, we *must* consume in order to live; it is fundamental to our lives as humans. For example, we can't survive without consuming food. We need raw materials for shelter, clothing, and warmth. And because life is more than just surviving physically, we also need to consume natural resources for the purpose of building relationships and community, for creating beauty, and for celebrating life.

The material world is good and using its resources is also good. The problem comes—as it usually does—when we get things out of balance. Our culture has made a god out of consuming. It encourages us to live in order to consume, rather than consume in order to live.

Or to put it another way, we have been indoctrinated to think that our lives find their meaning in the things we have. Things have become the goal, when they should only be the means to a much more fulfilling end.

The word that has been coined to describe this is "consumerism." Consumerism equates happiness with the purchase and consumption of material goods. It is really just the end game of what we were thinking about in the previous chapter.

In order to be happy we must consume. So we are told.

Naturally, the line between the two is not easy to determine. When exactly does "consumption" become "consumerism"?

The oft-quoted bumper sticker of the nineties—"I shop, therefore I am"—puts the finger on the matter in a profound way. (It is of course, a play on Descartes's famous statement, "I think, therefore I am.") When the practice of shopping dominates our aspirations and energies, it begins to shape our identity, who we are. Our very existence becomes defined by our consumption.

Rodney Clapp highlights the insidious and corrosive nature of consumerism when he observes that it has a much less obvious impact on us than a billboard has. It powerfully shapes our attitudes and behaviors, he suggests; and it does it by ever so subtly changing the "lenses" through which we see and experience the world.

That's why consumerism is much more than just the things we do—buying the gadgets, adding the accessories, filling the wardrobe. It is a whole way of life, an ethos, seducing us into lives of discontent, impulsiveness, and permission to fulfill every desire we experience. This is achieved "almost always with a velvet glove rather than an iron fist. It speaks in tones sweet and sexy rather than dictatorial, and it conquers by promises rather than by threats"[3]

The biblical virtues—such as self-denial, patience, and contentment—are out of place in the world where Consumerism is King. They restrict, they limit, they deprive. Or so consumerism tells us—with never a suggestion that they might instead free us, enlarge us, fulfill us . . .

Consumption as disease

It is interesting to note that like so many other words that have been redefined in the past few decades, consumption has morphed from being a state of potentially terminal illness to something desirable. Even enough to give our lives for.

Economist Jeremy Rifkin points out the surprising right-angled turn made by this word: "If you go back to Samuel Johnson's dictionary of the English language, to consume means to exhaust, to pillage, to lay waste, to destroy. In fact, even in our grandparents' generation, when someone had tuberculosis, they called it 'consumption.' So up until this century, to be a consumer . . . was considered a bad thing."[4]

The wasting away of the body because of the disease of TB is actually very powerful imagery for what happens if we allow consumption to become the driving force of our lives, our *raison d'etre*. We become a mere shadow of ourselves, unable to function to our potential. And eventually, left untreated, our consumption will "kill" us.

---

3. Clapp, *Border Crossings*, 127.
4. Quoted in de Graaf et al., *Affluenza: the all-consuming epidemic*, 134.

Section B: Culture

Our over-consumption wreaks havoc in our lives, in at least three ways...

It leads to addiction

Consumerism is an addiction. It involves unhealthy preoccupation and dependence on material possessions. This leads to compulsive behavior. We just can't live without having stuff! Lots of it. It may not be *substance* abuse, but it is certainly *material* abuse. For, "When pathological becomes normal, an addict will do whatever is necessary to maintain the habit."[5]

The fact that we speak approvingly of accumulating more and more possessions and use it as a badge of honor, a status symbol, is one indication of our "habit." We even joke that when someone needs a lift in life, they might engage in a bit of "retail therapy." And our addiction is intimated in comments such as, "I just *love* to shop" and, "I just *have* to buy this." People even proudly joke about their obsessive behavior by calling themselves "shopaholics."

There are other pointers to our irrational actions. Four will be touched on in following chapters:

- The muddying of the distinction between needs and wants. (Chapter 13)
- The excessive use of "credit." (Chapter 16)
- The habitual offloading of still useful clothes, appliances, and cars, in favor of new ones. (Chapter 13)
- The capitulation to style over substance. (Chapter 14)

These are all indications of our addiction.

Addiction is idolatrous. That is, it involves a giving of our allegiance or worship to something other than God. When we pin our hopes and dreams on what we own or what we intend to possess, it dictates our decision-making, priorities, and time.

The worship of consumerism is cultural—not just individual. This means that the problem is not simply our own personal obsession with possessions but our whole society's desire to build meaning and fulfillment through material means. "That millions share the same forms of

---

5. Ibid, 107.

mental pathology does not make those people sane," says psychologist Erich Fromm.[6]

We have normalized addiction to consuming. But in doing so, we cede control of our lives to an insatiable god—one that demands more and more from us.

It leads to environmental disaster

The end game of over-consumption is not just personal and cultural devastation. It's also environmental obliteration. Our whole way of life is built around taking more than we need from the earth and polluting it with the resulting waste.

Of course, this is getting a lot of press at the moment. And so it should. However, being aware of the fact that we are progressively devastating our physical world, and actually doing something significant enough to change our ways, are two different matters.

Canadian ecologist William Rees has recently stated that we are consuming 30 percent more material than is sustainable from the world's resources. Such a depleting of the essential elements obviously can't continue forever. However, addictive behaviour doesn't take into account the consequences. It only focuses on what we think we "need" right now. Addicts live in the present, not in the future.

One aspect of this is the vast quantity of waste we keep producing. Clive Hamilton and Richard Denniss are right when they point out that, "Dealing with ever-growing piles of waste is not an engineering problem: it is a psychological and social one . . . Waste does little for our wellbeing, but it is crucial to the health of the economic system . . . While governments urge us to 'reduce, re-use, and recycle,' manufacturers and marketers of consumer goods spend billions persuading us to do otherwise . . . The long-term solution to mountains of waste is not more landfill sites but fewer shopping centers."[7]

It leads to commodifying relationships, faith and God

We've already noted in chapter 10 the strong tendency our culture has to commodify things that should not be valued in economic terms.

---

6. Ibid, 36.

7. Hamilton and Denniss, *Affluenza: when too much is never enough*, 101–102, 111.

Section B: Culture

Consumerism has this effect. And it is fatal. For we become less than human when we allow it to happen. The truth is that "money alone cannot buy the deepest things we desire. Money never purchases love, or eternity, or God. It is the wrong means, the wrong road, the wrong search."[8]

Commodification deeply affects our relationship with God and the way we think about the Christian life. For example, while few would be able to consciously identify it, most of us approach church life with a thoroughly consumerist mentality. We unselfconsciously talk about "church shopping" and approach involvement in a faith community more on the basis of what it can do for us, than what we can contribute to it. This leads us to often relate to church leaders (and church leaders to us) as a kind of "provider of religious goods and services." This undergirds the way we think about pastoral care and Sunday services. It determines the unspoken expectations we carry of what our church community should provide. At its most raw, we are customers who expect certain services. Or in the case of pastors and church leaders, they are the ones attempting to keep their people happy and contented.

Unsurprisingly, our consumerism also filters into how we often engage in evangelism. The Good News is frequently viewed as something to "sell," as if it is a commodity people should choose because it meets some of their needs better than other products on the market. Our attempts to make the gospel as attractive as we can sometimes lead us to gimmicky sales techniques and a minimizing of the significant costs involved in following Jesus. But in marketing "JC" as just another brand, we prostitute the gospel and simply encourage people to transfer their consumerist expectations onto God.

Consequently, we subtly reinforce the perception that God " . . . is a tool we employ, a force we control, and a resource we plunder. We ascribe value to him (the literal meaning of the word 'worship') based not on who he is, but on what he can do for us."[9]

This reduces God, like everything else in life, to a commodity. Someone to be used for our own ends.

Clearly, this is not how we should live.

---

8. Guinness, *The Call*, 138.
9. Jethani, *The Divine Commodity*, 37.

Consumption

Up Close and Personal

1. Part of the problem is that many of the things we consume are perfectly legitimate needs. So just when does consuming become consumerism? Think of some specific practical examples where our "consuming to live" has moved into "living to consume."

   - For example, consider a cellphone. There are plenty of circumstances in which this "gadget" fulfills a useful purpose. Name some.
   - But there are also circumstances when it slips into "consumerism." Identify some.
   - Now list five other examples of products that push us to consume, and analyze where the line might be crossed.
   - Are there items you've seen that are pure consumerism with no merit whatsoever?
   - Are there actions of consuming which, when indulged in rarely, might be acceptable, but which when made a regular habit would be inappropriate? For example?

2. Read Matthew 26:6–1

   a. Can you come up with a scenario in which this scene described by Matthew might justify the reaction of the disciples?

   b. On what grounds do you consider the woman's actions as described by Matthew *are* justifiable?

   c. Make up a modern-day incident where consuming some precious commodity might be a commendable thing to do.

3. In this chapter I identify three ways in which over-consumption wreaks havoc in our lives—*addiction, unsustainability* and *commodifcation*.

   - Which one most affects you personally? Why?
   - Are there any other destructive results to consumerism you can think of?
   - In what ways do you see these issues in your (personal, family, church community, local community) patterns of living? Be as specific as you can.

Section B: Culture

4. Discuss the statement that: *God "is a tool we employ, a force we control, and a resource we plunder. We ascribe value to him (the literal meaning of the word 'worship') based not on who he is, but on what he can do for us."*

13

Need

"Yesterday's luxuries become today's necessities and tomorrow's relics."
David Myers

"There is enough for everyone's need, but there is not enough for everyone's greed."
Mahatma Gandhi

It's a little hard for me to believe now, but in my early years my parents did not own a car. And they were not unusual. Cars were in short supply. In fact, there were limits placed on the number of vehicles available in postwar New Zealand. This "closed market" kept prices high and out of the range of many people. Most travel was by walking, cycling, or public transport. This was not a great problem for families like our own, because most of our life was lived in fairly close proximity to home.

In such times, venturing further afield was an infrequent occurrence. The first family holiday away that I can remember was a weeklong trip to see our cousins in Wellington—about a five-hour drive from our home. In order to get there, we drove my Dad's new work car—a Ford Anglia—with all five of us squeezed into its small frame. Since that left little room for luggage, a roof rack was attached for the suitcases. The only problem was that halfway to our destination the rack gave way. Our belongings went scattering all over the road!

Section B: Culture

By my third year at university, I owned a car myself. It was a Ford Zephyr Mark 3. Admittedly, it was almost as old as I was and in not-so-perfect condition. Nevertheless, it gave me increased freedom and capacity to go where I wanted, *when* I wanted. Mind you, for a student the cost of fuel was a limiting factor. The fuel gauge was perpetually low. I worked out that the car would give me early indication of its impending lack of gas, by briefly stalling on the hilly roads of my university city. After a quick restart, I knew I then had about two miles of travel before emptiness became irrevocable!

Many years later, in 1995, I began importing into New Zealand secondhand vehicles from Japan. By this time huge volumes were flooding into the country. Prices dropped accordingly and made reasonable-quality cars accessible to almost everyone. Suddenly there were scores more models available to choose from. Plus, they had features not seen a lot before—power steering, air conditioning, remote central locking, and electric windows. Initially these were all treated as novelties. However, it wasn't long before such "extras" became "necessities"—items people couldn't possibly do without. So car manufacturers, determined not to lose their marketing edge, produced further features to fill their "surprise bonus" list. Things like Traction Control, airbags, CD players and variable valve timing (VVT) engines. Needless to say, we all soon learned that we just *had to* have these as well.

Occasionally I think about what it was like back in the "old days." How exactly did my Mum survive with small children and no car? And what was it like before power steering? Every so often I have seen some of the cars we drove in past years—Ford Anglia's and Hillman Hunter's, Zephyr's and AP5 Valiant's—and I've wondered, how did we do it? They were such *basic* cars. Now almost relics. And then I think of my grandparents' generation, and wonder . . . how on earth did they manage to live at all!

Let's face it, in the past few decades the advances in technology have been extraordinary. So fast that the rest of history is left gasping. The truth is that our free-market system has been remarkably effective at developing new goods and producing them in huge quantities, and the car industry is just one example of this rapid development. This, as we noted in chapter 10, is one of the key achievements of Capitalism. The resulting "economic growth" has been staggering.

What a fortunate and favored generation you and I were born into. Except...

Well, *is* there a downside? I only ask because I notice that my grandparents' generation seemed relatively content. More so than mine...

The growth of an appetite for more and better

Think about this. If such innovation and creativity is to continue and thrive, then the new goods and services need to be bought, and so do the next set of improved models, and the upgrades that follow that... and so on. If each new wave of fresh ideas and products don't find a market, then all our brave new innovations will soon come to a grinding halt.

There are two primary ways that such markets can be grown and expanded: either *we can either get people to buy the new products, and more and more of them*, or *we can get them to replace what they bought yesterday with newer and better ones today.*

The first solution requires an increasing of people's desire or appetite for the new, often fuelled by triggers such as the lure of greater convenience or freedom. The second entails dissatisfaction with what people already have. In promoting discontent with our current goods and services, we stimulate the desire to replace them with better and improved versions.

However, the key to both strategies is the same. Consumers must be convinced that what is being sold is something they really *must* have. Not just "want"... but "need." This goes to the very heart of our present economic system. It is by this muddying of the distinction between wants and needs that our purchasing habits have been accelerated.

If it's true that the language of need has replaced the language of want, and that "need" has become the great imperative—how did this come about? How did our thinking get changed?

"Greed" turns into "Need"

British sociologist, Tony Walter, has tracked the development of economic policies of most Western governments since the 1930s, to help explain the proliferation of material needs in the mid–twentieth century. He suggests that until the 1930s, thrift was a powerful motive in most people's lives. But as a result of the Great Depression, the Keynesian argument of "spending your way out of depression" became popular. "If somehow demand could be artificially stimulated, jobs would be created, people would have more money to spend and the economy would get going again."[1]

However, for people's attitudes to change, economies had to put a new spin on spending. Walter explains how it came about:

> Somehow they [people] had to be got to spend without feeling guilty. Advanced capitalism required people to be greedy if it was to continue to expand; yet it had bred generation after generation that disapproved of greed. The answer was to portray the new consumerism as a matter of spending to meet need rather than spending to meet greed. Which is not to say that manufacturers or advertisers or economic policies could create specific needs, but that the language of need replaced the language of greed in the market place.[2]

It's easy to see how talking of "needs" and "rights" makes us less uneasy about spending. Feeding ourselves the belief that we have a right to a higher standard of living eventually convinces us that our material wants are not a result of greed, but instead a need. In fact, Walter suggests, we've made it even more noble than that: we actually, and genuinely, believe that most of our purchases are done for the benefit of others—for our spouse, our kids, our grandparents . . .

This explains a curious human phenomenon: how we can so easily dismiss other people's wants as materialistic and excessive, without conceding that our own desire for luxuries is equally selfish, materialistic, or greedy.

Changing "needs"

The process of "luxuries" evolving into "needs" and eventually into "relics" (as in David Myers's quotation at the head of this chapter) happens incrementally. We hardly notice how our expectations have altered, nor how our lifestyles have adapted to the changing context. It evolves—rather like the well-known boiling frog experiment. When the water in the pot is heated very gradually, the frog doesn't pick up the subtle change in temperature until it is too late. It adapts to the varying conditions. So it is with us.

1. Walter, *Need—the new religion*, 30.
2. Ibid, 30.

For example, in the case of the motorcar, the accelerated development of mass–produced vehicles resulted in the allure of freedom. You could now go where you wanted, when you wanted and at the speed you wanted. Better still, no longer did you have to live close to your employment. You could escape from the noise and cramped homes of the inner city and live in a garden suburb, yet still enjoy the amenities and entertainments of city life.

Governments and businesses began to assume car ownership as the norm, and to plan accordingly. The development of extensive road systems was an automatic consequence. Not only could you now commute to work, but you could also visit Aunt Mary across the city. And your children's horizons were broadened too. New sports and hobbies became possible for them because you could get them to facilities that were further away. Put simply, people could now do much more with their week because getting from one place to another was so much easier and quicker.

But we humans seem doomed to live in the shadow of Murphy's Law. Just as we are reaching the heights of new freedom and opportunity . . . we're apt to discover that we've slid painfully into the crevasse of unexpected consequences.

Before we knew it, what began as a non–essential desire for greater freedom from the constrictions of the city, led to dependency. We (individuals and communities) had now built our lives around the new reality, so that it became increasingly difficult to imagine living without an up–to–date car . . . or two cars . . . or three!

And then as our collective habits changed, the problems began to appear. Since the car was so much more convenient, public transport declined. At first we didn't notice. Roads were empty; petrol was cheap. And then, to our horror, the roads began to seize up; the price of petrol began to soar. When public transport might have been a useful choice, it wasn't there, or it was so inefficient that it just didn't do what we needed. We spurned it and clogged our inner cities with parked vehicles, spending longer and longer each morning getting to work, and each evening getting home.

Then we realized that our life had sped up. And again the car was part of the problem. As well as spending longer getting to and from work, we were racing backwards and forwards across the city to meet our schedules. And not just the men in the work force.

Section B: Culture

One sociological analysis done in the 1980s discovered that the new labour-saving devices had indeed changed the tasks done by mothers. But it turned out that they hadn't simplified their lives at all. They still worked for the same length of time as their grandmothers had. Only now it was driving to shopping centers, standing in supermarket queues, and driving children to clubs and classes. Since that study was done, of course, mothers have also begun joining the paid workforce in ever-increasing numbers.

So now the car has become indispensable to our lifestyle. We can't do without it. It is now a "need." Walter suggests that this is what might be called an "addictive need"—something that began with a satisfying feeling and evolved into an "I can't do without this."

Planned obsolescence

One critical way of growing our appetite for new goods and services is by encouraging people to replace their old possessions with a newer, improved version.

Ordinarily, this replacement process would be a natural cycle. That is, purchasing a new product would only occur as the older one wore out. However, very early on in the consumer revolution, companies realized that innovation and technology were moving so rapidly that if they "waited" until their older products wore out they would have a very limited market in which to sell their updated goods.

As far back as 1929 an executive of General Motors, Floyd Allen, remarked that, "advertising is in the business of making people helpfully dissatisfied with what they have in favor of something better. The old factors of wear and tear can no longer be depended upon to create a demand. They are too slow."[3]

This has come to be known as "planned obsolescence"—"instilling in the buyer the desire to own something a little newer, a little better, a little sooner than is necessary."[4]

Obsolescence can be engineered in at least two ways. The product can deteriorate (i.e. not be built to last—like many toys). Or it can be

---

3. Salgo, "The Obsolescence of Growth: Capitalism and the Environmental Crisis," 32.
4. Brooks Stevens defined it this way in 1954.

superseded by a new or improved product that does a much more effective job than the old one (like all the computers you've ever owned).

Most people are not aware of how we have been programmed to believe the "obsolescence" line. Often it is expressed as a general feeling that it's time for a change. A change of bathroom, TV, stereo—or car.

In fact, it is in the world of automobile marketing that this practice has been honed to a fine art. Those "new features" that are trumpeted every year are not really very significant. Those "new improved" models are usually over-hyped. The truth is that you and I are being nudged into a carefully engineered trap. The whole point of the exercise is for us to think of our present car as "past it." So we're pushed into offloading that car long before its useful efficient life has reached an end. We just *need* a new one.[5]

Advertising

The role that the advertising industry has played in this fuelling of desire and need is clearly significant. However, it is not alone in arousing within us the imperative for new and updated products and services. As Walter notes, "Advertising has to appeal to needs that people already feel—for example for love, belonging, prestige, identity or escape—and then proceed to show how the product will meet one or more of these needs, so that the product itself becomes needed. Advertising does create needs, but not out of nothing. It confirms the needs we already feel."[6]

We'll explore this further in the next chapter.

Up Close and Personal

1. Confession time! Choose one of the following and unburden your soul before your friends who care about you! (If you're reading this book on your own, then you'll have to peer into the abyss by yourself. Make a strong cup of coffee before you start!) Then analyze the strange person that is you with the question that follows.

---

5. I can't claim any credit for this observation. Alvin Toffler pointed it out *40 years ago!*—in his book *Future Shock*, 62–63.
6. Walter, *Need*, 29.

Section B: Culture

- Own up to two items which you once "desperately needed" ... and which are now languishing unused at the bottom of a drawer or wardrobe or wherever.
- Do you have some gadget or tool or article of clothing that you constantly renew or replace or upgrade beyond reason? (In my case it's books. My library gets added to on a regular basis. Books I just *have* to read get purchased online. Most of them I do read. But others, sadly, lie languishing on the shelf for months.)
- Is there some shop (a secondhand shop perhaps?) or mail-order catalogue or internet site that you can't stop yourself going through again and again as you covetously eye the merchandise?

Question: Does this fascination make any sense to you? Why is it, do you think, that you are obsessed by the item you've identified? How do you feel now it's out in the open? Relieved? Embarrassed? Suicidal?

2. On to a more serious question. If it is true that all of us now find it difficult to determine where the line should be drawn between "need" and "want," what steps can we take so that we may find greater clarity?

3. Discuss Mahatma Gandhi's statement: *"There is enough for everyone's need, but there is not enough for everyone's greed."*

Personal Question: Observing yourself

4. Reflect on your own history. Have you, as Walter suggests, easily dismissed other people's wants as materialistic and excessive, without conceding that your own desire for luxuries might be selfish, materialistic, or greedy? Try to honestly assess whether you, like most of us, have applied this double standard. (Watch for this in yourself, whenever in the coming months you experience one of those spasms of judgmentalism that we all seem to go through.)

14

Brand

"Consumerism has created a culture that values style over substance, image over reality, and perception over performance."
Skye Jethani

Time: June 2003.
Place: a bus stop in the southwest of Philadelphia, USA.

The nineteen year–old boy waiting for a bus was Kevin Johnson. And what was distinctive about him was the "Allen Iverson" replica jersey he was wearing. So distinctive that a group of teenagers began hassling him and demanding that he hand it over. Johnson refused. This was not just any jersey; it was a valuable branded piece of clothing, named after the '76ers basketball star Allen Iverson. Such items cost a lot of money and carried a great deal of status.

The group of teenagers knew this. That's why they wanted it too. A few moments later one of the group shot Johnson, stripped him of his jersey and left him for dead. Except that Kevin Johnson did not die—at least not immediately. He survived for another three years, living as a quadriplegic, tied to a respirator. His death finally came, from complications, in 2006. Johnson was buried in a replacement Allen Iverson jersey—the very piece of branded clothing that got him killed. It meant *that* much to him.

Connected, however illogically, with this ugly murder, Iverson the basketballer offered to pay for Johnson's funeral. Clearly reeling from the absurdity of it all, Iverson explained his action: "It was tough to see

Section B: Culture

somebody die for something senseless like that, over a jersey, over something material. Life is way more precious than a jersey."

Time: March 2005.
Place: an alley in South Side Chicago.

The seventeen year-old boy found dying—and shoeless—was Steven Terrett. Apparently his last words were, "They set me up." Set him up for what? It was the brand new Nike Air Jordan sneakers he was wearing. Terrett was robbed and killed for his shoes.

His mother said the Air Jordan's were important to him because Michael Jordan was his favorite basketball player. But there was much more to those shoes than a bit of sports star adulation. Like numerous other teenagers, Steven Terrett was mesmerized by the status of the brand. He just *had* to have those shoes. Unfortunately his attackers felt the same.

What seems trivial to us had actually become a matter of life and death. Evidently those Air Jordan's were more valuable to the two teenagers who robbed Terrett than a life. And for the victim? Wearing the "right" shoes in public ended up getting him killed.

How on earth did it come to this? What twisted sense of value has brought us to murder for a trendy logo? Sadly, these are not two isolated incidents. Since Kevin Johnson and Steven Terrett, a number of other young Americans have been killed for their enviable clothing.

Is this simply the end game of the sport of marketing that now dominates our waking hours? Has advertising become so much part of our lives that it naturally becomes part of our dying too? How did advertising take over our culture?

As we have seen, the answer to that is not difficult. With so many goods and services being produced, ways had to be found to stimulate greater consumption. Developing a language of need was the solution. For this enables us to easily justify our acquisitions on the basis that they are essential, even indispensable, to our lives.

Convincing us of this has become the domain of the ad. It is therefore not surprising that billions of dollars are spent by businesses every year on advertising—and on researching what motivates us as consumers.

The advert is now an essential part of consumer culture. Most of us have a love/hate relationship with the ubiquitous ad. We all have our favorites. Some are very funny. Others are extremely clever. They can tickle our fancy, lighten our day, and even spark interesting conversations.

Of course, there are plenty of us who recognize the seduction of advertising—and consciously reject it. We mentally (and, with our television remotes, actually) switch off when the ads come. We recognize the false claims they make, and we are not affected by them. In short, when they turn their guns on us, advertisers are wasting their money.

Welcome to the innocent bliss of being naïve! For the very thing that gives the ad so much power is our lack of awareness of its impact. Some commentators suggest that we are actually at our most vulnerable when we nonchalantly drive by the billboard without giving it a second thought. For advertising is so pervasive that even if we resist the invitation to buy a particular product, we are nevertheless still immersed in its world and oriented to its mindset.

As sociologist Bernard McGrane puts it: "It's like breathing the air. You don't notice the pollution."[1] The crucial part is not the effect a *particular* advert has on us. It is the *cumulative* impact of living in an ad–soaked world. In essence, the sea of advertising around us powerfully shapes our worldview. It significantly determines how we see ourselves, what becomes important to us, and how we should relate to others.

Media critic Jean Kilbourne puts her finger on it: "Advertising sells products but it also sells a great deal more—it sells values, it sells images, concepts of love, reality, sexuality, and success . . . above all, [advertising] teaches us to be consumers. It teaches us that happiness can be bought, that there are instant answers to life's complex problems, and that products can meet our deepest human needs . . . because the individual ads are stupid and trivial, people assume that the whole phenomenon is stupid and trivial."[2]

From information to persuasion to socialization

How did we mold a culture where advertising wields so much influence and power?

Needless to say, offering your goods and services to whoever will buy them has been around for a long time. If you have something to sell then it is natural to find ways to inform people about it. However, it was around the second half of the nineteenth century when the simple advertisement began to gain a greater visibility in everyday life. At that stage,

---

1. Parallax Pictures, *The Ad and the Ego*.
2. Ibid.

most ads were informational in nature—telling the public details of the product, with perhaps a picture (usually a line drawing) alongside.

As we've seen, a new thrust appeared in the 1920s and 30s—the capacity to mass-produce. Goods in large numbers needed to be sold. To get the job done, ads morphed. No longer simply informational, now they sought to actively persuade people. Stimulating demand increasingly became the goal. And to do this well, you need to produce "consumers"—a process of socializing people into using not just a wide range of goods, but newer and brighter and better and cleverer models of the same goods.

Promoting discontent

Again, as we know, a key element for doing this was to promote dissatisfaction—with ourselves and with our lot in life. As Bernard McGrane explains: "One of the sub-texts of all advertising is: 'You're not okay the way you are. Things are bad. You need help. You need salvation.' In that sense, advertising is designed to generate endless self-criticism, all sorts of anxieties, and then to offer the entire world of consumer goods as your salvation ... In contrast, one message you'll never hear in advertising is, 'You're okay. You don't need anything. Just be yourself.'"[3]

We must acknowledge how incredibly effective this strategy has been. Perhaps its most visible success has been in the targeting of young women. We all of course, male and female, struggle with issues of self-confidence and self-image. But from an early age young women in our culture are conditioned to the ideal of what constitutes feminine beauty. In magazines and television and films, and in social (sometimes, unbelievably, parental) expectations, they are blitzed with the ultra-manicured glamour of models.

Set up against this freakish ideal, ordinary women are and always will be failures. Yet they are constantly faced with the tantalizing, though ultimately unachievable, goal of a perfect body shape, face, skin, hairstyle, if only they will buy product X. In this environment it is little wonder insecurity reigns to the degree it does, revealing itself occasionally in pathologies like anorexia, bulimia and depression.

3. Ibid.

From words to images

Of course, the link between product on the one hand, and beauty or perfection or happiness on the other, is not explicit in much advertising. The connection is merely hinted at. Key to this has been the evolution from using just words to creating images.

UBC professor, Richard Pollay, explains it this way: "[Most advertising today] creates an image or aura—a portrayal of lifestyle or contentment around the product . . . we don't process images the same way we process words. If I say something to you in order for you to file it in your memory, you can match it up with what you already know and determine whether it is true or not . . . but seeing is believing. The picture is an experience. It is not treated or processed in the same way. We still have this cultural pre–disposition to believe what we see. The photo does not lie."[4]

When a TV advert shows a family happily cruising the uncluttered roads of a beautiful countryside, not a word needs to be said. The scene unfolding before our eyes "speaks" to us—powerfully and alluringly. The messages are implicit; they tap into our longing for the freedom to roam the wide–open spaces on a clear day. They also suggest that if you own *this* car you too will be able to go to all the beautiful places you've always wanted, and experience the kind of contented, happy family holiday you've always desired.

As that micro–odyssey unfolds on the screen, it's the images that convince us—much more than words ever could. When a claim like that is made solely by words, we are more likely to question it, to consciously think it through, and to assess the merits of the argument.

From the image to the logo and brand

In recent decades the advertising industry has developed the use of images even further, using easily recognizable symbols to communicate its messages.

Of course, symbolism is very important to how we live as humans. Those of us who follow Jesus understand this. Our faith is full of symbols—from the Cross to the water of baptism, to the cup and the bread of the communion table. Symbols encapsulate meaning. They tell a story,

---

4. Ibid.

evoke emotions, recall memories, and experiences. A symbol can communicate powerfully, and do so with great simplicity.

The epitome of symbolism in our culture has been the development of the "logo"—with its instant promotion of a brand. Logos are everywhere. We now see hundreds of them every day. On our way to work, in the shopping mall, on the side of the road, in school—and even when we talk with other people.

They dominate the landscape. Almost no part of our lives is exempt. We all recognize and know what the Nike swish represents or the partly eaten apple, the "golden arches" or the "t" in a squashed circle on a car. Banks and corporations display logos. Food chains and car manufacturers multiply them, as do political parties, sports teams, and even many churches. Much of our clothing and footwear carries a logo. Often we can't even look at people without being aware of the brands they are wearing. They are literally walking advertisements.

What is being sold is not primarily a product or service. It's a brand—that is, in the words of marketing expert Colin Bates, just "a collection of perceptions in the mind of the consumer."[5] It is these perceptions that dictate what the customer is prepared to pay. The quality of the goods is not the issue; what sets the price is the emotional connection between the customer and the product, the level of "brand loyalty" that the marketers can create.

The trick is to link a logo with a set of feelings. For example, the Nike shoes Steven Terrett lost his life over carried connotations—in his and his attackers' minds—of power, success, and status.[6]

A brand will also "manufacture" or project a positive image regardless of the company's ethical behavior in producing such goods or services.[7]

The most "successful" brands will induce people to do quite irrational things. Like pay many more dollars for a particular branded product, compared to one that is of the same look and quality, but which is either unbranded or carries another (presumed) inferior brand. This illogical behavior is most on display in supermarkets, shoe stores, and car lots.

And tragically, as we saw at the beginning of this chapter, these brands can even lead people to kill. So great is the power of certain labels.

5. Noted in Jethani, *The Divine Commodity*, 49.

6. Jethani explains well this process of nurturing emotional ties with certain products, in chapter 3 of his book.

7. A point well amplified by Naomi Klein in her book, *No Logo*.

Why would people go to such lengths to possess certain products? Ultimately, because the world of advertising wants us to "define our identity and construct meaning for our lives through the brands we consume."[8]

The culture of our brave new twenty-first century hustles us to define ourselves as consumers. But it's not satisfied with that. With branding it goes a step further. Who we are is not based on consuming just anything. Our identity is built on consuming *particular* products and services. And we are trained to perceive these products as providing a sense of purpose, value, prestige, and self-worth to our lives.

Brands are the new religion. They are what we are encouraged to aspire to, and to build our lives on.

Up Close and Personal

1. Share your favorite advert. What was it that intrigued/amused you most about it?

2. Discuss Skye Jethani's statement, *"Consumerism has created a culture that values style over substance, image over reality, and perception over performance."*

    - To what extent is this true?
    - Can you think of specific examples where products or services you have purchased have had their price/value established more by style, image and perception than by substance, reality and performance?
    - Can you think of specific examples where you gave unthinking credibility to brands or logos?

3. Victorian Britain is commonly ridiculed for its "hypocritical" and "prudish" attitudes towards sexuality. Will future generations mock us for our gullible and mindless acceptance of advertising?

    - Is it true that, like fish, who take for granted the water they swim in, we have simply assumed that our advertisement-drenched world is normal?

---

8. Jethani, *The Divine Commodity*, 50.

Section B: Culture

- Examine your own life and identify ways that you have given thoughtless acceptance to specific forms of advertising. If appropriate, share this with your group.

4. Professor Edward Blaiklock used to say that the church reflects the sins of the community it lives in. What effect has living in an ad–soaked consumer culture had on our understanding of church and faith? For example, do we flock to churches that know how to promote (market) themselves?

   Have we reduced evangelism to a sales promotion program? If so, in what ways?

15

Choice

"Our culture sanctifies freedom of choice so profoundly that the benefits of infinite options seem self-evident."
Barry Schwartz

CEREALS ARE MY PREFERRED breakfast food. I'm particularly partial to a good muesli, though to be honest anything with grains, nuts and fruit is attractive to my palate.

At any given supermarket I can locate the aisle for cereals in mere seconds. It's hard to miss, given the length of the shelves these products occupy nowadays. In recent years there has been a nuclear explosion in breakfast cereals. Every possible combination of ingredients is lined up along those shelves.

Of course, cereals don't have this on their own. In fact, it's estimated that many supermarkets today display up to thirty thousand different items. But you can see my breakfast problem. Though I can reach the display area in a flash, once there I stall.

Choosing which particular cereal to purchase is not easy. Variety is for me the spice of life. So while at one level I'm a creature of habit, another part of me is intrigued with the variations available and can't wait to sample alternatives. My favorite cereal maker has over twenty options, let alone all the combinations made by other manufacturers. So once I've checked out five of the cereal boxes, I feel compelled to check out the rest—just in case I'm missing the best, tastiest, most nutritious, and most cost-effective option.

Having taken an extra ten minutes to do this, I make my decision (though invariably with a sense of regret for the ones I've left behind). What a complex process it has been. All for the sake of a box of cereal.

If that were the end of it, it wouldn't be so bad. But now as I move further down the aisle, I begin to look for the next item on my shopping list—and the decision-making process begins all over again. By checkout time I've made countless small and largely insignificant decisions, based on price, nutritional content, size requirements, ethical considerations (i.e. organic, free-range, free trade, etc.) and quality.

No wonder I feel exhausted when I go shopping.

The tyranny of small decisions

This curious modern problem is not an issue of poverty and want—which has been the ever-present struggle for ordinary people throughout the vast majority of recorded history. Instead, it's a problem (though that seems an odd word to use) of abundance. Stay with me while I enjoy my humble breakfast. It may give us an insight into how you and I might improve our quality of life.

In my supermarket forays I experience what has been called "the tyranny of small decisions."[1] By themselves, small decisions like this may not seem too big a deal. But when we're making these kinds of choice hundreds of times every day, we develop a weariness.

The worst element of our developing tyranny is not so much in the making of these countless decisions—products to buy, TV programs to watch, websites to connect to, color of paint for the toolshed, which utilities company to connect with (and on which particular plan), et cetera—but in the cumulative effect they have. Which adds to the load we carry when we then work through the much bigger and more important issues of life. These are the ones relating to education, training, employment, where we live, who we build friendships with, how we go about making our lives count, and so forth. These choices too have increasingly unlimited possibilities. Determining what to do with them demands a lot of energy—both because of the hugely expanded options and the importance they carry.

Of course, some of us delight in the challenge of becoming "savvy" consumers. We seem to excel in exploring all the different options on

---

1. Coined by economist, Fred Hirsch.

all the various products, services, and possibilities, so that we can then make the "best" decision. (Though it's a frightening thought that if we're spending a good percentage of the week trying to get the best deal, in the end our achievement is to become a "super-consumer.")

Aggravating our need to make multiple choices is the move to custom-made products and services. Needless to say, there's a lot good about this personalizing of our surroundings, but it does add still more to our load of choices. Once it was simply, "Will that be fries with that, madam?" Turns out that designing our own pizzas, sandwiches, buffet and smorgasbord meals was just training for the next step. In many industries the current trend is to cater for the huge variety of tastes and preferences our population has, along with a more individualized and customized sales approach.

So now customization has penetrated the music playlists we develop, the type of bank accounts we operate, the multiple insurance plans available to us, and the variations in the cars we can order.

Another layer makes our decision-making even more demanding and complex. Traditionally, there were some significant spheres of our lives sheltered from the kind of choices that consumerism thrusts on us. But increasingly even areas such as education, healthcare, and faith have been significantly annexed by the market. We now come to these decisions as consumers. For example, one writer has described the modern university as a kind of "intellectual shopping mall." Students are treated as customers, with a smorgasbord of competing options that can easily overwhelm them, but which may have significant implications for their lives.

Whether we realize it or not, that's the way we now live our lives. Choice is king. In almost every sphere of life.

The drive to increased choice

I've already described in earlier chapters some of the key drivers to the rapidly expanding options laid out before us. When creativity and innovation flourish and are rewarded, the sky is the limit. And competition allows other companies with similar products to get in on the act. Often the differences are only marginal—like my cereals—but they still add to the choice available.

For good or ill, then, you and I have inherited two modern notions for our journey through life. The first is the belief that freedom is found in having unlimited options. And since increased freedom is the road to increased happiness, more choices are viewed as *always* being in our best interests.

The second factor is that more is always perceived as better, bigger as always best. With this overriding philosophy, we're not inclined to impose limits on our decision-making capacity.

Is so much choice good for us?

But what impact does all this decision-making have on us?

The range of choices available certainly brings much to be thankful for. When I contrast my options with those of my grandparents, for instance, there's no way I'd trade places. To have such freedom to decide what work I undertake, where I live, and what and where I learn has been fantastic.

However, could it be that while *they* may have suffered from a lack of choice, *I* now suffer from too much choice?

There is a growing body of evidence that too much choice actually becomes debilitating, rather than liberating. When the options are unlimited we easily reach a point where our decision-making capacity becomes overloaded and closes down in response. Paralysis results, and with it the inability to make decisions. Or at least, to make *good* decisions.

You may already have recognized, at least dimly, the decision-weariness that descends when we are confronted each day by such a barrage of choices. This is what has been labeled *over choice*—"the point at which the advantages of diversity and individualization are cancelled by the complexity of the buyer's decision-making process."[2]

Barry Schwartz, author of the book, *The Paradox of Choice*, explains: "There is no denying that choice improves the quality of our lives . . . On the other hand, the fact that *some* choice is good doesn't necessarily mean that *more* choice is better . . . clinging tenaciously to all choices available to us contributes to bad decisions, to anxiety, stress and dissatisfaction—even to clinical depression."[3]

---

2. Toffler, *Future Shock*, 239.

3. Schwartz, *The Paradox of Choice*, 3. I'm grateful for the many helpful insights Schwartz highlights in this book.

Could our state of over choice actually be slowly killing us!

Put simply, too many options can clutter our minds and lives, add unnecessary stress and anxiety, and even immobilize us. Additionally, these multiple options on all the insignificant stuff will reduce the energy we have available to make the really important choices. We each live with a built-in limit of energy for daily decision-making. If most of this energy is consumed by the small and insubstantial choices, when it comes to the big stuff we will have already drained our decision-making tank and have little left. The more decisions we have to make, the more effort we have to expend. Freedom of choice is supposed to be an advantage; it's turning into a burden!

True freedom

At the heart of our culture's desire for more options is a misunderstanding about the nature of true freedom. For real freedom is not defined by the lack of restraints in our lives—that is, the throwing off of anything that might reduce our ability to choose what suits us. The political philosopher Isaiah Berlin has labeled this "negative liberty." It's a *freedom from* constraints.

In contrast, true freedom, Berlin argues, is a kind of "positive liberty"—that is, the *freedom to* make good choices that improve our capacity to live well. This positive liberty isn't dependent on having no boundaries or limitations. In fact, such limits often aid true freedom. The love experienced within the confines of marriage is just one such example. Intimacy and fulfillment are enhanced by the restrictions, not cramped by them.

Unlimited choices, then, are not good for us and don't lead to true freedom. Such is the insight of recent psychology. As I've delved into this rather surprising topic I've been impressed by how it neatly dovetails with an implicit message that is threaded through the Bible. We'll explore this further in chapters 21 and 22, but for the moment may I invite you to tease out the matter by mulling over these questions . . .

Up Close and Personal

1. Share your thoughts and feelings regarding some of the choices, big and small, you have had to make this past month.
    - What choice/s did you find easiest to make? Why?

Section B: Culture

- What choice/s did you find hardest to make? Why?
- Was there any decision where you felt overwhelmed by the choices available?

2. Suppose you were about to purchase a replacement car or washing machine. How would you go about the process of choosing one?
    - Would you consult anyone or any particular publication for help?
    - Would you be likely to feel any anxiety about the decision? Why?

3. Do you agree or disagree with the points made in this chapter about the destructive aspects of over choice?
    - Why or why not?
    - Share any experience you've had in limiting or simplifying choices.

4. The Ten Commandments specifically point to the faith-full life as involving limitations and restrictions. Discuss how these commandments promote a "positive liberty."

5. How do you think Jesus would describe "true freedom"?
    - Why? (What elements of the Gospels point toward this?)
    - Is there anything else in Scripture that might reinforce this view?

16

Credit

"The credit card is to someone suffering from affluenza what a bottle shop is to an alcoholic—a disaster wrapped in paradise."
Clive Hamilton and Richard Denniss

JOHN AND CHRISTINE ARE in their mid–twenties and have been together for three years. John works as a mechanic for a local car dealership. He left school early and finished his apprenticeship before he reached twenty. With overtime, he can earn over $1000 a week. Christine, his fiancée, was working in a local bank until six months ago. Recently she gave birth to a healthy baby girl.

They currently live with Christine's parents in an effort to get back on their feet financially.

Today they ruefully admit that they might have bought their own home by now, if it wasn't for the catalogue of bad decisions they made over the last three years. Their story is not untypical of many.

Not long after they got together John decided to buy another car, to replace his old Ford. He found a nice Mazda 323 through his boss, and managed to get it for a good deal. The only problem was, he and Christine didn't have the $9500 they needed. However, a finance company was happy to lend them the money, with repayments set for ninety dollars a week over four years. They figured that given their incomes they could easily afford this.

A couple of months later John and Christine found a new house to rent, with a little more room and closer to Christine's work. The landlord asked for a two thousand dollar bond. Fortunately they were able to

Section B: Culture

borrow this from The Money People—a street-front quick cash operation. Paperwork was minimal and repayments only fifty-five dollars per week. They barely noticed that the interest rate was 29 percent (plus fees).

To furnish the house, the couple bought a bed, lounge suite, washing machine, fridge/freezer, drier, TV, and DVD—from two big-box stores. The furniture shop was offering interest-free terms for twelve months, which was perfect for John and Christine. The appliances were all put on their credit card. While they maxed out the card limit, the couple felt they would be able to pay off reasonably quickly so weren't concerned about the 20 percent interest rate.

Several weeks later John decided to jazz up the car a little. He had spotted a good quality set of alloy (mag) wheels at work and decided to also put on a full body kit. While this set him back a tidy $2500, the car looked awesome!

When, a few months later, the shocks and brakes on the Mazda gave up, John wasn't too concerned. After all he could do the work himself and the parts were at trade. The boss was very relaxed about it. He was happy just to deduct some of John's wages every fortnight to pay for it all.

The letter in the post from the bank also helped cash flow. It stated that their credit card limit had been lifted from $5000 to $7500. Evidently John and Christine were good customers! This made all the difference for paying the bills and meeting the interest payments on the appliances, which had just kicked in after the twelve months interest-free.

However, it was the offer of a second credit card from another bank that made the real difference. This came in handy when John finally proposed to Christine some months later. He'd picked the perfect spot to pop the question—flying Christine to an island resort for the weekend and presenting the $1500 ring underwater while scuba diving!

When Christine discovered she was pregnant six months later, neither she nor John was too concerned. It's true that they were only just getting by financially . . . but why wouldn't things work out? They always did.

Christine stopped work at the twenty-eight-week mark. She had intended to continue longer but being on her feet most of the day while carrying such a large bulge got too much. Three days later the transmission went on the car. This coincided with John's boss telling him that there would be no more overtime, due to the economic downturn.

With over half of their dramatically reduced income going toward servicing the interest and principal on their debt, and three hundred dollars for rent each week, John and Christine found themselves with just over eighty dollars left to cover living costs. Well short of what they needed.

It took a couple of months for the crisis to register. When they received a Tenancy Tribunal notice from the landlord—their rent being four weeks in arrears—there was no longer any doubt. The couple realized they were in deep trouble; they were going backwards fast. Their A/P on the car payments had also stalled, and with all credit options exhausted the Mazda was repossessed. The eviction notice followed soon after.

With nowhere to go—credit had dried up with the credit crunch—the couple turned to Christine's parents for help. As it happened they too were under financial pressure, having recently bought a bigger house and increased their mortgage. Fortunately this turned out to be a win–win situation, because the young family was able to move in with Christine's parents and contribute a little to the costs.

Now, several months later, John and Christine have sought budgeting advice and are on the slow, painful road towards paying off their very substantial debt.

So much for the "good" times!

John and Christine's story could be repeated many times over. They are typical of countless people who have earned good money but have little to show for it except debt.

Through much of the first decade of the twenty-first century, the economic good times have been in full force. Western economies have grown consistently and consumer spending has been at all time highs. But here's the irony. Though we've experienced enormous prosperity and money has flowed liberally and freely, many individuals and businesses are now more in debt than ever before. This is even true of many Western governments—in particular, the US and the UK.

Debt is now king. For example, in New Zealand we have slid in a single lifetime from saving 14.6 percent of our household incomes in 1960 to spending, in 2006, 14 percent *more* than we earned.

Our household debts have ballooned from 50 percent of our after-tax annual incomes in the early 1980s, to 140 percent in 2004.

All this *before* the financial meltdown of 2007/8!

Section B: Culture

How debt became credit

What has brought about this bizarre situation? How is it that such debt could balloon in the so-called good times?

The roots of this go back, as we've already seen, to the onset of the consumer revolution last century. When greed and wants are reframed as "needs," when thrift is discouraged and when we are all encouraged to spend freely, it is no wonder that eventually people's financial habits change. However, another key shift in our attitude to money emerged with the advent of the credit card. It was at this point that the negative association with debt began to be eroded and replaced with the attractive allure of "credit." Of course, this is all smoke-and-mirrors territory. For the "credit" card should really be called the "debt" card. Its advent encouraged a radical paradigm shift so that people became eager to incur debt in order to buy what they wanted . . . *now*.

The concept of delayed gratification became a distant memory. No longer did we have to wait until we had saved for something. Nor did we even have to put it on "lay-buy" (set aside by the retailer until it was paid off) or "hire-purchase" (taken with a deposit and the balance paid off over a period of time). We could have it right now, with nothing more than a signature. That is, of course, until the monthly account arrived, reminding us that what we had purchased with plastic needed *real* money for paying it off!

The freeing up of such credit, particularly for the purchase of consumables (products and services that hold little or no value as assets) signaled the beginning of the slide into easy credit.

At first it was slow. Credit cards and loans were not that easy to obtain and credit limits were kept comparatively low. Even with asset classes likely to appreciate over time—such as houses and businesses—getting "credit" was not effortless. There was limited supply, and eligibility generally required stringent tests. Loans on depreciating assets such as cars often stipulated 66 percent deposits. And as recently as the 1980s a young couple wanting to buy a house could walk into their bank manager's office with no guarantee they would get a mortgage.

However, in the later part of the twentieth century the supply of money grew substantially. This was partly due to the relaxing of monetary regulations by Western governments.

The selling of "credit"

The availability of credit reached a tidal wave at the turn of the millennium. Banks and other financial institutions now had access to more money than they knew what to do with. As a result, within a few short years most of us went from having to beg in order to borrow . . . to being sent multiple letters in the mail pleading for us to take up the offer of cheap credit.

With so much access to money it was not surprising that financial institutions began to actively *sell* credit in ways and degrees that far exceeded what our economies had witnessed before. In fact, they redefined the way we understood and used debt, by actually marketing it and encouraging us to leverage debt against equity.

This "financialization" has taken several forms. One has been to foster the buying of second and third houses as investment properties with people using the equity[1] they have in their own homes as a security for their borrowing. While such "leveraging" is not new, the extent to which it has happened is. In particular, unprecedented numbers of middle-aged couples became investors—most doing so on the assumption that house prices would continue to rise.

And they did—for an extended time. But with credit available in this way, more people entered the market. That pushed prices up, which in turn encouraged others to get a piece of the action. The buying frenzy that resulted not only left many people with multiple properties, but also greatly increased debt.

In the USA, this took the form of a huge "sub-prime"[2] mortgage market, where people were encouraged to buy houses with no equity whatsoever, and with other incentives such as no or low interest for a period of time.

The next step was that those financial institutions which had sold these mortgages now parceled up bunches of them and sold the debt to institutions hungry for mortgage-backed securities. These were ascribed credit ratings according to where a particular CDO (collaterised debt obligation) was in the pecking order.

When the "credit crunch" came, the drop in house prices was particularly brutal in the USA. Many people just walked away from their

---

1. The part of the property that the person owns, and not the bank!
2. "Sub-prime" meant that they were high risk—based on the history of the borrower or the lack of security in the mortgage.

investments. But even worse, as the prices plunged the value of such "creative" financial investment products was found to be as flimsy as the paper they were printed on.

Death by debt?

Perhaps worse still has been the encouragement for people to use the money they have put into their houses for the sole purpose of consumption. Having extended their mortgages or taken out personal loans, many people simply spent the "credit" on overseas holidays, newer cars, home entertainment systems, and a more upwardly mobile lifestyle.

Meanwhile, in the world of education, young people were increasingly tempted to take out bigger loans to fund their tertiary study. In NZ this was further encouraged by the Labour Government's 2005 "election bribe," which abolished interest on student debt. This proved to be a disincentive for repayment and unsurprisingly has resulted in a ballooning of student loans. That we could allow this to happen to young people, who are generally not mature enough to understand the real value of money, is tragic. Coupled with our inability to model and teach the concepts of delayed gratification and moderation, this step has meant that many young adults are being slowly strangled by the noose of debt around their necks.

What happened to savings?

Along with all this came the erosion of centuries of thrift. Saving used to be considered a virtue. Not surprisingly, in most Western countries household saving has declined in the past thirty years. In fact, "By some kind of financial alchemy, 'saving' has become what we do while we are spending. Bargain hunters can easily 'save' hundreds of dollars in the post–Christmas sales, but in order to save a great deal we need to max out our credit cards. Perverse as it sounds, we have been persuaded that the only way to save a lot is to borrow a lot. The idea of going without seems to be a relic of the age of piggy banks and anally retentive middle-class thrift."[3]

---

3. Hamilton and Denniss, *Affluenza*, 71.

Credit as a way of life

All of this has resulted in credit becoming a way of life. In fact, for younger generations it is all they have known. Australian economists Hamilton and Denniss posit that: "Our dwindling ability to think carefully about what we really need and whether we can afford to buy what we want lies at the heart of our debt problems. For all the recent talk of improving our 'financial literacy,' [people] are increasingly prone to financial stupidity. [Those] who are permanently in debt exist in a 'money coma'—a state of vagueness and confusion about their financial circumstances."[4]

Clearly, such a way of living is unsustainable. Eventually we all must pay for the debt we've incurred—individually, corporately, and nationally.

Up Close and Personal

1. What points made in this chapter really made sense to you? Why?

2. What points made in this chapter do you disagree with? Why?

3. Think about your own history with debt over the years. Perhaps you've made it reasonably unscathed through the financial alarms of recent years. But how much of that is simply good fortune? Is there a period in your own life when you might have ended up like John and Christine if economic conditions had, at that time, gone into crisis? With the advantage of hindsight, might you have done things differently? What should you look to change at present?

4. Life is never simple. Pluses and minuses abound in every argument. I've identified serious dangers from our current debt culture . . . but is there any positive features of debt? If so, what might they be?

    Another way of asking this question is: are there any circumstances when taking on debt might make good sense? What factors might be important to take into account when you're deciding whether to go into debt or not? For example, try starting with the topic of mortgages. Hardly anyone can buy a house without borrowing money and therefore going into debt. Should that discourage a young couple from aiming to own their own house? What precautions should they take?

---

4. Ibid, 80.

Section B: Culture

5. What's your take on what the Bible says about debt? Here are a few passages to get you started. They provide a mixed report.

    On the one hand . . . read Deut 15:7–10; Luke 6:35; Matt 5:42.

    On the other hand . . . read Proverbs 6:1–5; 11:15; 17:18; 22:7, 26–27; Romans 13:8.

Remember to try and understand the context of all passages you examine. A vigorous discussion should result!

17

Affluence

"Greed has infected our society. It is the worst infection."
Dr. Patch Adams

IN THE EIGHTEENTH CENTURY a substantial revival occurred across Great Britain. Thousands of working class poor came to faith—people for whom the Church was a closed door and a completely alien environment. One of the leaders of this "great awakening" was John Wesley—an Oxford-educated Anglican priest.

When churches barred him from preaching his messages of new birth, he took to the fields and streets. This was a brilliant move. Most of his audience would never have been accepted and welcomed in the churches. It was a simple equation: he wasn't allowed to preach in churches . . . and the poor weren't in the churches anyway . . . so he would go to where they were. For Wesley, "the world became his parish."

But John Wesley was more than simply an evangelist. It was his genius to devise a system that turned converts into mature believers. He organized the growing numbers of the poor who were coming to Christ by grouping them into small communities (called bands and classes) where they began to be transformed by the gospel. These small groups were greenhouses for change. People who were previously completely ignorant of the gospel began to discover and work out a discipleship that transformed every area of their lives.

The movement mushroomed. Hundreds of thousands of working-class poor became Jesus followers. And as they did, some very significant social and economic changes occurred in the fabric of British society.

Section B: Culture

Their growing faith established a strong work ethic and a freeing from addictions such as alcohol and gambling. This made upward mobility almost inevitable. As they worked harder and spent less of their money on damaging and wasteful pursuits, families discovered they were able to save and dramatically improve their physical circumstances. Their thrift and work lifted substantial numbers of these Christians out of poverty and into a burgeoning middle class.

One could easily assume that John Wesley would have been well pleased with this upward mobility. After all, it showed that faith was making a demonstrable difference in people's day-to-day lives. And to a degree he *was* pleased.

But he also became increasingly disturbed. He noticed that with such upward mobility his converts' passion for radical discipleship mellowed. "Comfortable-itis" frequently took root, and the zeal they once had for following Jesus was replaced by a fading of their desire to live passionate, selfless lives of risk and faith. Their growing wealth began to undermine the vigor of their discipleship. In later life Wesley experienced moments of despair, because, " . . . wherever true Christianity spreads it must cause diligence and frugality which, in the natural course of things, must beget riches. And riches naturally beget pride, love of the world, and every temper that is destructive of Christianity."[1]

John Wesley's unease about the increase in disposable income and the impact it was having on his disciples presented a very real conundrum for him. And nothing has changed. Wealth has exactly the same effect on us too in the twenty-first century.

On the one hand, developing a good work ethic is very much a part of our call to follow Jesus. Our faith flows naturally into being industrious and conscientious, utilizing our gifts—creating, adding value, and making a difference. And of course the result is likely to be that we will earn more than we need. But what happens if (or when) this growing prosperity begins to corrode our values, lead us away from dependence on God, undermine community, and dull our sensitivities to the needs of the world?

---

1. Walsh, "John Wesley and the Community of Goods," 48.

Affluence

The word we increasingly use to describe the state of having more than we really need, is *affluence*. It simply means abundance or wealth. Or in the colloquial, we might identify affluent people as being "well-off," "well-heeled," or "loaded."

In some ways using the word "affluent" is a more helpful way to understand ourselves than saying we are rich or wealthy. That's because with the latter terms we inevitably compare ourselves to those who have more than us, and so automatically dismiss the idea that *we* are rich. Whereas affluence simply implies that we have excess income—more than we genuinely need.

There would be few who question that our Western societies are the most affluent in history. Disposable income is greater than in any previous generation. And, as we have seen, the range of choice has never been as wide.

And yet in the last chapter I claimed that many of us are drowning in a crisis of debt. Isn't this a contradiction? Are we indebted . . . or are we affluent? Shouldn't it be one or the other?

Well, the truth is that as a culture we are both at one and the same time. In fact, it is partly the easy credit that allows many people to live such affluent lives and to consume what they like when they like. Even for those deeply in debt, their negative net worth doesn't necessarily disqualify them from a lifestyle of affluence. As long as the "credit" continues to flow, our choices are not curtailed and our ever-rising aspirations to personal happiness through consumption are not diminished.

Of course, living in this way is ultimately a fool's paradise—because a day of reckoning must come, both for the individual and also for the culture. Indeed, it *has* come for some as a result of the recent global financial crisis. None has had a more spectacular crash than highflying investment specialist Bernie Madoff—or for that matter, the nation of Iceland.

Indebtedness does not preclude affluence, though it certainly does make the crash more dramatic. In fact, our system often seems incapable of limiting the conspicuous-consumption lifestyles of those who are most heavily in debt. High fliers go bankrupt, but remain driving luxury cars and living in expansive mansions. Disgraced entrepreneurs quickly claw their way back to borrowing other people's money again, as if the first failure never occurred.

Sadly, indebtedness and affluence are *not* mutually exclusive.

Section B: Culture

Is affluence good or bad?

So how should we treat our cultural and individual affluence? Should we be as pessimistic as John Wesley about the effects of our affluent lifestyles?

John Schneider, a professor of theology at a Christian college in the US, argues that there are lots of positive benefits to affluence. His book *The Good of Affluence: seeking God in a culture of wealth,* is much more subtle and articulate than those of the prosperity doctrine variety (which he considers vulgar and extreme).

Schneider's thesis centers on the goodness of creation and God's ultimate plan for humans. The abundance (affluence) of the Garden of Eden and of the Promised Land are very much part of God's intention for us.

Though Schneider is much more positive about Capitalism than I am—and about the biblical connection between wealth and God's blessing—on one point we certainly agree: being affluent is not bad in itself. To have more money than we need, to be able to choose what we invest our time and our resources in—these are good things. And as we observed earlier in the book, wealth *can* be used well.

Nevertheless, affluence does present some pitfalls—particularly for those of us seeking to follow Jesus. Wesley wisely discerned that growing affluence could be both a blessing and a curse.

Affluenza

Even for our wider culture, affluence is apt to produce unfortunate side effects. The last few chapters have identified some of the dis-ease that can easily occur when we have too much of a good thing. We become obsessive and compulsive in our behavior. Greed and gluttony end up driving our consumption. When this happens, our affluence is likely to develop into "affluenza."

Coined a few years ago, the word "affluenza" pictures the downside of affluence as an illness—a social disease. John de Graaf and his colleagues popularized the term in the late 1990s, through their public broadcasting TV program, *Affluenza* (which was followed by a book of the same name). In it, they explored the high social and environmental costs of materialism and over-consumption. Here's how this "disease" was defined:

> *Affluenza, n.* a painful, contagious, socially transmitted condition of overload, debt, anxiety, and waste resulting from the dogged pursuit of more.[2]

Several years later, Australian economists Clive Hamilton and Richard Denniss developed the definition a little:

> *Af·flu·en·za, n.* 1. The bloated, sluggish and unfulfilled feeling that results from efforts to keep up with the Joneses. 2. An epidemic of stress, overwork, waste and indebtedness caused by dogged pursuit of the [Western] dream. 3. An unsustainable addiction to economic growth.[3]

These descriptions don't sound much like the "good life" our culture has signed us up for. In fact, as we've seen in recent chapters, while our economic system has brought great prosperity to significant numbers in our society, it has generally not led to those people being happier, more fulfilled or liberated. In fact, quite the opposite. Rather than liberate us, our affluence tends to weigh us down with ever-increasing desires and wants masquerading as needs, as well as with high levels of debt and over choice. Plus, being more affluent tends to produce much more effluent. The waste our wealth produces is killing our planet.

So the great Western dream promises much but delivers little. The disease of affluenza is really just the sickbed of the Capitalist vision.

An alternative vision?

But is there an alternative to the vision and values of Capitalism? Or are we stuck with the obvious problems inherent in our system?

Our overview of the Bible's view of money in the first part of this book pointed to an economic vision very different to that promoted by our culture. At its core it is the dream of shalom. We saw that God's intention to bless humankind very much includes the economic side. The earth has an abundance of resources for all, *if* managed sustainably and shared equitably.

The people of Israel were instructed to develop an economic system that provided built-in checks and balances to ensure that *all* people were able to live well off the land. They were called on to be vigilant in

---

2. de Graaf et al., *Affluenza: the all-consuming epidemic*, 2.
3. Hamilton and Denniss, *Affluenza*, 3.

protecting those who might be marginalized through the circumstances of life. The biblical vision of shalom is built around a community in covenant relationship with God and solidarity with each other. Within this framework, the underlying dream of relational harmony—between God and humans, humans and others, and humans and creation—leads to a sustainable and just future for all, where economic considerations play a critical but not dominant role in how people live.

But just how might we be able to live this way? Is it even possible for followers of Jesus to be faithful to this alternative vision when we live in such a powerfully driven consumer culture, committed as it is to a very different goal and values? Or is it necessary to extract ourselves from the economic system we are a part of? Do we need to abandon our market economy altogether and "go bush"?[4]

I firmly believe that it is possible, indeed it is critical, to chart a different course, pursue a different vision, while still living *within* our culture and participating in our market economy. We don't have to capitulate to Capitalism's values. Or, in the lingo of John 17, we *can* "be in the world but not of it."

The Bible offers values and practices that can assist us to live counter-culturally. They act as a compass, setting a course for a different destination than the one towards which our society is taking us. They can anchor us firmly to a biblical worldview—helping us to live out God's vision for shalom.

So this is where our attention will now turn for the remainder of the book. It's an economic vision with thrilling potential.

Up Close and Personal

1. Do you consider yourself affluent? What are some of the indications that lead you to your conclusion? How do you think your friends view themselves?

2. For someone seeking to follow Jesus faithfully, what might be some of the positives of growing material affluence?

3. Discuss John Wesley's conundrum. How can we stay hungry for and passionate about God, while having more than enough for living?

---

4. "Go bush" is a Kiwism. In New Zealand "the bush" means forest, woods, wilderness, etc.

Affluence

4. Looking back over the first two major sections of the book...

- What are the most striking points of contrast for you, between how the Bible views money and how our culture sees it?
- Can you identify any points where the Bible and our culture are closely aligned?

Section C

Counter–Culture

Eight practices that enable us to pursue
an alternative vision

As followers of Jesus we are called into a new covenant with God that involves *Trusteeship* of all our resources. *Gratitude* for God's gifts to us leads to *Generosity* towards others, and this brings *Contentment*, both with what we have and with who we are. Focusing on the most important things of life leads to a *Simplicity* in priorities and use of resources, and a commitment to *Sabbath*—the regular ceasing from productivity and striving, trusting God for his provision. *Hospitality* also marks our lives—particularly the welcoming of those who are marginalized. This kind of counter-cultural life is best expressed within *Community*–committed companions who share our aspirations and lifestyle.

18

Trusteeship

"The earth is the Lord's and all that is in it, the world and all who live in it."
Psalm 24:1 (NRSV)

"From everyone who has been given much, much will be demanded; and from the one who has been entrusted with much, much more will be asked."
Luke 12:48 (NIV)

Tom and Sue are in their mid–forties, live in what real estate agents call "a desirable home in a good suburb" and have three teenage children. Tom works for a multi–national as a senior manager, while Sue is a nurse. They're involved in a church and take very seriously their commitment to follow Jesus.

Nevertheless, when Tom and Sue look at their lives they feel uneasy about the ongoing pressure to earn more in order to cope with their increasing expectations of consumption. Not that their workmates or Christian friends ever think of Tom and Sue as particularly extravagant. The way they live is fairly normal within their social context.

However, looking back both Tom and Sue recognize that many of their choices were poor, and are part of why they now have limited options. At the moment they're in the most resource–poor period of their lives. Raising teenagers, they've discovered, is incredibly expensive! As

Section C: Counter-Culture

Sue says, "If I'd realized the costs we'd meet at this stage of family life, I wouldn't have been so keen on shifting. Having more money for the teenage years would've taken away some of the pressure."

Tom has a similar comment. "The problem," he explains, "is that even though we've always wanted to serve God, we've never really understood that our money was not just ours to do with as we pleased. Don't get me wrong. We've been faithful tithers and we've given where we could. But we've always taken it for granted that we should regularly replace our car with the latest model, or every now and then upgrade our fridge even if the old one was running okay, or get new furniture whenever we could afford it. And Sue's right. Shifting three years ago to a bigger house in a better part of town was not a good call. It just put more pressure on us financially. It gave us a bigger mortgage for one thing—and then we had to buy more furniture to fill the house!

"Truth is, we'd simply grown tired of our surroundings. And most of our friends were doing it, so we just assumed it was a good idea. Sue saw this really nice house across town one day, and next minute we found ourselves moving!"

Sue agrees. "Yes, it's quite ironic really. I thought having such a dream home would make our lives easier. But quite the opposite! And it's not just financially. Shifting tore us away from the people we'd been getting to know in our old suburb and church—our network of relationships.

"Because our lives are so hectic, with both of us working fulltime and the kids involved in all kinds of activities, I regularly 'buy time' by using pre-prepared foods. Plus, it isn't uncommon for us to eat out or have takeaways two or three times a week. We're on the run so much that it's the convenient thing to do."

Both Sue and Tom also agree that their loose patterns of spending have spilled over into other areas as well. "I'm horrified at it now," says Sue. "It's no wonder, looking back, that we feel we're always struggling financially—all the stuff we convinced ourselves we needed, the expensive holidays we thought we required because we were so exhausted and needed to spoil ourselves a little. Really, we've been caught in a vicious cycle—spending most of our income simply to maintain our lifestyle. If we'd dropped our expectations earlier, we would have released a lot more money for other purposes. And again, it's not just the money. It would have freed up time and energy too."

Like many of us, Tom and Sue are struggling with how to manage their resources. They genuinely want to live in a way that extracts them from the traps and dead-ends of our consumer culture, but they're not sure where to begin. It all seems just so overwhelming.

Back to the beginning

We don't have to read far into the Bible's pages to discover how God intended us humans to relate to the material world. And what we find there is very different from the lies our culture has sold Tom and Sue and many others like them.

Right in the very first chapter of Genesis, hard on the heels of God's master act of creating humankind, come these words to the first man and woman: "God blessed them: 'Prosper! Reproduce! Fill Earth! Take charge! Be responsible for fish in the sea and birds in the air, for every living thing that moves on the face of the Earth.' Then God said, 'I've given you every sort of seed-bearing plant on Earth and every kind of fruit-bearing tree, given them to you for food. To all animals and all birds, everything that moves and breathes, I give whatever grows out of the ground for food.'"[1]

Often referred to as the "creation mandate," this statement sets the tone for the whole of Scripture. It articulates God's original intention for his relationship with humanity. And for our role in God's world.

We are commanded to prosper, reproduce, fill the earth, take charge, and be responsible for the material world we inhabit. Some might say that as humans we've done a decent enough job. Look at the agriculture and animal husbandry we've developed. But others argue that we've gone too far the other way. "Taking charge" (or in other translations "subduing the earth," "ruling," "controlling," or "taking dominion") has often been viewed as licence to do whatever we like. Frequently this has meant raping and pillaging the earth, plundering its key resources in an unsustainable way.

But now, with the all-too-visible signs around us of our many excesses, the charge to proactively care for the earth is a sharp reminder.[2] The message of the Genesis story is that God delegated the day-to-day management of the Garden to Adam and Eve. They were to view themselves as caretakers or guardians of the created order and all within it.

---

1. Gen 1:28–29.

2. Referring to Genesis 1:28 ("Fill the earth and subdue it . . . have dominion . . . over every living thing . . . "). Loren Wilkinson notes that, " . . . stewardship rather than domination best describes the human relationship to creation." See Wilkinson, 'Ecology,' *TCBEC*, 328.

Section C: Counter-Culture

Versions of this concept can be found in many indigenous cultures. For example, as I noted in the chapter on Land, New Zealand Maori traditionally view themselves as *kaitiaki*—guardians of the land, sea, rivers, and sky. At their best, they take seriously the managing of the natural resources.

A question of ownership

Biblically, this guardianship is of course built on the principle that ultimate ownership of everything we have and inhabit is not ours, but God's. King David emphasizes this point in his prayer in front of the people of Israel, at the establishment of the Temple building fund: "Everything comes from you; all we're doing is giving back what we've been given from your generous hand . . . GOD, our God, all these materials—these piles of stuff for building a house of worship for you, honoring your Holy Name—it all came from you! It was yours in the first place!"[3]

David had it right. He understood that all of our resources are given to us by God. We have no right to claim absolute ownership of them.

Our role as stewards

In a long-established tradition, English translations have used the word "stewardship" to describe our role in taking care of God's resources. In the New Testament, this concept of stewarding is a feature of a number of the parables of Jesus. The most well known is the Parable of the Talents, in Matthew 25:14–30, which we briefly considered in chapter 8. But there are others such as the Parable of the Unrighteous Steward in Luke 16:1–13 and the Parable of the Corrupt Tenant Farmers in Luke 20:9–19.

Jesus's widespread use of the role of stewardship in his parables reflects the frequency of this position in both Jewish and Greco-Roman society. The Greek word for steward most often used in the NT is *oikonomos*—the person in a large household who was responsible and accountable to the master for the running of that household.[4] This person was frequently a bond-slave, but a highly trusted one. Bear in mind that the typical well-off Roman household contained scores of people—a kind of

---

3. 1 Chr 29:14–19.

4. A second Greek word is sometimes used which also means steward or manager—*epitropos*. See Fee, *The First Epistle to the Corinthians*, 159.

extended family, including slaves. Managing the master's affairs could be a substantial role.

Trustees

However, you may have noticed that this chapter is entitled "Trusteeship" and not "Stewardship." There are good reasons why I think the word "trustee" is more helpful.[5]

First, in spite of attempts by many to widen the scope of stewardship, the term in our general church use still suffers from a narrow interpretation; it is seen as only really concerned with the way we use our money. In particular, stewardship often refers to fundraising and financial matters within local church life. But in the scriptures we are called to steward much more than just our money; when the Bible uses the word it extends far beyond what is in our wallets.

Second, the only stewards we now have in our contemporary society are those who look after us when we are flying, or at the racecourse! While the name carries a residue of meaning, neither of these activities greatly helps us to appreciate and understand the biblical role of a steward.

In contrast the word "trustee" has recently become very much part of our vocabulary, and most closely mirrors the sense and use of the word *oikonomos* in Scripture. In practice the term "trustee" may function slightly differently from one country to another, but the main point in all its uses is the responsibility that goes with looking after someone else's resources or affairs.

My role as a trustee

In New Zealand, trustees are the people ultimately responsible for managing the affairs of a "trust"—a legal, non–profit entity. Three main types of trust exist: family trusts, charitable trusts, and school trusts.[6]

Having been a trustee in all three entities, I have developed a good appreciation of the role. It means working on behalf of others, managing *their* resources as if they were my own. These "others" are the beneficiaries

---

5. On this, I agree with Leonard Sweet who argues that the term "steward" is now both anachronistic and loaded. See "Freely You Have Received, Freely Give."

6. We also have "trustee companies" whose actual business revolves around managing others' affairs.

in the case of a family trust; the disadvantaged people being helped by a charitable enterprise; or the staff, students, and community of a school. To work on their behalf, I am expected to take seriously the "trust" that has been placed in me. Along with other trustees, I am accountable to these people for how I manage their resources.

Wide decision–making powers rest with the trustees. We are given a great deal of freedom to act, but this must always be in the best interests of those we serve.

Being a trustee has not been easy. Not only will I see things a little differently from other trustees on some issues, but working out the specifics of what constitutes "the best interests" of the trust is not always straightforward. I can think, in particular, of my work as a school trustee, where we were often faced with hard choices. The money and personnel we had available were often far short of what was needed for the many worthwhile projects we contemplated.

As a trustee I do not operate on my own. In fact, in NZ law trusts require multiple trustees. This means that the responsibility is both collective and individual. Having other trustees working alongside me acts as a counterweight, balancing out any temptation I might have to act in self–interest. It also broadens the limited perspective I carry on an issue—for none of us have 20/20 vision.

The scope of Christian trusteeship

I've learned some important lessons from my position as a trustee, regarding my bigger role as one of God's trustees. One relates to how broadly the scope of Christian trusteeship extends. We are trustees of *all* the resources at our disposal. These include our:

- Time
- Money
- Possessions
- Gifts and abilities
- Environment (that we are to cultivate, to conserve, and to co–create.)
- Heritage
- Relationships

And another lesson I've learnt is the wisdom of involving others in this process. As with so many parts of our Christian lives, we miss out on too much when we do it on our own. Having close friends who walk with us can provide not only support but also perspective, and give a model of what trusteeship is all about.

Greater resources mean greater responsibility

The truth is that we are not all entrusted with the same number of resources (as the Parable of the Talents reminds us). Some have more material wealth. Others are time-rich or full of talents and gifts, much more than the average. Still others have a supportive heritage, having been given a great head start in life—from a well-off family, or a mind-expanding education, or supportive friendships and a strong community. Even the physical environment we live in varies; some regions are places of great beauty or full of rich resources—fertile soil, abundant rainfall, good growing climate, copious seafood, or lots of mineral deposits.

And resources apply not just to individuals. Whole nations may enjoy better opportunities than others.

The scriptures teach an important principle in this regard: the greater the resources we are responsible for, the greater the accountability. We are to be faithful with what we have been entrusted with.[7] As one writer puts it, people in positions of power and wealth have no increased privilege—just increased responsibility![8]

Jesus picks up on this accountability theme when he ends his teaching on the Wise Steward by stating, "From everyone who has been given much, much will be demanded; and from the one who has been entrusted with much, much more will be asked."[9]

God's resources for God's purposes

The practice of viewing ourselves as God's trustees is a foundation block for working against the excesses and mistruths of our culture. Until we think through this biblical concept we're likely to take it for granted that our resources are for us to do with as we please (once we've paid our dues

---

7. See for example, Luke 12:42 and 1 Cor 4:2.
8. Blomberg, *Neither Poverty nor Riches*, 84.
9. Luke 12:48b.

to God, of course!) and that the way we use our money is no one else's business.

Of course we all need to consume some of our resources just in order to live; and of course we are personally responsible for what we have. But all too often we stop there. Generally we Christians in the West don't take seriously enough the call to maximize the use of our resources for God's kingdom.

What applies to us as individuals also applies to the groups we are part of. By virtue of our birth into affluent nations, our families and churches have rich resources. We need to take seriously the call to manage and invest them for God's wider purposes. Yet we often limit ourselves to our immediate surroundings. So much of our collective money and time is tied up in maintaining our own lifestyles and houses or church facilities.

In saying that our resources are not to be viewed primarily for our own use and enjoyment, I'm not indulging in some fussy caution against wasting money, or some dry lecture about learning to do without. The principle of trusteeship is no cramping limitation of our lives. Its intention is that we should dramatically expand our lives; that we should join God as partners in both the creative and redemptive aspects of his mission to the world. It is an invitation to participate in God's vision and purpose for the universe he created.

In the language of the New Testament: to help bring about the kingdom of God.

Maximization

In this book you and I have looked closely at the place of money in our lives—lives that at every point are deeply enmeshed in the market economy of our western culture.

When all is said and done, both our market economy and God's economy are about the *maximization of resources* for the benefit of the owner. The difference is in who we consider the "owner" to be.

Our consumer culture is primarily about maximizing monetary profit for the shareholders. However, in God's economy, our role as trustees is to maximize the use of resources for the work of building God's kingdom—the transformation of the world. We have been called to participate in this cause with all the resources at our disposal.

Trusteeship reminds us *who* we are working for and *what* we are working toward. It centers us in a new economy, a different dream—one framed by God's agenda for this world; and by God's agenda for you and for me.

So…

In summary, we can say that:

- Biblically we are to view ourselves as trustees of all of the resources we have.
- Trusteeship reminds us that these resources are not ours to do with as we please. They are God's.
- God has entrusted us with great responsibility *and* freedom regarding the investing of these resources.
- Discovering what is in "God's best interests" and how to be faithful in investing what we have been entrusted with, is not always easy.
- While individual responsibility is important, collective trusteeship is also part of the deal. We share our role with others. Families, churches, communities, and nations are accountable for how they manage God's resources.

A Trustee's Prayer

Lord, we remind ourselves today—all we have is yours; not ours.
So help us to manage your gift of time well.
Help us to invest your gift of money and possessions wisely.
May the unique personality, skills, experiences, and abilities entrusted to each of us Be well nurtured, developed, and used, for your purposes.
May we appreciate the gift of loved ones you've placed around us.
All of creation is a gift to be stewarded.
Let us be your servants this day—not abusing or misusing, always treating with care.
Lord, help us to know what to do with what you've given,
That you may be glorified and your kingdom built.
In the name of the supreme example of trustees—Jesus.
Amen.

Section C: Counter-Culture

Up Close and Personal

1. Discuss the following statement by CS Lewis:

   "Does it not make a great difference whether I am, so to speak, the landlord of my own mind and body, or only a tenant, responsible to the real landlord?"

2. Make an inventory or list of all the resources you have been entrusted with. If it is helpful, you may want to list them under the following categories. (Suggestion: focus on one category per day over the course of a week, so as to evaluate your personal situation at some depth.)

   - Time
   - Money
   - Possessions
   - Gifts and abilities
   - Heritage
   - Relationships
   - Environment

   Some of these resources will be more tangible than others. However, once you've done your best to write your list, spend some time reflecting and praying about where you see yourself.

   If you are doing this in a group, remember to talk about the areas of *common* responsibility you have over these resources.

3. What particular resources do you find hardest to consider yourself a trustee of, and not an owner? Why?

4. Can you think of any particular practices that you might develop in order to remind yourself that these resources are entrusted to you for a wider purpose?

19

Gratitude

"What do you have that you did not receive?"
1 Corinthians 4:7 (NRSV)

"You have given so much to me. Give me one thing more—a grateful heart."
A prayer of George Herbert

VICTOR HUGO IS ONE of the great French novelists; his works are shaped by a strong Christian faith. In 1862 he wrote *Les Miserables*. It is one of my favorite novels, and like many other people I have also greatly enjoyed the brilliant musical based on the book.

Les Miserables (French for "the wretched/poor ones") is set in the early part of the nineteenth century in France. Life is dreadful for a large proportion of the population; in fact, it is a matter of survival. Re-entering this world for the first time in nineteen years is Jean Valjean, Hugo's central character. The year is 1815 and Valjean has just been released from prison on parole. As the story progresses, we discover he was originally arrested for stealing a loaf of bread as a last resort to feed his family. His initial term was for five years; it was progressively extended for several escape attempts.

The hard labor of Toulon prison has taken the best years of Jean Valjean's life, but he remains a strong and fit man in mid-life. However, he quickly discovers that re-establishing a meaningful life for himself on the outside is nigh impossible. At all times he must carry the yellow "ticket–of–leave" (passport) wherever he goes. By law he must present this to potential employers and landlords. Marked forever as a convict, Valjean is trapped and condemned to be an outcast in his own country. No one wants to know him. No one wants to hire him. No innkeeper will even let him stay at his inn.

So in desperation late one night Jean Valjean knocks on the door of the Bishop of Digne. Much to his surprise the bishop invites him in, feeds him and offers him a bed.

However, embittered by years of hardship, Valjean repays the bishop's kindness by stealing his silver and leaving in the middle of the night. Caught by the police a few hours later, the paroled convict is brought before the bishop in chains. The police expect to be congratulated by the bishop for recovering his stolen silver. Instead a remarkable thing happens. Much to everyone's consternation, the bishop lies to the gendarmes in order to save Valjean from life imprisonment. He tells them that he has given Valjean the silver, and is only angry with him because he failed to also take the silver candlesticks as the bishop had instructed him to!

Valjean is overcome. This supreme act of grace causes him to turn his life around. He is blindsided by the inexplicable generosity of the bishop. The rest of the story hinges on this one watershed event. Several years later we discover Valjean having established himself as a successful businessman and living under the pseudonym of Monsieur Madeleine.

There are many more twists and turns to his story but it quickly becomes clear that the remarkable act of grace by the bishop has thoroughly transformed Jean Valjean. In deep gratitude he has committed himself to a life of serving God and others.

Gratitude

Gratitude is a response to grace—perfectly demonstrated in *Les Miserables*. When we realize that what we possess is undeserved, we cannot help but offer deep thanksgiving. Indeed, gratitude really should be our first response to God.

Karl Barth, one of the leading theologians of the twentieth century put it this way: "Grace and gratitude belong together like heaven and earth. Grace evokes gratitude like the voice and echo. Gratitude follows grace as thunder follows lightning."

This must have been how King David felt when the prophet Nathan told him of God's future for him and his offspring. Overwhelmed with such unbelievably good fortune, David cried out in thankfulness: "Who am I, my Master GOD, and what is my family, that you have brought me to this place in life?"[1]

A culture of ingratitude and entitlement

In contrast, there's something very ugly about ingratitude. When a child throws a tantrum after opening a birthday present and finding it is not what she wants, we quite rightly put it down to immaturity. But that sort of response is not limited to children.

The inimitable Bart Simpson, asked to say grace at the table, announces, "Dear God, we pay for all this ourselves. So thanks for nothing." Bart's attitude typifies much of our culture's twisted take on life. We have so very much to be thankful for, yet we often respond as spoilt brats, completely unappreciative of all that's been given to us.

Behind these responses lies a self-confident sense of entitlement—as if we are somehow "owed" something. Such behavior betrays an inflated view of our own importance, and a very limited awareness of gift, grace and good fortune in our lives.

Gratitude as an antidote to commodification

Gratitude is a healing act. It cuts across our culture's obsession with reducing anything and everything to a commodity that can be bought or sold. When there's a price tag on relationships, experiences and acts of kindness, then getting something for nothing – something quite undeserved and unrepayable – doesn't quite fit. We're tempted to blurt out "How could I ever repay you?" in the hope we'll find some way of dealing with the sense of indebtedness we feel. Of course, the answer is that we can't possibly repay a true gift. That's why it's called a gift. It's an act of grace.

There's no way, for example, that children can ever repay their parent/s for all they have given them. (Notice how we often betray our cultural norms by using a phrase from the marketplace – for all that their parents have *invested* in them.)

1. 1 Chr 17:16.

Section C: Counter-Culture

The destructive power of coveting

One of the things that so often prevent us from experiencing gratitude is our tendency to be envious. It's easy to spend our time begrudging others for what they have, rather than being content and grateful for what *we* have. As we've seen, our culture feeds this envy. We are liberally encouraged to compare our lot in life with others, and to "keep up with the Joneses."

This attitude is something that God takes seriously. In fact, it is clearly a big enough problem of the human condition to be noted in the Ten Commandments. There we are warned: "No lusting after your neighbor's house—or wife or servant or maid or ox or donkey. Don't set your heart on anything that is your neighbor's."[2]

The older translations call this "coveting"—desiring, craving what others have.

And it's not just the things they "possess" and the people in their lives. It's fair to assume that God is also warning against coveting the circumstances and abilities of others. We're not talking of ambition here, but of that craving for the wealth or power or popularity of someone we envy.

I used to think that the reason coveting made the Big Ten was because of its potential for social anarchy. And it's true that if we allow ourselves to crave after what others have or are it will cause enormous social damage. Broken marriages, unsafe streets, distrustful relationships, barbed-wired homes . . .

However, the results of such envy go much wider and deeper in their damage. It also wreaks havoc on our capacity to be content with our own lot in life.[3] We become incapable of recognizing God's amazing grace toward us and of expressing this in genuine gratitude and worship of our Creator and Provider.

For if we live with an ongoing sense of the unfairness of life, always looking over our shoulder at what others have, we really treat God's gifts with disdain. We effectively give him the one-finger salute.

All this reminds me of the parable which Jesus tells about the workers in the vineyard. On first reading, the story reeks of unfairness. A landowner hires workers at different times through the day, but at the end of the job he chooses to pay them all the same—regardless of how

---

2. Exod 20:17.
3. We'll reflect on contentment in chapter 21.

many hours they may have worked. This is a case ripe for our Employment Court!

Yet in answer to the complaint of a worker who had labored the full day, the landowner says: "Friend, I am not being unfair to you. Didn't you agree to work for a denarius? Take your pay and go. I want to give the man who was hired last the same as I gave you. Don't I have the right to do what I want with my own money? Or are you envious because I am generous?"[4]

That was the landowner's prerogative, surely. And so it is with God's treatment of each of us.

Sheer grace

Of course it's easy to convince ourselves that what we have is solely—or even mainly—a result of our own hard work, intelligence, or creative genius. The reality is quite the opposite. I've come to recognize that it's way more good fortune than good management that caused me to be born into a loving family, into a prosperous country, into a church and faith that followed Jesus, and with gifts and abilities that have allowed me to grow and develop and serve so freely.

To be brutally honest, our habit of feeling superior to those who live in poverty or suffering is pretty ridiculous. For crying out loud, the fact that I am a person of substantial resources, living in a land of such abundance, is not exactly a result of my own brilliance! What would have happened if I was born in a slum in Dhaka, Bangladesh? Or to abusive parents? Or in a society and religion that knew nothing of the liberating love of Christ?

I don't pretend to understand the mysteries and inconsistencies of life. Nor can I get my head around *who* or *what* determines one's initial circumstances. Did God orchestrate my positive start in life? And if so, did he also arrange for someone else to be born into a deprived and crushing slum? I honestly don't comprehend the apparent inequity of it all.

But this I *do* know: so much of who I am, and of what I've been able to experience, and of what I believe, has absolutely nothing to do with anything I have brought about. It is sheer gift. Maybe even sheer good fortune?

4. Matt 20:13–15 (NIV).

This is a more healthy and biblical perspective. It's not just being modest. It's being truthful.

As the Apostle Paul asks the Corinthians: "Isn't everything you *have* and everything you *are* sheer gifts from God?"[5]

Sheer gifts indeed. And such gifts call for a response, one that we'll consider more in the next chapter.

Cultural shortsightedness

It's not just individuals who can be taken in by the lie (or at least, half-truth) of being "self-made." Culturally we can also develop an arrogance that believes we are superior to other nations and ages because of our technological sophistication and advancement. It's easy to think that previous generations were so "primitive" and even simple. We "moderns" and "post-moderns" are proud of how clever we are. But as Bernard of Chartres famously expressed it in the 12th century, " . . . we are like dwarfs on the shoulders of giants, so that we can see more than they, and things at a greater distance, not by virtue of any sharpness of sight on our part, or any physical distinction, but because we are carried high and raised up by their giant size."

So much of our immense understanding of the universe, so much of what we benefit from in our lifestyle today, if we are truly honest, is built on the work of those who have gone before us. We may take it for granted. Yet an honest assessment will lead to humility and gratitude to those who have paved the way.

Interestingly, psychologist Martin Seligman, whose work on happiness I mentioned in an earlier chapter, lists "gratitude" as one of the key attitudes or attributes that happy people possess. And this gratitude, Seligman suggests, can be cultivated by recognizing that much "goodness" that comes our way, does so independent of our own actions. Happy are those, it might be suggested, who when good things happen ask, "Why me?"

Unfortunately we normally ask that question only when bad things happen to us.

5. 1 Cor 4:7.

The practice of gratitude

Gratitude then, is our first and foundational response to God's grace. And its practice has the potential to change the way we view and treat our material possessions, let alone all the other resources entrusted to us.

Our life's road, then, has brought us to two signposts; they point in opposite directions. The culture we belong to encourages envy, acquisitiveness, and a sense of entitlement. Jesus looks for gratitude and generosity and a sense of contentment.

Up Close and Personal

1. In what ways does our economic system encourage us to covet/envy what others have?

2. When it comes to coveting, what is it in others that you are most susceptible to?

Their fame, power, influence, money, popularity, good looks, sexual attractiveness, gifts and abilities, marriage partner, house, car, employment, friendships, leadership skills, capacity to relate to others, biblical knowledge and understanding, children or grandchildren?

3. Where does the line lie between admiration and envy?

4. How does understanding ourselves as trustees help us to nurture/develop gratitude?

5. Discuss my statement that *it's easy to convince ourselves that what we have is solely—or even mainly—a result of our own hard work, intelligence, or creative genius.* Do you agree or disagree? In what ways?

6. Make a list of all the things for which you can be grateful to God and to others. Spend some time reflecting on these.

7. Consider writing a letter to someone you know who has been an agent of grace in your life.

20

Generosity

"You have been treated generously, now live generously."
Matthew 10:8

"Gain all you can; save all you can; give all you can."
John Wesley

I MET HER AT our annual high school prize-giving. We were sipping wine in the Principal's office before the ceremony, so I introduced myself as a board member and then inquired in what capacity she was there. And so began her story. She had travelled from another city especially for the occasion, to present a newly established scholarship she and her husband had donated to the school. Many years earlier she had been a student at the college. But only for a brief time. Curious, I asked why such a short involvement in a school many years ago and hundreds of miles from where she lived now would cause her to donate such a hefty sum of money on an annual basis to a graduating student who showed potential.

Her reply was sobering. She had had a troubled childhood and was a renegade student. If memory serves me correctly, she ended up at this school as a kind of last resort. According to the woman, that's when her life trajectory took a dramatic turn for the better. At school she was befriended by a teacher, who saw through her hard exterior and found ways to inspire, challenge, encourage and believe in her. In a word, she was loved.

Looking back, it was a watershed experience. Here she was, years later, happily married and a successful businesswoman.

So what was it that caused her to contact the school several decades later?

It was a profound sense of gratitude. You could tell it in her voice. She carried an overwhelming thankfulness, even indebtedness to the teacher and school who had rescued her from a downward spiral. This woman knew that it was pure grace and gift that had been extended to her. And this is what drove her generosity.

Gratitude leads to generosity

While it's true that too great a sense of indebtedness to people can cripple us, generally our sense of thankfulness will lead us to express generosity toward others. For when we are truly grateful and aware of how much grace has been extended to us, we are liberated to be thoroughly generous in our praise, our time, our money, and our relationships. In the words of Jesus himself: "You have been treated generously, so live generously."[1]

True gratitude wells up in us like a volcano that just can't help but explode and blow the top off our own self-centeredness—overflowing to all around us.

This is exactly what happened to the churches in Macedonia. According to Paul, they spontaneously gave to the church in Jerusalem: "Fierce troubles came down on the people of those churches, pushing them to the very limit. The trial exposed their true colors: They were incredibly happy, though desperately poor. The pressure triggered something totally unexpected: an outpouring of pure and generous gifts . . . They gave offerings of whatever they could—much more than they could afford!"[2]

This generosity was a direct result of God's work of grace among the Macedonian believers. It " . . . flowed out of the purposes of God working in their lives."[3]

Encouraging the church in Corinth to join in contributing to the love gift, Paul uses the example of Jesus as his central motivating reason:

1. Matt 10:8.
2. 2 Cor 8:2–3.
3. 2 Cor 8:6.

"You are familiar with the generosity of our Master, Jesus Christ. Rich as he was, he gave it all away for us—in one stroke he became poor and we became rich."[4]

Why are we to give? It is because the One whom we follow modeled generosity to us.

Justice and fairness

Paul continues his challenge and encouragement to the Corinthians through the rest of chapter 8 and into chapter 9. These verses are the fullest articulation of the Bible's approach to giving that we find in the New Testament.

In verses 13–15 of chapter 8, Paul argues for a degree of equality to exist within the Church—backing up his point by using the experience of the people of Israel with the manna in the desert: "Nothing left over to the one with the most, nothing lacking to the one with the least."[5]

For Paul, this is an issue of equity and fairness. He's not contending for a complete equality between rich and poor. However, his line of thought suggests that there are extremes of both wealth and poverty that are intolerable in the Christian community.[6] What is at stake here is the condition of those brothers and sisters who find themselves unable to provide for their basic needs. If those who have a surplus don't respond to such extremity, one gets the feeling that Paul would consider this scandalous. And just as with the Jews in the desert, any hoarding should be viewed as futile. Those who "have" should share with those who "have not." This is fundamental for Paul.

All of which is—or should be—immensely challenging to us as wealthy Christians in a global world, where so many of our brothers and sisters go without the means to survive on a day-to-day basis.

Lives of joyful generosity

In chapter 9, Paul continues with his argument. He emphasizes that our giving should be characterized not just by generosity, but also by joy. We should give because we want to, willingly—out of the overflow of a

---

4. 2 Cor 8:9.
5. Paul is quoting Exod 16:18 here.
6. I am grateful to Craig Blomberg for this insight.

thankful heart. "Remember: A stingy planter gets a stingy crop; a lavish planter gets a lavish crop . . . God loves it when the giver delights in the giving . . . This most generous God who gives seed to the farmer that becomes bread for your meals is more than extravagant with you. He gives you something you can then give away, which grows into full-formed lives, robust in God, wealthy in every way, so that you can be generous in every way, producing with us great praise to God."[7]

Generosity, according to Paul, is far more than just what we give financially. It is a whole way of living. And a life of generosity will lead to our becoming "wealthy" in the full sense of the word.

The chapter closes with Paul coming full circle by giving thanks to God for the ultimate gift, that act of grace which should be the core motivation for our own generosity: "Thank God for this gift, his gift. No language can praise it enough!"[8]

Why we don't give more

In many ways, generosity is actually an antidote to our cultural addiction to debt. In an ironic twist, when we recognize our *absolute* indebtedness to God, our response is to give generously to others. We can't help but do so.

So why is it that so often we are reluctant or stingy givers, lacking in the kind of generosity the Bible talks about? Why is it that, within the Church in the West, the level of giving has dropped over the past few decades even though our wealth has dramatically increased?

Has something been chipping away at our sense of gratitude? Has our appreciation for God's grace and gift been diluted? Perhaps, as John Wesley perceived, the culprit is that old enemy, wealth. Our modern affluence seems to have weakened our concern for others. But why should this be?

I've long puzzled over this problem. Some possible reasons are:

---

7. 2 Cor 9:6-7, 10-11.
8. 2 Cor 9:15.

Section C: Counter-Culture

1. We're giving most of our resources to another dream

In chapter 11 on "Happiness," I suggested that our culture promotes a seductive dream—complete with a landscape full of consumption and "stuff."

This dream takes a great deal out of us. If we pursue it, it will suck us dry of time, money, and ambition. The reality is that we simply can't have both this dream and the "kingdom dream." They pull in opposite directions and both demand *all* of our energy and resources. We need to make a choice. One or the other.

Tom Sine says it well when he writes: "I believe a major reason so little of our total resources or time are invested in the mission of the church is that we have such heavy demands on our lives to carry out another mission. Other peaks and mountains have our attention, resources, and commitment."[9]

2. We don't really believe we are trustees of all of our resources

Instead of singing "All to Jesus, I surrender," many of us are still singing from the alternative song sheet—"One tenth to Jesus, I surrender." When we receive our pay packets we put aside a percentage for giving and then subconsciously assume that the rest is ours to do with as we please. However, as we've seen, this is not biblical. Everything is God's. So rather than asking, "Where should I give *your* portion, God?" we should be asking, "What portion will *you give me* to live on, Lord?" There is a subtle but very powerful difference.

This is one of the problems I have with the practice of tithing. In a world of such unequal distribution of resources, 10 percent is absurdly small for those of us who are affluent. Often all it does is to mislead us into thinking we have somehow fulfilled our duty. Anything we give over and above often makes us feel extra sacrificial. And it fails to take into account the non–material resources we have been entrusted with.

While we may not be happy to follow to the letter the ascetic practices of John Wesley, nevertheless we should be challenged by his example and his maxim—"Gain all you can; save all you can; give all you can." Wesley certainly understood himself as a trustee of all of his resources. Even though his income grew dramatically over the years (mainly from

---

[9]. Unfortunately I can't remember the particular book or article Tom Sine has written this in!

royalties on published works) he maintained his lifestyle at the same level throughout his lifetime, consistently giving away the surplus. Wesley took great delight in ensuring there wasn't much left over when he died!

3. We're not close enough to the real needs

Those of us who are affluent face a real problem. High-fenced houses, air-conditioned cars, a circle of friends that is limited to our own socio-economic group, and a church similarly restricted—all these conspire to keep us trapped in our wealthy enclaves. Those who have little are effectively banished from our world.

This means we often have minimal or no relationship with those who struggle financially—either at home or abroad. Our understanding of their plight and of their issues is limited by the distance between them and us.

However, when we get to know "the poor" in person, up close, our perspectives can change. Our vision focuses. Hearing their stories, seeing their plight, realizing that we have much to learn from them and that we also have much in common—these all contribute to a very different view of the world and of ourselves. And when we make choices and decisions about the use of our money, those who might benefit from it suddenly jump into sharp relief. The poor are no longer just faceless numbers. They now come with particular names and particular stories. Real people with real needs and real lives.

We've already seen earlier in this book that some of the Old Testament's wealthiest—people such as Boaz, Job and Nehemiah—built relationships with those who had less. They mixed with them every day. And this contributed to their generosity.

4. Familiarity breeds contempt

In contrast, we can sometimes be more like the wealthy person in the parable of Lazarus—unmoved by the real needs before us. This is a very sobering parable, for here there *is* proximity—at least of a geographical nature. The rich man would have walked past Lazarus every day, for Jesus tells us that the beggar lived right at his gate.[10]

---

10. See Luke 16:19-20.

However, to all intents and purposes, Lazarus does not exist in the eyes of the rich man. He is a "nothing" and there is no attempt by the rich man to treat him with dignity and develop a relationship. His attitude is so different to Job's (revealed in Job's rhetorical question regarding the worth of his servants)—"Didn't the same God who made me, make them? Aren't we all made of the same stuff, equals before God?"[11] But in the case of the parable, the sight of a desperate Lazarus failed to soften the rich man's heart.

Like the rich man, we can only too easily allow our hearts and emotions to be hardened to the needs around us. When we fail enough times to consciously respond or acknowledge, even if the need is right in front of us, after a while we become indifferent to reaching out.

Jesus, in contrast, lived and breathed compassion in his firsthand encountering of the poor.

Three Greek words used in the New Testament can be translated as "having compassion" (or "pity" or "mercy") though the one that is used most often regarding Jesus is *splanchnizomai*. Literally it means, "to be moved in one's bowels."[12] For instance, we might say these days, "I was moved from the very depths of my being" or, "My heart went out to her." The compassion Jesus felt for people invariably resulted in acts of mercy and love. Empathy, yes. But much more than just *feelings*. He acted. He responded.

5. Compassion fatigue

For many of us, one of the most difficult issues to resolve is not just *how much* I should give, but *where*? We genuinely want our giving to make a difference, but often find ourselves confused. Sometimes this is because there is just so much need out there. It can become overwhelming for us, leading to decision paralysis.

Other times we may become de-motivated when we give and later discover that nothing has changed; or that what we provided is not really achieving what it was intended to. A more recent (and legitimate) concern is whether our giving is actually causing more problems than

---

11. Job 31:15. This whole chapter gives us real insight into how Job interacted with the poor in his community.

12. Of course compassion is a major theme of the Old Testament as well—particularly God's *hesed* (compassion or loving-kindness) toward his people (e.g. Ps 103:17; Ps 106:1).

solutions for its recipients. Often such "help" is paternalistic or creates unhealthy dependency, rather than genuinely empowering the target community.

Even worse is if we find out that our gift didn't actually get to the people or project targeted. Sadly, when some Christian organizations, churches, and individuals promote causes, their claims can be exaggerated and overblown. We in the Church are not immune to being hoodwinked by the same marketing and spin-doctoring that occurs in our wider society. Some questionable charities even rely on the naivety of Christians when they trundle out their promotional machine. Getting the truth can be difficult. Certain organizations and individuals don't appreciate probing questions. They fail to respond to requests for financial accounts and/or external assessments of effectiveness.[13]

As a result, the work involved in overcoming all these challenges can create a kind of "compassion fatigue." It is striking that in the middle section of Paul's exhortation to the Corinthians, he spends quite some space explaining the steps he has taken to ensure integrity and honesty in the delivery of the love gift. In doing so Paul was "taking every precaution against scandal." He didn't "want anyone suspecting us of taking one penny of this money for ourselves."

Such care and transparency really helps to increase confidence and motivation for giving. Sadly, finding projects and people we can really trust and believe in is not as easy as it should be. However, they are around. We may just need to do a more little work to discover them.

Giving as a counter-cultural practice

Giving generously is deeply counter-cultural. Considering both the power that money has over us and the way in which our surrounding culture has institutionalized its worship, giving can be an act of defiance to the god of consumerism. It can bring liberty—freeing us from enslavement to Mammon.

Jacques Ellul, a French theologian who wrote a great deal about the power of money, describes perfectly how to offend our culture's greatest god: "There is only one act par excellence which profanes money by

---

13. A reluctance could be an indication that maybe this group is not going to use our gift with the integrity it deserves.

Section C: Counter-Culture

going directly against the law of money, an act for which money is not made. This act is *giving*."[14]

Up Close and Personal

1. Can you think of a situation where too great a sense of indebtedness to people has crippled someone/you?

2. We are commanded by Jesus to "live generously." What kind of ways can we express this over and beyond our money and possessions?

3. Why is it that we (the Church in the West) allow Christian brothers and sisters to go without the basics of life?

4. Of the five reasons raised for not giving much, do any strike a chord with you?

    - Which ones, and why?
    - Can you think of any other possible reasons for reduced giving?

5. We certainly face difficulties in deciding where to give our money, or to whom. There are some complex issues involved. In fact, many of our choices are not either/or's; they span a continuum. Below are listed some of these ranges of options. Discuss how you determine where to give. What are some of the issues involved?

    organizations..individuals
    local..overseas
    relief (handout)......................development (hand–up)
    social justice..evangelism
    cross-cultural missionaries..........indigenous missionaries
    partnership..donor

---

14. Ellul, *Money & Power*, 110.

21

Contentment

"Keep your lives free from the love of money and be content with what you have . . . "
Hebrews 13:5 (NIV)

"There are two ways to get enough: one is to accumulate more and more. The other is to desire less."
GK Chesterton

A CAPITALIST WAS HORRIFIED to find a fisherman lying beside his boat, smoking a pipe. "Why aren't you out fishing?" he asked.

"Because I've caught enough fish for the day."

"But you could be catching more," the capitalist persisted.

"Why?" asked the fisherman.

"So you can earn more money. Then you could have a motor fixed to your boat and go into deeper water and catch more fish. That would bring you money to buy nylon nets, so more fish, more money. Soon you'd have enough to buy two boats . . . even a fleet of boats. Then you could be rich like me."

"What would I do then?"

"Then you could really enjoy life."

"What do you think I'm doing now?" responded the fisherman, refilling his pipe.[1]

---

1. Apocryphal story as told by Mike Riddell, *Godzone: a travellers guide*, 55. I have edited it slightly.

Section C: Counter-Culture

There is something deeply ironic about our economic system. For decades we were told that "the good life" was just around the corner. Soon we would be down to three-day working weeks and would have more time for "leisure" than we knew what to do with. The catalyst for all this? Rapidly improving technology making more efficient productivity.

Apart from the questionable assumptions involved in this nirvanic vision (like: more leisure and less work is a good thing, technology is always positive . . .), the sting in the tail is that what has actually occurred is the opposite. Workers are, on average, spending longer at their jobs than they did forty years ago. For example, a Harvard economist, Juliet Schor, estimates that Americans are now working 160 hours more every year than they did in 1969.[2]

What is "enough"?

In chapter 10 I suggested that one of the problems with Capitalism is the inability of the system to put limits on our production and consumption. When economic growth is a god, the prospect of restraining ourselves, of limiting our economic options, is not particularly digestible. Yet our unchecked appetites have not led to liberty. Instead they have entrapped us.

What is true of the system is also true for us individually. We have seen that our inability to place limits has led to ever-expanding "needs," over-choice, and high levels of indebtedness. No wonder we feel we must work longer and harder in order to maintain and grow our lifestyle. It becomes a treadmill that all-too-surely runs faster and faster.

When I was younger and battling over deciding whether or not to have another helping at the meal table, my father (who had learned the discipline of self-control) would say to me, "*I know when I've had enough!*" My flippant reply—"I do too, and it's not now!"—came back to haunt me in the following years. As a youngster I had still to learn that too much of a good thing is *not* always a good thing. And that overeating would eventually result in bloating, stomach cramps, and a bulging waistline!

When greed and gluttony are proclaimed as economically good, the word "enough" is not invited to the party. The demand for "more" overrides any hint of self-control or self-imposed limits.

---

2. Noted in de Graaf et al., *Affluenza*, 42.

The dream of "shalom"

In contrast, as I've noted frequently, the Bible presents an alternative dream. It's one that isn't locked into the "more is always better" treadmill.

As I noted in earlier chapters, that vision is contained in one of the profound words of the Old Testament: *shalom*.

Shalom is what the Jews thought of when they reflected on God's vision for them and his world. It's well-known as the Hebrew word for peace, used as a greeting by Jews. But it's an even richer concept than that. Shalom in the Old Testament is an overarching term summing up the well-being in life when God is at the center of things. This well-being is meant in the widest sense of the word—prosperity, bodily health, contentedness, whole relations between people and between nations.

Shalom touched all areas of life because everything was interconnected and found its right place when God was at the center of things. The Jewish worldview saw life in its entirety—a panorama of wholeness.

This was the Hebrew dream. It was what salvation was about. God's wholeness, complete well-being, and harmony—socially, emotionally, economically, environmentally, and spiritually. In such a world of shalom there is always enough. For everyone.

Contentment

This vision of "enough" is threaded through the Scriptures. Learning to be content and satisfied with what we have is a life-enriching goal. For example, the writer of Proverbs pleads: "Give me enough food to live on, neither too much nor too little. If I'm too full, I might get independent, saying 'God? Who needs him?' If I'm poor, I might steal and dishonor the name of my God."[3]

Paul, in his first letter to Timothy, contends that: "A devout life does bring wealth, but it's the rich simplicity of being yourself before God. Since we entered the world penniless and will leave it penniless, if we have bread on the table and shoes on our feet, that's enough."[4]

And in his letter to the Philippians, Paul puts it personally: " . . . for I have learned to be content with whatever I have. I know what it is to have little, and I know what it is to have plenty. In any and all circumstances

---

3. Prov 30:8. The NIV puts it this way—"Give me neither poverty nor riches . . . "
4. 1 Tim 6:6–8.

Section C: Counter-Culture

I have learned the secret of being well-fed and of going hungry, of having plenty and of being in need. I can do all things through him who strengthens me . . . And my God will fully satisfy every need of yours according to his riches in glory in Christ Jesus."[5]

This is a much-quoted scripture—at least, the last sentence is. But I am sad to say that it's a sentence that is too often taken out of context and used to justify excesses that would have dismayed Paul. "Every *need* of yours" has been twisted to mean any lifestyle choice the speaker happens to aspire to.

Let's put the words back in context. First, the church in Philippi was not a wealthy congregation. It mainly consisted of people with "genuine, basic needs, not 'wishes.'"[6]

God was not offering to give them swimming pools; he was promising to provide for them in the day-to-day struggle to survive.

Second—and remarkably—Paul was in detention (we don't know whether he was under house arrest or in prison) as he wrote those words. He was depending on others to provide for *his* basic needs. Now, with that context in mind, let's hear Paul's bold confession again, this time as it appears in the words of *The Message*: "I've learned to be quite content whatever my circumstances . . . I've found the recipe for being happy whether full or hungry, hands full or hands empty. Whatever I have, wherever I am, I can make it through anything in the One who makes me who I am."

That's true contentment. For Paul to express this while awaiting trial is extraordinary. He really was content whatever the circumstances in which he found himself. And he had a supreme confidence that God would provide his real needs.

Of course, this contentment went much deeper and wider than just Paul's material circumstances. It penetrated his whole being. Nor was it just a reluctant resignation to his "lot in life"—a kind of fatalistic *Que sera sera* ("whatever will be will be"). Rather, Paul had come to terms with who he was and wasn't, his own limitations and failings, the reality of his situation, and who God was. He was at peace. He had "enough."

Why was he content? Because he had developed an implicit trust in God. Paul believed God was in control and quite capable of knowing what he needed.

---

5. Phil 4: 11b–12,19 (NRSV).
6. Keener, *The IVP Bible Background Commentary—New Testament*, 567.

Contentment of this type is a powerful antidote to greed and the constant desire for more. It also subverts the interminable restlessness and discontent we feel about ourselves and our situations. For unlike the Philippians and Paul, most of us don't know what is "enough." Our appetites have been trained to always desire more. Our senses have been tuned to respond to stimuli that suggest we are not okay just as we are. In reacting this way, we betray our fundamental unwillingness to trust God—to trust not only that he is aware of our needs, but also that he knew what he was doing when he created us the way we are.

So not only does our culture cause us to long for a good life that can't deliver on its promises, but it also plants the seeds of discontent about who we *are*—not just about what we *have*. As a consequence, we are rarely comfortable in our own skin.

To be fair, this is not just a result of our culture; it is part of the ongoing effect of the Fall. So part of our growth and maturing as sons and daughters of God is learning to nurture that acceptance in our own lives. Achieving that sort of contentment—not just with what we have but also with who we are—is a lifelong task.

How do we go about achieving it? As I've already noted, contentment as a spiritual practice and virtue goes well beyond the material world. But because the focus of this book is on money and possessions, my comments here will be largely limited to the financial area of our lives.

Who determines what is "enough" economically?

It would be much easier for us if God mandated the limits of our consumption. For example, imagine a manual that defined for us what we could and couldn't have:

Each person shall be allowed twenty square meters of living space.

One automatic washing machine, fridge/freezer, and microwave per five people. Each appliance must be purchased for the best quoted price within a fifty-kilometer radius.

A vegetable garden of at least ten square meters is required for every single dwelling house. 90 percent of its space must be used for a minimum of 75 percent of the calendar year.

Food budget must not exceed fifty dollars per person per week.

Allotment of three-and-a-half weeks holiday per year. Must be taken within a five hundred kilometer radius of home.

Accommodation must be three-star or less. Limited to one hundred dollars per day total spending . . .

Okay. So it wouldn't be that easy! For a start, each command would raise as many questions as answers —"What about this? How about that?"

Plus, it would take a whole library to contain all the stipulated allowances. We'd all spend so long looking up answers to particular scenarios, we wouldn't get anything done! And the "answers" would quickly go out of date or become irrelevant. All in all, such an approach would be a nightmare.

If we're looking for some clear line or straightforward guide we won't find it. Not only that, but our circumstances are all very different so rules can't possibly fit every situation.

Given that none of us have a true gauge on what is sufficient and what is excessive, and taking into account that being content with enough will look different in varying contexts, what do we do?

Walking with other Jesus followers

One starting point is to learn to ask more regularly the "what for?" question. What is this product for? Why should I use this service? Not just the factual question: what does it do? But rather: what is the need for it? Why should I commit energy and resources to procuring it?

It's not a question that advertisers will ask for us! And we are often not sufficiently objective to ask the question for ourselves. We need help from others who share our longing to seek real contentment in our following of Jesus—people who can ask us questions that help clarify our motives and uncover our genuine needs.

Now for sure what we don't need is some sort of church inquisition who thinks it's their job to tell us what to do, or to judge our eventual decisions. God is in the business of helping us grow in spiritual maturity. That's why he has *not* designed a hierarchy of spiritual bosses to do everything for us—giving us orders and telling us what the right answers are and checking that we're doing what we're told. We must learn for ourselves what is right and best. That is the only way we'll grow spiritually.

But what I'm suggesting is that we don't have to do it *alone*. If at all possible, we need friends who aspire to similar goals, who are struggling with the same issues, who experience the same difficulties. In an accepting and encouraging relationship with "significant others" like this, we will find it easier to learn *together* what is enough, what are God's true riches, what is contentment. (In chapter 25 on Community we'll explore this more fully.)

Walking with people who are struggling with genuine basic needs

During the months when I was writing this book, my wife Jill and I regularly attended a dinner once a week for homeless and semi-homeless people in the city of Vancouver, where we were living at the time. Each week we would sit at tables for a couple of hours, engaging in conversations with men and women who were struggling with the very basic needs of life. For most of them, this grinding existence revolved not only around the lack of a suitable place to call home, but also around issues of unemployment, addiction, isolation, worthlessness, and identity.

At first my stuttering attempts to connect with such people were filled with awkwardness, embarrassment, and long silences. I wanted so very much to relate, but our worlds seemed a million miles away from each other. How could I ask them, "So, where do you live?" "What kind of work do you do?" "Tell us about your family." The realization that such normal starting points were at best inappropriate and at worst insensitive, made me re-evaluate how I could begin to build rapport with folk who seemed so very different to me.

Even so, with God's help I learnt to find ways of reaching out. A smile here, a small act of service there. An acknowledging laugh at a joke someone made. There were some weeks where simply being a presence among these people was all I could offer. But more often than not conversations *did* spark into life, and it was then that I began to hear something of their own stories. For most of these men and women, it soon became clear that like me, they were desperate for someone to listen and to genuinely take an interest in them.

Often it was hard to tell where fiction and reality met, but nevertheless I found myself drawn into their worlds, marveling at their courage, resourcefulness, and resilience, even in the face of considerable obstacles. Sometimes, I even found that my initiative in asking questions sparked a whole table of strangers, sitting together, into varying levels of interaction with one another. It was then that I most felt the presence and smile of God. Disconnected people engaging with other human beings . . . lonely souls finding themselves valued . . . broken lives reveling in the sense of belonging . . .

Even if it was just for a fleeting moment or hour, it was worth it. We were experiencing together a small taste of God's shalom.

All of us who are "well-off" need such relationships. For the more we mix it with people who are relatively resource-less, the greater will be our chance to gain insight into our own needs. When we develop friendships with the poor, we hear their stories and observe their lives in a way that throws perspective on our own choices, dreams, and lifestyles.

We have much to learn from such folk. In fact, they can become a real gift to us for a number of reasons. Not least is that we soon find they have things to teach us—often about being resourceful, celebrating life, and not being concerned about status and excessive material acquisition. Their circumstances have often long since caused them to offload pretensions of grandeur. But we also discover how much they are just like us—broken people living with disappointment and the consequences of their own choices, yet still with hopes and dreams for a better life.

Perhaps most of all their lack of some of the basic needs of life can cause us to evaluate ourselves more carefully. When we look at them we might be more objective about our own possessions—and how content they allow us to be.

Walking with the Holy Spirit

It might seem obvious to suggest that our journey to material contentment is greatly aided by the Holy Spirit's work in our lives. And to a degree it is. However, let me approach this subject of the leading of the Holy Spirit in a different way. It's this: If we expect God's Holy Spirit to tell us *exactly* what we should and shouldn't do, we are barking up the wrong tree.

Ultimately God wants a love relationship with us, not a legal contract. Growing contentment is not about finding out where the line is between what we are "allowed" to have and what we can't have. Such an approach misses the point completely. God wants us to make good choices because we love him and love others. When we increasingly become passionate about what God is passionate about, it will lead us to see material possessions and money in a different light. And it will lead us to grow in contentment. The Holy Spirit is there to help us discover God's priorities and perspectives. This will lead us to make better choices with our use of resources.

Finally . . .

One thing is for sure. When we begin to learn when enough is enough, being content with what we have and who we are will result in an increasing simplicity in our lives. And this will, in turn, bring great freedom.

Simplicity is another important Christian practice in the journey to living counter–culturally, one that we'll consider in the next chapter.

Up Close and Personal

1. Discuss GK Chesterton's statement: *"There are two ways to get enough: one is to accumulate more and more. The other is to desire less."*

2. Think about yourself. In what ways do you struggle most to be content with:

    - *Who* you are (abilities, personality/temperament, etc.);
    - *Where* you are (work roles, living situation, communities you are part of, etc.); and
    - *What* you have (money, possessions, education, etc.)?

    If you are in a group, share with the others some of your joys and struggles.

3. To what extent do you think our consumption and our desire for more material possessions are fuelled by our aching lack of contentment with *who* we are?

4. Discuss Shane Claibourne's statement: *"I would suggest we need a third way, neither the prosperity gospel nor the poverty gospel, but the gospel of abundance rooted in a theology of enough . . . After seeing plenty of poor folks forced into economic crimes by their poverty and after seeing plenty of rich folks so content in their riches that they forget they need God or anyone else, I think we are all ready for something new."*

5. What relationships do you have with others who are:

Section C: Counter-Culture

- Seeking to grow contentment?
- Struggling to provide for their basic needs?

How important do you think it is to nurture these kinds of relationships?

What practical steps might you take to build them into your life?

6. We've seen that part of the challenge is knowing what is "enough."

    - Can you think of any helpful guidelines for doing this?
    - What specific things can you do to discern what is sufficient; to know when you don't need more?
    - What plans can you adopt so that these values do not wither as the years pass, and as the wider culture continually pressures you to think as it does?

7. This chapter has centered on developing contentment. But following Jesus also involves a healthy measure of dis–contentment. What elements of our life and discipleship do you think we should be discontented with? Discuss ways in which we can hold these two in tension.

22

Simplicity

"Steep your life in God-reality, God-initiative, God-provisions. Don't worry about missing out. You'll find all your human concerns will be met."
Matthew 6:33

"Simplicity enables us to live lives of integrity in the face of the terrible realities of our global village."
Richard Foster

THE TWENTIETH CENTURY WAS a period of prolific inventions, and we're apt to think of the private motorcar as one of the greatest of the conveniences it bequeathed on us. That's certainly true. But equally true is the unexpected by-product of that convenience. Stress!

Constant use of the car can "up" the frenetic pace of our lives simply because we are able to get to more places, do more things, and see more people in a day. Plus, city traffic being what it is, our stress levels often increase while we're driving. Mine do, anyway!

In short, the car makes our lives busier. One of the habits I have developed to counter this hectic pace, has been to walk where I can, or even take public transport. (That's a challenge for me as an ex-car dealer!) Walking slows me down. It fills my lungs with air, my nose becomes sensitive to the smell of trees and flowers, I see things that I miss at fifty kilometers an hour, and I meet people I would normally drive straight past. It gives me time to think, reflect, pray, and relax.

Walking is an undervalued and under-utilized act of simplicity. Sadly, today it tends to be a last resort.

The call to simplicity

We live in a fast and furious world. Our lives are cluttered—with things, choices, desires, and activities, some of which are not helpful when it comes to living faithfully as disciples.

The Christian discipline of simplicity is one response to this. Simplicity enables us to major on what is *most* important. It brings clarity and a straight-forwardness to our lives. It brings a direct and uncluttered relationship with God, with others, and with the physical world.

Richard Foster comments that: "Contemporary culture is plagued by the passion to possess... Christian simplicity frees us from this modern mania... It allows us to see material things for what they are—goods to enhance life, not to oppress life. People once again become more important than possessions. Simplicity enables us to live lives of integrity in the face of the terrible realities of our global village."[1]

Simplicity of purpose

At the heart of simplicity is single-mindedness in attending to God and his kingdom. In Matthew chapters 6 and 7, Jesus talks extensively about developing this kind of devotion. First he emphasizes our need to pray with simplicity—so that our focus moves to God and what is important to him, and away from ourselves.

Then Jesus goes on to clarify things by presenting two ways—alternative purposes for our lives. There are two treasures before us, one earthly and one heavenly. There are two gates through which we may enter, and two ways we may build the house of our lives. In short, there are two different ways our eyes may look at life.

By framing the options the way he does, Jesus is calling for a simplicity of purpose to our lives. And a simple trust in God's capacity to provide what we genuinely need.

1. Foster, *Freedom of Simplicity*, 3.

Simplicity

This could easily be misinterpreted as being simplistic. However, Jesus is not suggesting that "all you have to do is this..." as if following easy steps will deal to the central issue. That would be shallow and naïve, and is not (as we've already seen) God's way. Rather, Jesus points out that we need to see our alternatives for worship through the stark simplicity of worshipping *either* Mammon *or* God. Getting to the heart of the matter is this central question: "*Who* will you worship? Who will you give your primary allegiance to?" Jesus is being as straightforward and uncomplicated as possible. And in the course of his examples he clarifies things further, by stating:

> If you decide for God, living a life of God-worship, it follows that you don't fuss about what's on the table at mealtimes or whether the clothes in your closet are in fashion. There is far more to your life than the food you put in your stomach, more to your outer appearance than the clothes you hang on your body... What I'm trying to do here is get you to relax, to not be so preoccupied with getting, so you can respond to God's giving... Give your entire attention to what God is doing right now, and don't get so worked up about what may or may not happen tomorrow. God will help you deal with whatever hard things come up when the time comes.[2]

So how might developing this kind of simplicity affect our lives in practical and economic terms? Three expressions of simplicity come to mind—choices, lifestyle, and aspirations.

Simplifying our choices

In chapter 15 we looked at the issue of "over-choice"—where too many options in too many areas of life eventually immobilize us and sap or energy. Rather than aiding us to live freely, they end up imprisoning us.

There are no easy answers to the state of over choice we find ourselves in. However, Barry Schwartz suggests that we first determine which choices matter *most*. That's where our primary energy should go. By implication this will mean restricting our options with the less important choices.

---

2. Selected portions of Matt 6:25-34.

Section C: Counter-Culture

If we learn to accept "good enough" in many smaller decisions—we simplify our lives enormously and free energy to give to the more critical ones that involve our values, faith, and life-direction. Schwartz also suggests that these multiple small decisions be non-reversible. By this he implies that we often second-guess ourselves, asking the "what if?" question, and in doing so we just add another layer of complexity and angst to our over choice.

My experience has been that when I try to exhaust all the options I am generally being driven by the fear that I will regret not doing so—because I might miss the very best option. Dropping my expectations and accepting that in many cases a "good decision" is good enough—it doesn't have to be the *absolute* best—helps me cope with my fear.

Which decisions will I deal with quickly, and to which decisions will I give much more time and attention? My criterion is the *implications* of my choice. Those decisions that have minimal consequences either way, I try to treat with little energy. The bigger, more critical decisions should, of course, be given significant attention. With them I aim to take more time and consider a greater number of options.

I suspect that most of us would say the same sort of thing . . . in principle! But in practice have you—as I have in the past and still occasionally do—wasted far too much time and energy deliberating over small matters? A month or a year later they are exposed for what they were: minor decisions with no long-term consequences. Or choices which may have an influence in a small way, but where each of the possible outcomes has a mixture of strengths and weaknesses. Yes, the final result of my choice does lead to a different consequence, but each of the advantages is useful to me and each of the drawbacks can be lived with.

Choosing a cellphone is perhaps a good example. You can spend weeks analyzing, comparing, and contrasting different models. No two are identical. Each has some functions that appeal, others that are doubtful. If your cellphone will be the main tool of your professional life, something around which your whole mode of working will be adapted, yes, then you may well take pains over it. For the rest of us, several models will do the job. We'll adapt to the style of the one we end up buying. It doesn't deserve endless scrutiny.

Simplifying our lifestyle

The move to simplify our lifestyles is for the benefit of both ourselves and others. Doing so will reduce the "clutter" and help bring greater clarity to the way we live. We will likely find that in many circumstances "less is more."

For when we surround ourselves with "stuff," we can spend an inordinate amount of time and energy simply maintaining and looking after it all. With bigger houses to clean and fix up, cars and boats to wash and service, holiday homes to look after, multiple appliances to repair, and recreational equipment to maintain . . . we can find ourselves ending up just like Mike and Sarah in chapter 12. No wonder we feel so short of time!

However, the other reason for simplifying our lifestyles is for the sake of those whose lives are at most risk. For if we are to pursue a more just world, we can't assume that the volume of resources we consume is unrelated to the lack of resources available to the poor of the world. If we have the means to do so, doesn't our faith demand that we consume less in order to give more to those who live without?

Many of us can actually live on substantially less with very little pain. Buying a house in a cheaper area of town and then resisting the desire to "upgrade"; buying a secondhand vehicle that has already depreciated substantially but still has good life in it; settling for mainly secondhand furniture; eating out only occasionally; choosing cheaper forms of entertainment and holidays; keeping one's wardrobe to a minimum and wearing clothes till they are well-worn—these are some of the practices Jill and I have pursued over the years. And they have reduced our cost of living substantially.

Simplifying our aspirations—downward mobility

Developing the practice of simplicity will also affect our aspirations—what we want to achieve, what we want to possess, who we want to be. Our supreme example here is, of course, Jesus. We are challenged by Paul to:

> Think of [ourselves] the way Christ Jesus thought of himself. He had equal status with God but didn't think so much of himself that he had to cling to the advantages of that status no matter what. Not at all. When the time came, he set aside the privileges

Section C: Counter-Culture

of deity and took on the status of a slave, became human! Having become human, he stayed human. It was an incredibly humbling process. He didn't claim special privileges. Instead, he lived a selfless, obedient life and then died a selfless, obedient death—and the worst kind of death at that: a crucifixion.[3]

Central to Paul's line of thinking is the development of humility that leads to considering others better than ourselves: "Don't push your way to the front. Don't sweet-talk your way to the top. Put yourself aside, and help others get ahead. Don't get obsessed with getting your own advantage."[4]

Gordon Fee clarifies: "it is not so much that others in the community are to be thought of as 'better than I am,' but as those whose needs and concerns 'surpass' my own."[5] This is exactly what the example of Christ teaches us (see verse 8). When Paul writes that he "humbled himself" he is referring to Christ's obedient decision to sacrifice his own needs for our sake.

This is a difficult challenge to face for those of us who are rich. Everything about our culture's deference to people in positions of wealth and power seduces us to believe that our needs really *are* more important than the needs of others. That we are somehow entitled to live at the level we do.

Nevertheless, we too are to "pour ourselves out," as Paul has already asked the Philippians in verse 4. Jesus is our paradigm. It is his "attitude" or "mindset" Paul is asking the readers to emulate. So the question is asked, "How can we 'empty ourselves'?" While the answers will vary for different disciples, there can be little doubt that for those of us who are well off, there will be economic implications.

In our culture, "upward mobility"—working toward a higher level of lifestyle (what we like to call "standard of living") is applauded. Working hard to "better one's economic and social status" seems consistent with the Protestant work ethic. However, is this example of Jesus not a call to the well-to-do disciple to be engaged in "downward mobility"?[6]

---

3. Phil 2:6–8.
4. Phil 2:3.
5. Fee, *Paul's Letter to the Philippians*, 189.
6. Interestingly, Craig Keener notes that the call to Simon Peter and Andrew to follow Jesus (Matt 4:20) was very much a call to downward mobility because they paid a price economically to follow Jesus. See Keener, *Matthew*, 98–9.

With this focus, "looking to get ahead" may well be replaced with "looking to prefer and serve others." With that as our guiding principle, we might prefer to downgrade our house, car, and furniture, rather than upgrading them. The idea may sound outrageous—and it is—but if we take seriously the example of Jesus, might it not lead us in that direction?

A call to resourceful living

For many years now there has been an informal movement within and outside of the church promoting simple living.[7] As I've argued, it has much to commend it, but for those who follow Jesus, simple living should not be an end in itself. I suggest that our aim would be better thought of as "resourceful living." Let me explain.

As trustees we have responsibility to manage *all* of the resources God has entrusted us with. This includes our money and possessions. But it also involves our time, gifts and abilities, and relationships. For each of us has a whole bundle of resources we are responsible for—not just money.

We are called to obey God by using *all* these resources for God's purposes. This means that sometimes we might spend money resources in order to save time resources, or so that we can make better use of our gifts, or to facilitate relationships and community . . .

If simple living were the goal, offloading as many items of technology as possible would be a possible choice. However, if resourceful living is the goal, there may well be, for example, many labor-saving devices that actually assist us to maximize our resources for the kingdom. An automatic washing machine costs more financially than hand washing, but having one is more resourceful in stewarding our time. Similarly, I've written this book on a laptop computer. Without it, the process would have been incredibly slow and definitely more challenging.

For most of us resourceful living will certainly mean simpler living—a decluttering of our lives. However, this (simple living) should not be the goal, per se. Living resourcefully is an act of simplicity. It enables us to concentrate on what is most important as we follow Jesus. Getting first things first.

---

7. In the wider culture, these people are sometimes called "downshifters"—often with the goal of achieving more balance in their lives.

Section C: Counter-Culture

A "poverty mentality"?

On occasions over the years I have encountered people who are unhappy with the idea of simplifying our lifestyle and becoming downwardly mobile. The criticism they have expressed is that it advocates what they call a "poverty mentality."

I've often wondered what they mean by this phrase. It's unlikely they think I'm advocating that we should all give away what resources we have—become "poor" ourselves, as if I thought there's something morally superior or good about living in poverty. At least I hope that's not what they think I'm saying!

So I wonder if the phrase is really code for believing that they're being made to feel guilty for what they own—guilty for spending on anything more than bare necessities. Does it conceal a mentality that thinks talk about simplifying or limiting our consumption is tantamount to being a party pooper or spoilsport?

Christians who think this way often make a claim that goes something like this: *God is extravagant in blessing us with abundance. God wants us to enjoy these good gifts.*

Well, yes—and no. Yes, God delights to shower us with his blessings and good gifts. Yes, we seriously misrepresent God if we think of him as some kind of moral policeman "tut-tutting" every time we eat out at a restaurant or buy a lovely ornament. Yes, as far as I can tell most of us are not called to undertake a vow of poverty.

There's no doubt that what God asks of us will differ according to our situation. My world is not your world. The lifestyle that is appropriate for me has a lot to do with my personality, preferences, and interests, to say nothing of where I live and who I live amongst. My vocation and my income are factors too. So we are not talking about a new legalism here. Just because some of my friends live in tiny shacks without running water, doesn't mean I ought to do the same.

However, there is another side. Let me be clear here: wealth *does* carry with it increased responsibility. To whom much is given, from them much is required. Our good fortune is not meant all for us. And when we remind ourselves that the world we live in is grossly unequal and unjust, surely this must significantly shape what is appropriate regarding our consumption of resources and the employment of our energies? As New Testament scholar Gordon Fee recognizes: "In the new order, brought about by Jesus, the standard is sufficiency, and surplus is called

Simplicity

into question . . . Indeed, in the new age unshared wealth is contrary to the Kingdom breaking in as good news to the poor." [8]

Christians have always had to resist being seduced by the dominant cultural values of their age. We followers of Jesus in the twenty-first century are vulnerable to self-centered consumption. If I feel guilt pangs sometimes this may well be the Spirit prompting me to change my ways, to adjust my lifestyle. An active and responsive conscience is a good thing. Not all guilt is false guilt.

So is it a "poverty mentality" that I'm arguing for? No, not at all. The description I personally prefer is "responsible trusteeship."

Some examples of simplicity

Living a life of simplicity is all about seeking to be faithful and obedient to what we feel God is asking of us at the time. Nothing more, nothing less. There are no rules here. No compulsion to do certain things or not own certain things.

Here are just a few examples of how some people express the practice of simplicity—at least as far as their money and lifestyle is concerned. Each example challenges me to be faithful and obedient to God's call to simplicity.

John has chosen not to own a cellphone. He is not anti-technology; his decision to do without what might these days be considered an essential device is driven more by a desire to simplify his days. He simply does not want to be regularly interrupted from his core priorities. For many years he did carry a mobile phone, partly because of a small business he ran. Those days are gone. One bonus is that he now has to plan his time and connections with people, enabling him to establish a better daily rhythm.

Mary and Rob have always been "go-getters"; high achievers. For many years their schedules were packed full of responsibilities and activities. And this spilled over into the lifestyle of their children. However, a heart attack caused Rob to reassess what he was giving his life to. As a couple they made a decision. Their compulsion to respond to every need and opportunity that came their way was destructive.

The effect on their lives has been staggering. They are no longer driven to "save the world," taking on responsibilities beyond both their

---

8. Fee, *The Disease of the Health & Wealth Gospels*, 10.

Section C: Counter-Culture

energy and time resources, and often outside their sense of personal vocation. They now take more time to discern where God is leading them, and how they should contribute to God's kingdom.

As an odd side effect, the impact on their finances has been surprising too! They've realized that by their frantic lifestyle they actually consumed and spent much more than they needed to.

Diane and George have instituted a "simple food day" in their family life. Every Monday they eat as simply as possible. Dinner consists of rice and vegetables, often eaten with their hands—just for fun! After the evening meal they pray as a family for the country of Burma. The money they save from their limited Monday diet is set aside and given to a mission working with the people of Burma.

The Callendar family enjoys present–free Christmases. They no longer buy gifts for each other. However, what used to be spent on family gifts they now contribute toward a Christmas love gift—to a charity of their choice. The result is that the Advent/Christmas season is no longer cluttered with the stress of purchasing gifts for everyone and anyone. This simplification has enabled them to concentrate on the real centrality of the Christmas story and to celebrate well. Hospitality is a feature of their household through this time, including inviting all of their immediate neighbors to a meal at their place on the Sunday evening preceding Christmas. This is a real highlight in the street, so much so that neighbors take pains to ensure they don't miss it each year.

Jerry is a corporate "high flyer," earnestly seeking to serve God as CEO of a large publicly-listed company. He mixes with movers and shakers and his daily decisions have implications for thousands of employees. In Jerry's world, excessive (and often reckless) living is the norm. To counter this tendency, Jerry and his wife have placed a limit on their consumption—seeking to live on 20 percent of Jerry's income (he earns $1.5m a year, so this is remarkably easy!) and placing the remainder in a charitable trust which then distributes the income earned from its invested capital to mission projects here and abroad. Jerry and Sue are trustees, along with several friends. They spend a day together six times a year, discussing, praying, and considering what to give and to whom. Jerry and Sue live in an apartment close to Jerry's office, in order to reduce commuting time. It's a very nice pad, without being ostentatious, enjoying a view of the harbor. They are patrons of the arts so the walls are lined with delightful pieces of work, which often become talking points with the many guests they entertain. Jerry has several routines that enable him to regain focus in the often frantic, high-pressure world of business. Sundays are sacrosanct, as is a daily walk he takes around the local park early morning. So too is a fortnightly lunch with four other men seeking to follow Jesus in the marketplace. Amidst the complexity of life, these rhythms allow Jerry to slow down and re-center on the simplicity of trusting and obeying Christ.

Up Close and Personal

1. Discuss the concept of simplicity. What images does it trigger for you?
2. Use Matthew chapter 6, beginning at verse 5, for a meditation (individual or group), taking *simplicity* as your focus. That is, in each topic he addresses, how does Jesus "unclutter" our lives for the purpose of deepening our spiritual growth?

Simplifying choices

3. What kinds of choices are most important to you and call for as much effort as possible?
4. What kinds of choices are secondary and could be given less energy and attention?

Simplifying our lifestyles

5. Can you think of other examples than the one given (automatic washing machine) where seeking to live resourcefully might mean a different choice to that of living simply?
6. What kinds of questions might be helpful in assessing what is the most resource-full response in a particular situation?

Section C: Counter-Culture

Downward mobility

7. Do you think the example of Jesus (Philippians 2) in being downwardly mobile might have potential economic implications for us/you? Why or why not?

8. Do you know anyone who has made a conscious decision to de–accumulate, to live on less? If so, what are your observations regarding how this has affected their capacity to follow Jesus?

23

Sabbath

"Observe the Sabbath day, to keep it holy. Work six days and do everything you need to do. But the seventh day is a Sabbath to GOD, your God."
Exodus 20:8

IN MY EARLY YEARS, Sunday was a special day in our house. Mornings would revolve around church and Sunday school, followed usually by a special family roast dinner. After that we might all have a rest for an hour or so, and then we might visit or host grandparents, cousins, or friends, or even go for a "Sunday drive" to the beach, the countryside, or just around town. The whole day was relaxed and unhurried.

Of course this rhythm was greatly aided in those days by the almost total absence of anything commercial on Sundays. In the New Zealand of the 1960s virtually everything bar the local convenience store and the gas station was closed. Very little, if any, competitive sport was played on the Sabbath, there were no adverts allowed on TV, and the central city resembled a ghost town. Sunday was definitely different to every other day of the week and as children growing up we all recognized this—even those not involved in church life.

In my teenage years (the 1970s) things began to change, ever so gradually. I remember in my last year of high school being selected for a representative sports team but then discovering it would involve practices and games on Sundays. Turning down such an opportunity was not easy—in fact, my school coach was completely bemused by it—but engaging in competitive sport still seemed to our family out-of-step with the "day of rest." Sunday was different from every other day of the week. It was special.

The compulsion to produce—and consume

One of the features of our consumer culture is our compulsive work habits. It's as if we are on a treadmill which keeps getting faster and faster. As we produce more we are then compelled to consume more, which in turn leads to having to work harder to produce even more. Growing demand and expectations create a vicious cycle for us. As Gordon MacDonald says: "The more we want, the more revenue we must produce to get it. The more revenue we must produce, the longer and harder we have to work. So we build larger homes, buy more cars, take on added financial burdens and then find ourselves having to work harder to pay for it all. More work, less rest."[1]

In the midst of this compulsive madness, finding true rest is not easy. Gone are the days like those of my childhood when Sunday was largely a non-producing day. Not only is our culture full on, 24/7, but technology has conspired to increase the acceleration. Now we can take our cellphones and our laptops—and our work—anywhere and everywhere; we can toil away at any time of the day or night.

What is Sabbath?

Sabbath literally means "to cease." To stop. To pause. In the Genesis 1 story, that's exactly what God did. He took a break from his activity. No doubt he reflected on what he had created—and appreciated it. It was good. Very good, in fact.

Subsequently, God commanded the emerging people of Israel to establish a weekly Sabbath. It was part of their covenantal responsibility—a day to focus and re-center on God, to celebrate life. We know it as the fourth "commandment," but in reality it was given in order to keep the people of Israel liberated. For the call to "lay down the tools" for one day a week was a discipline intended to break the relentless demands of work. It was a kindness; an example of God's care.

The Jews were to take a break, to pause from their work and productivity. In such a rigorous and demanding agrarian life this can't always

---

1. MacDonald, "Rest Stops."

have been easy. Particularly if the crops failed or the rains didn't come. To produce enough in six days to live on for seven would have required both faith in Yahweh and good planning.

Why we need Sabbath

We too need rest from our labor, from the need to always be doing "stuff." Establishing regular time-out enables us to re-focus and regain equilibrium.

Sabbath is a regular repudiation of the desire for "more." It's a statement to ourselves that there are other things in life besides producing and consuming. And that there is more to our identity than what we do or what we produce.

Sabbath is an act of trust. It dares to suggest that we can place our confidence in God's provision for all our needs. As the Israelites discovered in the wilderness, " . . . [GOD] fed you with manna, something neither you nor your parents knew anything about, so you would learn that men and women don't live by bread alone; we live by every word that comes from GOD's mouth."[2]

Taking a Sabbath is a reminder that ultimately life depends not on our hard graft, but on God's provision and grace. It also liberates us from thinking that our choices are the only determining factor in how life turns out. We are enabled to trust again in the providence of God—in the role he plays in leading and directing and working in our lives. His choices—not ours—become the focus again. For a few hours each week, a Sabbath can slow us down enough to bring this realignment.

For all these reasons, Sabbath is deeply counter-cultural and much needed.

Sabbath and our possessions

One of the kinds of "ceasing" Marva Dawn suggests Sabbath is about, is the ceasing of our possessiveness.[3] She notes that the relationship of Sabbath-keeping to possessions is a paradoxical one. Citing the Jewish experience, Dawn writes: "On the one hand, the Jews would choose gladly to live more frugally during the week in order to enjoy the

2. Deut 8:3.
3. See Dawn, *Keeping the Sabbath Wholly*—particularly chapter 5.

special foods and candles of the Sabbath. On the other hand, the Torah commanded them to refrain from any buying and selling on that day. Thus, both a special appreciation of possessions and a desire not to be dominated by them are part of keeping the Sabbath holy."[4]

In other words, the special use of certain items on the Sabbath was a reminder of the sacredness of the material world and the fact that such things are a gift from God. At the same time, it was not a day to accumulate more or to engage in trade. By ceasing from such things the Jews were shifting their hearts and desires away from what *they* wanted to what *God* wanted.

One way of loosening the grip of possessiveness in our lives is to view Sabbath as a time of giving away. That is, practicing generosity. This can take many forms, of course. For example, we could use it to give financially to someone/something else, and/or to give hospitality. The second of these forms of generosity we'll consider more extensively in the next chapter.

Whatever we do, Sabbath can allow us to get our possessions in their right perspective. It can remind us that we do *not* live by bread alone; that we are *not* worth the sum total of our bank accounts; and that what property we do "own" is only entrusted into our hands by the owner, and is for the purpose of serving God and others.

How we practise Sabbath

Let's be honest. Our world is very different to that of the ancient people of Israel. It is even radically changed from the world of our parents. There are no longer any society-wide practices that help us to Sabbath well. The shops are open seven days a week. In fact, our traditional day of rest (Sunday) is often now the busiest time of the retail week and the focus of the professional sports calendar. More people work on Sundays than ever before. The hustle and bustle of Monday to Friday continues unabated through the weekend.

Even if we do manage to refrain from the scurry of buying, selling, and producing for one day a week, the reality is that consumer culture has invaded virtually all spaces in our world. On our way to gathering for corporate worship or going to have a meal with friends we pass billboards or other marketing messages. We turn on the radio or TV and are

---

4. Ibid, 36.

confronted with adverts promoting products or services we just *have* to have. Even at our church services we are not safe! The message that we are consumers of religious goods and services will likely be subtly reinforced.

So it is not easy to create "commerce-free" space. Nevertheless, with a good deal of intentionality and planning it can happen. A regular rhythm of work and rest can be established.

I acknowledge that I haven't always been good at doing this myself. While creating space for rest has been something I've generally managed well, consistently putting aside a full day of Sabbath weekly has been more challenging. But there again, this is not a practice that we need to feel has to be lived out in any legalistic way. I am convinced that as long as we intentionally make space for regular Sabbath, we have the freedom to individually and communally determine a shape and form that fits our own context. This might mean, for example, that we straddle our Sabbath over two days—as the Jews do—beginning on Saturday dinner time and finishing at Sunday dinner. Or if one whole day is not realistic (perhaps because of church leadership responsibilities) then maybe we could find two half days or a day during the week?

A Sabbath from . . .

There are several elements of the practice of Sabbath that might be of benefit to us. One is making times when we take a break from some part of life (a useful idea this for loosening the grip of consumerism). For example, setting aside a no-go slot for making choices . . . or buying things . . . or using certain forms of technology (in my case, my laptop) . . . or motorized transportation (yes, me again with the car). This "ceasing" could coincide with our normal weekly Sabbath, or we may feel it helpful to create special days or weeks or periods of time (the season of Lent is the model here) where we intentionally take a break from certain activities or foods.

Imagine a day, for instance, where you choose not to buy anything. The now annual international "Buy Nothing Day" is one example. It makes a statement to ourselves and those around us that we are pushing back against the invasive influence of shopping and consumerism in our lives.

Section C: Counter-Culture

Sabbaticals

One form of Sabbath that is not practiced very often—except by university professors and church pastors—is the sabbatical. For the people of Israel, this was ceasing every seventh year from work and productivity. And it included the land. Pasture and cropping fields were to lie fallow in order that they might rejuvenate.

I am a strong proponent of, where possible, building sabbaticals into our lives. In fact, I am writing this book while on sabbatical. My wife Jill and I have taken six months out from our normal responsibilities and environment. We've based ourselves in a different city in a different country, and temporarily joined two new communities.

A sabbatical is not an extended holiday, though it will contain aspects of rest and relaxation. Generally it involves activity and work but of a different type and at a slower pace to what we normally engage in. A change of daily and weekly rhythms often enables us to re-assess how we normally live.

For example, most of our sabbatical has been without the use of a private car (see, I *am* trying), which has enabled us to be refreshed by going everywhere by walking and using public transport. We've also enjoyed doing without any telephones—either landline or cellphone (though our email and Skype facilities on our laptop have been well employed!).

This is not the first sabbatical we have had during our working lives. Each time we have planned well in advance, leaving behind commitments and ongoing relationships for a period. Taking a sabbatical has often been financially costly for us. We've had to set aside savings to cover some or all of our living costs.

However, there's no doubt that these times of extended Sabbath have enriched our lives considerably, helping to illuminate our future direction, and enabling us to see God, ourselves and life in a new light.

Sometimes I've heard people say, "It's alright for you, but I couldn't take a sabbatical." When I ask why not they generally mention reasons like not being able to get time off work or to leave their business for a period. Undoubtedly there are challenges for many of us. However, if we're employed we may have the option of taking long-service leave, or leave-without-pay, or even resigning if we think our season in the position is coming to an end.

The point is, sabbaticals don't just happen. We need to be intentional in planning them into our lives. And embarking on an extended period of ceasing will probably cost financially. We can save for such eventualities—just as the Jews were instructed in the Law to set aside a portion of their produce to cover particular Holy days.

Summary

Sabbath can be expressed in a variety of shapes and forms. The act of ceasing from work, productivity, and the imperatives of consuming can re-center us on God and his priorities for our lives. To do this is to trust in the abundance and provision of God, much as the people of Israel learnt in the wilderness with the daily manna from heaven. Sabbath is something we desperately need if we want to resist the corrosive elements of our consumer culture. It can be a liberating experience.

Breathe fresh life into your Christian walk. Catch the adventure of Sabbath!

Up Close and Personal

1. If you grew up in the church, describe what part Sabbath played in your early life—how was it expressed in your family and church context? Then think about how this has changed now—both in your understanding and practice of Sabbath.
2. Discuss the reasons raised in this chapter for Sabbath being important to us. Do you agree or disagree? Why?
3. What (if anything) do you find most difficult in establishing a regular rhythm of Sabbath? Why?
4. What kinds of "ceasing" have been (or might be) relevant for you and your situation?
5. Have you ever had the opportunity for a sabbatical? Share your experiences, the lessons you learnt, or the things you would do differently next time.
6. Discuss creative ways of making space and time for sabbaticals.

24

Hospitality

"So reach out and welcome one another to God's glory. Jesus did it; now you do it!"
Romans 15:7

"Jesus' gracious and sacrificial hospitality—expressed in his life, ministry, and death—undergirds the hospitality of his followers."
Christine Pohl

THE MOVIE *BABETTE'S FEAST* is the story of a small, remote Danish village in the nineteenth century, where a tiny Christian sect seeks to live out their faith. It's a very austere existence and life is hard, but they live with purpose and dignity, and in harmony with one another.

One night a young French woman arrives seeking refuge. She has fled from danger in Paris at a time of civil war, and a friend of hers has given her the name of two sisters who live in the village. Though they possess little, the sisters take Babette in. She offers to work for them in exchange for board, and it is agreed that she will cook and help them. While the meals they eat are very basic and bland, Babette gladly prepares the food and serves her hosts, without complaint.

Many years later, Babette is still working for the two sisters when she receives word from a friend in Paris that she has won a large sum of money in a lottery. The friend has faithfully bought a lottery ticket each year on Babette's behalf.

About the same time the two sisters decide to organize a special meal to celebrate the birthday of their long deceased father—who was the founding pastor of the sect. Babette offers to cook and to pay for the celebration.

Though the sisters don't know it, in her former life Babette was one of the top Parisian chefs. She uses her former contacts to send for the very best ingredients; they are shipped all the way from France—quails and turtle, the very best wine.

The feast is sumptuous and lavish, way beyond what any of the villagers have ever experienced. But it's not just the food and the wine that is extravagant. So too is Babette's heart for the people she is serving. She uses up all her lottery winnings for this one meal. It is really an overflow of deep gratitude to the villagers for their hospitality over many years.

Babette, who came as the guest, has now become the host. And the money that might have taken her back to Paris to re-establish herself has been sacrificed in one generous act of hospitality.

Hospitality

What do you think of when you hear the word "hospitality"? Your mind may jump to cups of tea, cucumber sandwiches, and dinner parties. Or perhaps tourist companies, restaurants, and hotels—what is often called the hospitality industry.

In the Christian tradition, however, hospitality is a very different affair. It involves the welcoming of strangers. In fact, the most common Greek word used for hospitality in the Bible, *philoxenia*, literally means "love of the stranger" (*philo* being a Greek word for love, and *xenia* for stranger). Our English word "hospitality" comes from the same root as hospital, hospice, hostel, and hotel—but more about this later.

So who is a "stranger"?

A "stranger" is someone who is disconnected from the basic relationships that give a person a secure place in the world—separated from family, community, church, work, and culture. A stranger is very obviously different from us. He or she knows it—and we know it.

You become a stranger when you find yourself in totally alien or foreign surrounds—knowing no-one, not being familiar with the way

Section C: Counter-Culture

things are done, having no prior history, and few if any resources to survive. As a stranger, you feel intensely vulnerable.

Many of us can remember a time in our lives when we were in a strange place. It may have been an overseas trip to a culture thoroughly different from our own—with completely different language and cultural traits. Or it may have been a time when our whole world seemed to disintegrate before our very eyes—a loved one dying, a dream evaporating, a relationship turning ugly. All of these are times when we had little, if any, internal resources to cope with what we were experiencing. We were impoverished.

The world of a stranger contains a fair measure of disorientation, displacement, and disillusionment. This is particularly so for refugees; for them most of what was familiar is now all gone. But it's also true for the foster child, psychiatric outpatient, prisoner, homeless person, and immigrant.

Jesus himself was very much a "stranger" at various times in his life. At birth he was a homeless infant. Then he became a refugee child in a foreign land—Egypt. In early adulthood he became homeless again—with "no place to lay his head." And at the end of his life he was a despised and condemned convict.

The point is this: Jesus knew what it was to be a stranger. These experiences would have shaped the way he related to other strangers—those on the margins of his society. In fact, he built a community that "did not judge, categorize, or label people based on any external commodity."[1]

As I noted in earlier chapters, the people of Israel were specifically commanded to care for strangers—widows, orphans, and foreigners. These were the groups of people most vulnerable, powerless, and marginalized in their society. They were the poor.

And here's a curious twist: God instructed the Jews to view *themselves* as "strangers in a strange land." Even when they inherited the Promised Land, the Jewish people were not allowed to forget that they were sojourners.

God's welcome

Why this emphasis on the welcoming of strangers?

---

1. Jethani, *The Divine Commodity*, 147.

Its origin, surely, is in the very nature of God—self-giving and other-receiving love.[2] This remarkable quality is expressed by the way each member of the Trinity relates to the others. They (Father, Son and Spirit) are a perfect community. In fact, their relationship is reciprocal—that is, each of their identities and completeness is dependent on the others.

It is into this open and welcoming community that God invites humans. We might say that this is really the ultimate act of hospitality—the trinitarian God (Father, Son and Holy Spirit) inviting us to be a part of their fellowship. This is particularly radical when we consider that as humans we have made ourselves the enemies of God by our willful rebellion. We have put up barriers between us and God—and between one another. Theologian Miroslav Volf describes this astonishing action: "We, the others—we, the enemies—are embraced by the divine persons who love us with the same love with which they love each other and therefore make space for us within their own eternal embrace."[3]

It is, of course, the work of Christ that makes this possible. Because of him, our pattern of excluding God and others is broken. Now God can welcome us in. The Apostle Paul notes: " . . . God put his love on the line for us by offering his Son in sacrificial death while we were of no use whatever to him."[4]

The table of welcome

Our most visual and tangible expression of this gracious and generous act of hospitality is communion—the Eucharist. The "Lord's table" is central to our faith. It is a table of radical welcome and a foretaste of the "great banquet table." Everyone is welcome. No one is excluded from participating in the meal that celebrates God's hospitality.

And the message it speaks, loud and clear is: "As we (Father, Son and Holy Spirit) welcome you, so you are to welcome one another and all who are estranged." Paul puts it this way: "So reach out and welcome one another to God's glory. Jesus did it; now *you* do it!"[5]

---

2. This is how Miroslav Volf expresses it in his book, *Exclusion and Embrace*, 127.
3. Ibid, 129.
4. Rom 5:8.
5. Rom 15:7.

Section C: Counter-Culture

The return of the Prodigal Son to the waiting and open arms of the father is perhaps the gospel story that best illustrates God's welcome.[6] We see that in spite of good reasons for the father to reject his recalcitrant son, or at least place conditions on his return, he reacts in a thoroughly counter-cultural manner. Not only does he run to meet the son (very unbecoming of an elder), throwing wide his arms to embrace, but he also treats him to an almighty party—a banquet of celebration. Full of grace and graciousness, the father withholds any judgment or expectations on the son. This is true hospitality.

Christian hospitality[7]

It makes sense then that hospitality—the welcoming of strangers— is fundamental to what it means to follow Jesus.

Two key gospel passages in particular shape the distinction between conventional and Christian hospitality—Luke 14 and Matthew 25. They mark out Christian hospitality as a radical act of love.

In Luke 14 we find Jesus sharing a Sabbath meal with one of the leading Pharisees. In the middle of the conversation he turns to his host and says: "The next time you put on a dinner, don't just invite your friends and family and rich neighbors, the kind of people who will return the favor. Invite some people who never get invited out, the misfits from the wrong side of the tracks. You'll be—and experience—a blessing. They won't be able to return the favor, but the favor will be returned—oh, how it will be returned!—at the resurrection of God's people."[8]

Jesus then goes on to tell the parable of the man who threw a great dinner party—which most of the invited guests chose not to attend, using all kinds of excuses. So the host told his servant to go out to the "city streets and alleys" and invite "all who look like they need a square meal, all the misfits and homeless and wretched you can lay your hands on . . . "

The distinctive quality of Christian hospitality is that it offers a generous welcome to the poor and "the least among you"—to the very people who are unlikely to be able to "return the favor."

---

6. Luke 15: 11–32.

7. I'm grateful to Christine Pohl, whose teaching and writing on the ethics of hospitality has been very helpful to me. See her book *Making Room*. I recommend it.

8. Luke 14:12–14.

This is also evident in Matthew 25: 35–40—a passage we've already looked at in chapter 8. Here Jesus presents the final judgment according to how two groups of people (the "sheep" and the "goats") have cared for the marginalized. When the "sheep" react in astonishment—wondering why Jesus would think that in being hospitable to the sick, the hungry, the homeless, and the imprisoned they were welcoming him, he replies: "Whenever you did one of these things to someone overlooked or ignored, that was me—you did it to me."

These perspectives deeply shaped the way the early church lived and related to its surrounding culture. Welcoming the stranger was viewed as welcoming Jesus. This gave a real moral imperative to the church to extend radical hospitality to the poor.

It is little wonder then, that it was the Christians who:

- Rescued abandoned (exposed) babies on the streets of the Roman Empire and took them into their homes.
- Frequently entered epidemic-wracked cities and nursed those dying from the plague.
- Established the early hospices and hospitals.

They took seriously the words of Jesus in his Sermon on the Mount: "I'm telling you to love your enemies. Let them bring out the best in you, not the worst. When someone gives you a hard time, respond with the energies of prayer . . . If all you do is love the lovable, do you expect a bonus? Anybody can do that. If you simply say hello to those who greet you, do you expect a medal? Any run-of-the-mill sinner does that."[9]

The meal table: doing life together

The most visible expression of hospitality around the world is the act of eating together. In fact, the meal is central to almost all cultures.

And yet in our own consumer culture the place of the table has been deeply subverted. The advent of fast foods, TV dinners, and "eat-all-you-can" smorgasbord/buffet restaurants, to say nothing of the increased pace of life, has resulted in the meal table becoming little more than a work-surface in many homes. When it *is* used for eating, it is mainly functional—a place for "gobble-and-go" meals.

---

9. Matt 5: 43–47.

Section C: Counter-Culture

We often come to the meal table the same way we approach much else in life—as consumers rather than participants, as autonomous individuals rather than as friends sharing community.

To recover the place of the meal table we need to ask ourselves questions such as "Is our home—our table—really a place of welcome?" and "Would a stranger feel comfortable here?"

We may need to make some deliberate lifestyle changes like, for example:

- Allocating significant periods of time to eating together as families and churches, viewing it not as an optional extra but as core to doing life together.
- Considering physical ways we could make the kitchen and dining spaces in our homes and church buildings more conducive to shared meals.
- Eating out less, in favor of spending more resources on home-based hospitality.

Part of recovering the place of the meal is finding ways to celebrate regularly and well.

Good celebration does not have to cost a lot of money. Nor does it require expensive foods or wines to do so. Extravagance *can* involve fine dining (like Babette's feast) but it can just as easily be expressed through thoughtful and resourceful creativity. In other words, spending a lot of money is not a pre-requisite. It may even be counter-productive—subtly shifting the focus from the celebration itself to the means of celebrating. And it may also cause guests to feel uncomfortable and inadequate.

Celebration was, of course, core to the life of the people of Israel. They made gala events of festivals and holy days, where their identity was collectively remembered and where they celebrated being God's people.

We too, can nurture such times of celebration. And it is possible to do this in a way that includes those who are not part of our faith community. Imagine if we became known as people who knew how to party well and often. People who were great to be with. Who knows? We too might be accused of being drunkards and gluttons!

Hospitality—a counter-cultural practice

The more we understand and appreciate God's generous hospitality toward us, the more we will naturally want to welcome others.

As we've seen, hospitality (or welcome) has a subversive, counter-cultural element to it. It is counter to the human tendency to exclude those who don't fit our view of how they should be. In fact, the radical nature of Christian welcome is only evident when we are hospitable to those we have no natural reason to embrace—our enemies, those substantially different to us, and those who are undervalued by society.

There is no right or wrong way to practice this type of hospitality. Our circumstances and contexts are all very different. Some of us live in the inner city, others in the suburbs, still others in rural or provincial environments. Some are single; others have young families or teenagers, or are empty nesters or retired. Some of us live in single dwelling houses, others in community houses, still others in apartment buildings.

All these and other factors will influence and shape what forms of hospitality we are able to express. We will also need to look around us and observe the people who are living and working in our neighborhoods, workplaces, and communities. Which of them are in some way "strangers"? Some of us will find these people in our already existing worlds. Others of us may be called to re-locate or re-arrange our lifestyles in order to associate with "strangers" more regularly and naturally.

Depending on our context we may find people who are homeless, lonely, elderly "shut-ins," prison inmates (and their families), refugees or new immigrants, people with mental health issues, those who are physically disabled, at-risk young people, teenage moms, those caught up in the prostitution trade, or the local gay community.

When it comes to where we express hospitality and to whom, we need to take all these factors into account, as well as our own gifts and passions. We need to ask the Spirit to lead us regarding which particular "neighbors" to welcome.

Taking hospitality seriously will make a radical difference to the way we use our resources. Here are four short examples of how this can happen:

Ken and Diane have fostered children over the past decade. They wanted a way to welcome the stranger that meshed well with their own life stage and circumstances. Having three sons of their own, they knew the demands of raising a family; furthermore, fostering was one way their

Section C: Counter-Culture

whole family could embrace the call to hospitality. As a result, their own boys have shared in the "welcoming of strangers" and have grown up seeing this type of care as a normal part of the Christian experience. There has been a cost to the fostering—both financially and in time. Diane has foregone paid employment; and the demands of caring for other children have often meant that avenues they would like to have explored have been out of the question.

Neroli has recently moved to South East Asia to be part of a small Christian community, with the aim of helping the internally displaced people and refugees of civil–war–torn Burma. She is involved particularly in befriending children who have lost their parents and who are deeply traumatized as a result. The military junta's regime has had a brutal impact on the tribal groups of eastern Burma. Neroli's journey started when her church became aware of this and began building a connection to a Burmese Christian community. The journey then became, for Neroli, a literal one. She has re–located to be with them and to partner them. Meanwhile her home church provides financial commitment, prayer, and the provision of key resources.

Janet and Mike, along with Sarah, have covenanted to live together in a large house. Janet, Mike and Sarah intentionally looked for a house that would be suitable for such living. The place they found was old but had multiple bedrooms and two large living areas. Currently resident with them are two adults who would struggle to live by themselves—a guy who suffers from a mild form of autism and a woman with multiple sclerosis. Members of the home eat together every night of the working week, with one of those nights given to a "house night." They also host a community meal once a month for their neighbors—including several elderly folk and a man next door who struggles with his mental health. The monthly gathering is complemented by many other informal interactions with these people, and neighbors often drop in for a coffee and chat, which frequently results in staying for a meal.

John and Fran lead a home group that has, over the past two years, taken on the challenge of helping three refugee families settle. Two of the families are from Africa and the other is from the Middle East. In each case specific group members have taken on the role of primary support people, while everyone contributes to the care in various ways. This might involve taking one of the refugee family members to an appointment, helping buy equipment to set up home, or having them over for a meal. On special occasions—such as Easter, Mothers' Day, Thanksgiving, and Christmas—the home group has a big celebration meal where these refugee families are invited to be a part. They love these times, and though there is often some reflection around the Christian significance of the occasion, this is always done in a very inclusive way, so much so that their refugee friends eagerly look forward to the next celebration.

These, then, are just a few ways in which Christian hospitality can be expressed. The range of possibilities is really as wide as the various circumstances, gifts, and creativity of the people involved.

For when we are captured by the vision of welcoming the "strangers" around us—particularly people who are normally excluded—there is no limit to the ways it can be done. I like how Skye Jethani puts it: "Our homes are to be hospitals—refuges of healing radiating the light of heaven. And our dinner tables are to be operating tables—the place where broken souls are made whole again. In our churches people should find rest from their battle for acceptance and release from the lie that they are nothing more than the goods they possess."[10]

And not only in our churches should this happen . . . but in our homes as well. This is true hospitality.

Up Close and Personal

1. Can you recall a time when you were a "stranger"?
   - What was it like?
   - In what ways did you feel vulnerable or helpless?
   - Was there anyone or any group who helped you through this?
2. Can you recall a time when you welcomed a stranger? Share your experience.
3. What aspect of hospitality mentioned in this chapter most appeals to you? Why?
4. Are there any barriers or challenges you can think of that might make it difficult for you (individual and group) to become more hospitable to strangers?
5. Think about your local community. Make a list of the kinds of people living or working close to you, who are excluded or marginalized in some way—those who might be considered "strangers." To do this,

10. Jethani, *The Divine Commodity*, 154.

Section C: Counter-Culture

you may have to do some asking around or research. Then begin to reflect and pray on how you might begin to explore reaching out, and with whom.

25

Community

"By means of his one Spirit, we all said good-bye to our partial and piecemeal lives. We each used to independently call our own shots, but then we entered into a large and integrated life in which he has the final say in everything."
1 Corinthians 12:13

THE 2006 MOVIE *AMAZING Grace* tells the story of William Wilberforce, the British MP who spearheaded the movement to abolish the English slave trade (and eventually slavery itself) in the late eighteenth and early nineteenth centuries.

In the late 1780s much of the wealth of the British Empire was dependent on the trading of slaves from West Africa across to the New World. In fact, it would not be overstating matters to say that the growing power of "Great" Britain occurred on the backs of slaves.

Challenging this immoral trade inevitably pitted the proponents of abolition against enormous and very powerful economic interests. This helps to explain why the anti-slavery movement had to battle for decades before they succeeded in stopping it. It was not until 1807 (a full twenty years after the campaign began) that the slave trade was abolished, and then a further twenty-six years until slavery itself was made illegal. Appealing to politicians, who were themselves profiting significantly from the trade (either directly or indirectly) or were backed by the barons of industry, required more than just pointing out the immorality of such treatment. For the truth is that so often when we think our livelihood

Section C: Counter-Culture

is threatened, any ethical concerns are relegated to the too hard basket.[1] Money does indeed rule.

The movie paints this long battle well—as it does the forces of opposition, abuse, and ridicule that the abolitionists had to endure. However, what is less obvious is that Wilberforce was one of a group—men and women working together to bring change. He was not acting alone. Nor was he the only leader. Wilberforce was really just the most public face of a community of people who came to be known later as the Clapham Sect.[2] It was this group of remarkable individuals and families who were the nerve center of the anti-slave trade and anti-slavery campaigns.

It began in the village of Clapham, on the edge of London,[3] where a banker named Henry Thornton lived with his family. It was the Thorntons who invited young MP William Wilberforce to move there in the late 1780s.

Soon Thornton had gathered together others of like mind, who shared a passion for taking their evangelical faith boldly into the world of English society. Many of this group came to live in Clapham—such as John Venn (the vicar of the local parish), lawyer James Stephen, long-time campaigner Granville Sharp, gifted researcher and writer Thomas Clarkson, and the former Governor-General of India, Lord Teignmouth. Then there was Zachary Macaulay, a fellow of the Royal Society whose brilliant mind was applied to preparing evidence and reasoned arguments. (When the group needed an answer to a question, Wilberforce would sometimes joke, "Let's look it up in Macaulay.") Other members of the community lived at some distance, while still being relationally connected and committed to the group's endeavors—people like the writer Hannah More, influential clergyman Charles Simeon, and the President of Queens College, Cambridge, Isaac Milner.

The Claphamites were not a clearly delineated group. Nor would they have viewed themselves as anything more than evangelical Anglicans with a passion for "Christianity in action." Nevertheless, at its core, Clapham became a vibrant center of community, with families living out

---

1. Another major challenge was the French Revolution, an unsettling upheaval which sparked enormous fear in England of something similar happening in Britain and was effectively manipulated by those arguing for the status quo on slavery.

2. This phrase was never used by the Clapham community about themselves, but likely coined some time after the group's existence.

3. These days Clapham is very much part of metropolitan London – far from the peaceful village retreat it was in the days of the Sect.

of each other's homes, daily prayers, and collaborative projects developed over the kitchen table and in Thornton's library. In today's terminology they might be described as a "missional community."

While the slave trade campaign was the core issue at the heart of the Clapham Sect's mission, they spearheaded numerous other attempts to bring transformation. Their political conservatism was sometimes criticized—particularly because of their reluctance to support increased democratic rights, trade unions, or anything else that might undermine the social order of their society. Nevertheless, the group was passionate about many of the great injustices of the day, initiating campaigns for penal reform, the abolition of the press gang, relief of chimney boys, education for all, and the regulation of factory conditions—which in their day were appalling. They established numerous organizations ("voluntary societies") to assist and relieve the poor. Additionally, they fought to stop indecent literature, abolish the lottery and the cruel animal sports of the day, and to promote the Sabbath as a day of rest. To give some idea of the breadth of their interests, William Wilberforce was a member of no less than sixty-nine of these voluntary societies!

Claphamites were also key initiators in the founding of the Church Missionary Society (CMS), the British and Foreign Bible Society, and the Sunday School movement, as well as in the creation of Sierra Leone as a colony in West Africa for freed slaves.

Viewing themselves as trustees of the resources God had given them, the men and women of Clapham strategically pooled their time, abilities, spheres of influence, and money, to the causes they gave themselves to. They worked at the political level—agitating for change, using their organizational and writing skills to mobilize public opinion. And they gave their considerable financial resources to fund numerous causes.

Macaulay is reputed to have given away all of his vast fortune, dying a poor man. Wilberforce's "generosity was warm-hearted and impetuous," while Thornton was more calculating and planned but no less generous.[4]

Though we live in very different times, Clapham is a powerful example. It shows how a community of privilege and wealth was able to apply their resources to the pursuit of a vision—a vision that was different to the values of the society around them. The result was striking: they

---

4. Furneaux, *William Wilberforce*.

Section C: Counter-Culture

were leaders in inspiring their society to new values—values that persisted for a century and more, in Great Britain and far beyond its shores.

Money and Community

Someone once told me that the two subjects of conversation that have the potential to break apart a Christian group or church are: parenting styles and money.

I wasn't surprised when I heard this. In our individualistic culture both are seen as intensely personal or private issues. Talking openly about such matters is somewhat daring and apt to be frowned upon. But what is even more dangerous than discussing these topics is our predilection for telling others *how* they should use their money and how they should raise their children—as if *we* know better than they do. As one writer shrewdly puts it: "We are surrounded by communities based on the practice of 'setting each other straight'—an ultimately totalitarian practice bound to drive the shy soul into hiding."[5]

It's not surprising then that most of us in the church steer well away from matters like these. Better to avoid hot topics that could provoke ill feeling, get people's backs up, and erupt into outright hostility.

Or is it? Is there a way of talking about money matters with others in our faith community, without being tempted to try and determine everyone else's decisions? I say yes! It's possible—and it's necessary. However, it's not easy. To do so requires us first to get over the sense of taboo we feel when we enter such conversations, and then to deal with our remarkable delusion that we know better than others how *they* should live.

For it is not just having the freedom to talk about money that matters. We must also give others the freedom to respond and own their own choices, *without them feeling we are in any way judging them.*

We can't do it alone

God knows we need others with whom we can work out our faith—particularly when it comes to our money and resources. If we want to live counter-culturally, resisting the pressure to give in to consumerism and all its variations, we'll never manage it on our own. It's like swimming upstream in a fast-flowing current. Maybe salmon can do it—but we can't.

5. Palmer, *Let Your Life Speak*, 92.

Community

Pursuing a goal that is an alternative to the great Western dream requires an alternative community. A group of people who can seek, with God's help, to set their hearts on shalom—God's kingdom—here on earth.

Community is both a *goal* of God's dream for us and the *means* for producing this shalom. Christianity is a communal faith through and through. While our relationship with God is very personal, it can only be lived out in the context of interdependent relationships with other followers. We are called to live interconnected lives—with each other, in dependence upon God. Paul writes in 1 Corinthians 12:13: "By means of his one Spirit, we all said goodbye to our partial and piecemeal lives. We each used to independently call our own shots, but then we entered into a large and integrated life in which *he* has the final say in everything."

Everywhere we look in the New Testament there is what Brian Dodd calls "a theology of 'we.'"[6] Following Jesus means not only being joined to God, but also to his other disciples; not only working with God, but working with each other, in partnership, creating a community that brings to reality his kingdom.

It's no surprise that Jesus, living here on this earth, gave us a model of this partnership.

In the gospels we see him forming a small community (made up of a diverse and disparate group) and pouring his life into these men and women, eventually entrusting them with the responsibility of his ongoing mission.

Community is also clearly evident in the writings of Paul. We could easily think of this great missionary leader of the early church as being a solo operator, a lone ranger. But if we read carefully through the New Testament we see that the way Paul operated couldn't be further from the strong, independent, archetypal leader. Paul is a *team* leader and a *team* player through and through.

So why does the Bible have such an emphasis on living and working in community with others?

The Trinity—perfect community

To answer this question I want to explore a rather deep theological issue. Fasten your seatbelt. We're about to enter an area of verbal

---

6. Dodd, *Empowered Church Leadership*, 106.

turbulence. For the next few minutes Greek words and theological terms are likely to strike from all angles. But relax, it's all by way of clarifying some basic Christian insights . . . and anyway, you won't have to sit an exam on it!

Primarily, the importance of working together, so evident in the early church, derives from the core of God's identity. Once again we're brought back to the very nature of God.

God is the ultimate community. God the Father, God the Son, and God the Holy Spirit relate and work in complete harmony with one another. This interrelationship models for us the way *we* are called to relate to one another.

You see, the Trinity is not three independent agents doing quite different things, but rather three co-equal persons within the Godhead who all have unique identities and roles, but who in the same breath cannot be separated from one another. This is because *who* they are and the work they do is inseparable from their relationship with the other members of the Trinity.

This is the God we worship and serve—a community of three whose very nature and identity is so interconnected that operating "solo" is unthinkable.

At the core of our faith, then, is a God of "we." The Trinitarian God invites us to join this community—living and serving with God, and with each other.

Co-workers

The Apostle Paul uses several words to refer to the people he works with, but the most frequent is *synergoi*—meaning "co-workers." These people are both co-workers *with God*[7] and co-workers *with himself*.[8] In the thirteen letters Paul writes, he refers by name to nearly one hundred co-workers or partners. That's a large community!

Synergos (the singular form of the word) simply means "working together." *Syn* is a prefix meaning "with" or "together," while *ergon* means "work." This is the source of our word *synergy*, which means the "interaction or co-operation of two or more organizations, substances or other

---

7. See for example, 1 Cor 3:9 and 1 Thess 3:2.
8. For example, Rom 16:3 and Phil 2:25.

agents, to produce a combined effect greater than the sum of their separate effects."⁹ Listen to this:

> A famous illustration of this is the study done on two horses. The first one could pull ten thousand pounds on a sled behind. The second could pull fourteen thousand pounds. What would you think they could pull harnessed together in the same direction? Most people would guess something like twenty-four thousand pounds, but the answer is forty-nine thousand pounds! The sum is greater than a combination of the parts. Of course, there is a negative implication too. If the horses were allowed to pull in different directions, the total amount they could pull is less than what they could pull individually.[10]

The Trinity is the ultimate in synergism. But we too can experience something of the fruit of this living and working together. Particularly as it relates to the employment of our collective resources—our money, possessions, abilities, etc.—in seeking to bring about God's kingdom vision for his world. When we discover ways of valuing and channeling the various contributions of members, the results can be awe-inspiring. God takes the contributions of all the individual parts and weaves them into something much greater than the sum of each person's individual resources.

This was exactly the experience of the Claphamites. One writer catches it beautifully: "Wilberforce needed the others to make him what he was; but the others needed Wilberforce to make a river from a group of pools."[11] The sum total of Clapham working together was much greater than the individual parts.

Partners

Another term the New Testament uses—one that's more familiar in Christian circles—is the word *koinonia*. Often we translate this "community" or "fellowship."

Koinonia was a well-used word in the Greek world. It referred to "having something in common with someone." However, the New Testament use of *koinonia* has an emphasis on *active participation*—having a

---

9. Concise Oxford Dictionary.
10. Dodd, *Empowered Church Leadership*, 105.
11. Howe, *Saints in Politics: The 'Clapham Sect' and the growth of freedom*.

share in something rather than just being associated with it. "Sharing in" is partnership. So when Paul writes about *koinonia* it's all about active participation. There is . . .

- The sharing (*koinonia*) of Christ's sufferings,[12]
- The financial contribution (*koinonia*) of the churches to the poverty-stricken church in Jerusalem that we looked at in chapters 9 and 20,[13]
- The Philippians' partnership (*koinonia*) in the gospel.[14]

In all of these cases, Paul challenges his churches to be working partners with himself, with each other and, of course, with God.

Now here's the point. While following Jesus means the extraordinary privilege of joining the family of God, this sharing does not exist just for its own benefit. Engaging in *koinonia* means taking part in God's mission—his vision for this world. It is outward-focused.

And this *koinonia* includes sharing our money and possessions. As we've seen, Paul's request to the Philippians makes that clear—but of course, this emphasis is repeatedly made throughout Scripture. God asks for the wholehearted commitment of ourselves and all that we have and own.

I have a dream . . .

With apologies to Martin Luther King Jr., I have a dream. It is the vision of counter-cultural communities seeking to live out the values of the kingdom of God in the midst of our consumer culture.

Communities who, refusing to be seduced by the Great Western Dream, are committed to following the dream of shalom . . . the dream of a world where there is enough for everyone, where well-being and harmony exist socially, emotionally, economically, environmentally, and spiritually.

Communities who understand the dark side of money. Who handle their money with care—knowing that it has the potential to do a great deal of good, but that it can also be corrosive and destructive. People who

---

12. See 1 Cor 10:16-21.
13. See 2 Cor 8.
14. See Phil 1:5.

are actively choosing to serve God, not Mammon; who appreciate and resist the addictive and insatiable power of money.

Communities who are learning to read Scripture with fresh eyes. People who model themselves after Abraham and Job and Boaz and Nehemiah, not after Solomon and Ahab. Who don't presume that their affluence is a sign of God's blessing but who treat their economic wealth as a responsibility and privilege, not a right.

Communities who know that their resources—both individual and collective—are not their own, but are God's; who take seriously the call to manage and invest the money, possessions, abilities, and relationships God has entrusted them with, for the kingdom dream, not their own dream.

Communities who live and breathe gratitude to God, knowing that all they have and are is completely gift and grace—not a result of their own cleverness and hard work.

Communities who express this gratitude in lives of generosity and grace toward others; who are always on the lookout for opportunities to give out of their abundance. Communities for whom giving has become a way of life—an attitude that affects how they relate to all people, to rich and poor, immigrant and indigenous, those who follow Jesus and those who don't, those in their own street and those on the streets of Kolkata and Nairobi . . .

Communities who know when enough is enough; who are content with who they are and what they have; who don't spend their time forever accumulating more (or dreaming of doing so). Communities who shun greed and hoarding and are helping their members learn to live within their means and to differentiate between wants and genuine needs.

Communities who are learning the practice of simplicity—both inward and outward. Communities working at de-cluttering their lives, so that single-hearted devotion to God and the things that are important to God take priority. People who, because of this desire for simplicity, willingly limit their choices, their consumption, their lifestyle, and their aspirations.

Communities who know that the most important things in life can't have a price tag put on them. People whose priorities and values demonstrate that economics is a *part* of life—not the *whole* of life and who place clear limits on their consumption. Communities who don't view each other as consumers, or see the church as a "provider of religious goods and services," but instead seek to relate as partners and co-workers in God's mission.

Communities of welcome. Groups of Jesus followers who express radical hospitality—particularly to those who are on the margins of society—the poor and the stranger in their locality and beyond. Communities who always have room for one more at the table, one more to stay over.

Communities who know how to rest and to celebrate well. Groups who have developed a regular rhythm of Sabbath, which reminds them that life is not all about producing and consuming—that they are much more than what they possess or achieve.

Communities who are working for true justice (including economic justice) locally, nationally, and globally; groups who are merciful to those most vulnerable, and who seek fairness for all.

Communities who are prepared to pay the cost of following Jesus with all of their lives—including their homes and their bank accounts.

Working toward the dream

What about you? Do you share this dream? Is it one worth giving your life for?

If so, I challenge you to actively explore the implications of faithfully following Jesus in our consumer culture . . . and to find others who can help make this dream a reality.

Up Close and Personal

1. What do you find most challenging or scary about the potential economic implications of living *koinonia* and *synergos*?

Creative communal responses to consumer culture

2. Brainstorm some practical ways to resist *together* the consumer culture of our world. Your list might range from things as simple as sharing a lawnmower or a car, to as complex as living in community with others or working together on an issue of economic justice.

3. Begin to prayerfully consider what might be a good starting point for you personally.

Final reflections on the book

4. What is one thing from this book that you've found most challenging? Why?
5. What is one thing from this book that you disagree with or need more time to think about?
6. Share with others an area of your attitude or use of money that you want to change as a result of reading this book. Pray for each other.

Bibliography

Blomberg, Craig L. *Neither Poverty nor Riches: A Biblical Theology of Material Possessions*. Grand Rapids: Eerdmans, 1999.
Brown, Colin. "Righteousness, Justification." In *The New International Dictionary of New Testament Theology Vol. 3*. Edited by Colin Brown. Grand Rapids: Zondervan, 1986.
Bruggemann, Walter. *Interpretation and Obedience*. Minneapolis, MN: Fortress, 1991.
Clapp, Rodney. *Border Crossings*. Grand Rapids: Brazos, 2000.
De Geus, Marius. *The End of Over-Consumption*. Utrecht: International Books, 2003.
De Graaf, John, et al. *Affluenza: the all-consuming epidemic*. San Francisco: Berrett-Koehler, 2002.
Dawn, Marva. *Keeping the Sabbath Wholly*. Grand Rapids: Eerdmans, 1989.
———. "Whom Do You Serve?" *Sojourners*, May, 2008.
Dodd, Brian. *Empowered Church Leadership*. Downers Grove: IVP, 2003.
Ellul, Jacques. *Money and Power*. Downers Grove: IVP, 1984.
Fee, Gordon D. *The Disease of the Health & Wealth Gospels*. Vancouver, BC: Regent, 1996.
———. *The First Epistle to the Corinthians*. Grand Rapids: Eerdmans, 1987.
———. *Paul's Letter to the Philippians*. Grand Rapids: Eerdmans, 1995.
Fergusson, Niall. *The Ascent of Money: A Financial History of The World*. New York: Penguin, 2008.
Foster, Richard. *Freedom of Simplicity*. New York: Harper & Row, 1981.
———. *Money, Sex and Power*. London: Hodder & Stoughton, 1995.
Furneaux, Robin. *William Wilberforce*. Vancouver, BC: Regent, 2006.
Guinness, Os. *The Call*. Nashville: Word, 1998.
Hamilton, Clive. *Growth Fetish*. Crows Nest, NSW: Allen & Unwin, 2003.
———, and Denniss, Richard. *Affluenza: when too much is never enough*. Crows Nest, NSW: Allen & Unwin, 2005.
Howe, Ernest. *Saints in Politics: The "Clapham Sect" and the growth of freedom*. Crows Nest, NSW: Allen & Unwin, 1952.
Jethani, Skye. *The Divine Commodity*. Grand Rapids: Zondervan, 2009.
Keener, Craig S. *The IVP Bible Background Commentary*. Downers Grove: IVP, 1993.
———. *Matthew*. Grand Rapids: IVP, 1997.
MacDonald, Gordon. "Rest Stops." *Life@Work Journal*. Vol 2, No.4.
Mackenzie, Alistair, and Kirkland, Wayne. *Just Decisions*. Christchurch: NavPressNZ, 2008.
Palmer, Parker. *Let Your Life Speak*. San Francisco: Jossey-Bass, 2000.

Bibliography

Pohl, Christine. *Making Room: Recovering Hospitality as a Christian Tradition.* Grand Rapids: Eerdmans, 1999.

Riddell, Mike. *Godzone: a travellers guide.* Auckland: Reed, 1992.

Salgo, Harvey. "The Obsolescence of Growth: Capitalism and the Environmental Crisis." *The Review of Radical Political Economics* 5 (October 1973) 26–45.

Schwartz, Barry. *The Paradox of Choice: why more is less.* New York: HarperCollins, 2004.

Seligman, Martin. *Authentic Happiness.* New York: Free Press, 2002.

Sider, Ronald J. *Rich Christians in an Age of Hunger.* Downers Grove: IVP, 1997.

Stigers, Harold. "sedeq —justice, rightness." In *Theological Wordbook of the Old Testament Vol. 2.* Edited by R. Laird Harris et al. Chicago: Moody, 1980.

Sugden, Chris. "Poverty and Wealth." In *New Dictionary of Theology.* Edited by Sinclair B. Ferguson and David F. Wright. Downers Grove: IVP, 1998.

Sweet, Leonard. "Freely You Have Received, Freely Give." No pages. Online: http://www.leonardsweet.com/article_details.php?id=23.

Toffler, Alvin. *Future Shock.* New York: Random House, 1970.

Volf, Miroslav. *Exclusion and Embrace.* Nashville: Abingdon, 1996.

Wallis, Jim. *The Soul of Politics.* London: Fount, 1995.

Walsh, John. "John Wesley and the Community of Goods." In *Protestant Evangelicalism: Britain, Ireland, Germany and America c.1750—c.1950*, edited by Keith Robbins, Oxford: Blackwell, 1990.

Walter, J.A. *Need – the new religion: exposing the language of need.* Nottingham: IVP, 1985.

Williams, Paul. "Free markets do foster the decline of virtue." *Christian Week.* April 13, 2007.

Wilkinson, Loren. "Ecology." In *The Complete Book of Everyday Christianity.* Edited by Robert Banks and R. Paul Stevens. Downers Grove: IVP, 1997.

Wright, Christopher. *God's People in God's Land.* Grand Rapids: Eerdmans, 1990.

Wright, N.T. *Matthew for Everyone.* Louisville: WJK, 2002.

www.ingramcontent.com/pod-product-compliance
Lightning Source LLC
Chambersburg PA
CBHW062014220426
43662CB00010B/1327